THE HEART OF THE MATTER

John Chamberlain

THE HEART OF THE MATTER

The Diary of a School Year

Ginger Plum Press
SANTA FE, NEW MEXICO

ALL RIGHTS RESERVED

COPYRIGHT 2001

John Chamberlain

PHOTOGRAPHS COPYRIGHT 2001

Jackie Mathey

FIRST EDITION

ISBN: 0-9710998-0-4

FOR INFORMATION AND ORDERS:

fayette@cybermesa.com

PRINTED AND BOUND IN CANADA

on permanent paper which meets
American Library Standards

Contents

Acknowledgments	IX
Foreword by Ken Richards	XI
Preface	XIV
PROLOGUE: The End of Summer Introduction of staff and description of school.	1

First Ten Weeks — 7

WEEK ONE: Love — 8
Foundation of Fayette's philosophy. Swinging in the Big Elm. First view of curriculum.

WEEK TWO: Safety — 15
Principles of safety. First steps in algebra. Our program for beginning readers.

WEEK THREE: No Textbooks — 23
Reasons we avoid textbooks. Enjoying Robert Burns and William Shakespeare.

WEEK FOUR: Marianne's Studio — 33
Mapping each child's neurology. Interactions with students testing the school rules.

WEEK FIVE: Games and Animal Friends — 40
Pets around the school. Shakespeare performed in the Big Elm.

WEEK SIX: Autumn Climbing Week — 49
Learning while thirty feet above the ground suspended by nylon ropes.

WEEK SEVEN: Writing 57
Techniques for teaching writing. Lectures on behavior.
Two folk singer guests.

WEEK EIGHT: Latin, Greek, and French 64
Language courses. A bicycle crash. "Spirit Sing" for Halloween.

WEEK NINE: Soccer and Court 71
Fayette soccer rules. Mock court. Techniques for
phoneme awareness.

WEEK TEN: Cube Roots and Student Manners 78
Complex mathematical operations. More court lessons.
Dealing with adolescence.

Seven Nonacademic Weeks 87

WEEK ELEVEN: Parents' Week 88
Parents running the school.

WEEK TWELVE: The Head Elf 95
First week of needles, thread, and beads. Rehearsal for our
Winter Concert.

WEEK THIRTEEN: Tolerance and Sensitivity 104
Pagan, Jewish, and Islamic rituals. Lessons in understanding
the beliefs of others.

WEEK FOURTEEN: Winter Concert 111
Our public concert. Reading of the birth of Jesus. Secret Santa.

The Hard Nine Weeks 121

WEEK FIFTEEN: Hard Nine Weeks 122
Bible. Constitution. Scientific notation. Alumni visits.

WEEK SIXTEEN: Gravity and Patriarchs 130
Book of Genesis. Questions of foreskins. Equations for free
falling bodies.

WEEK SEVENTEEN: Newton and Moses   138
Newton's Laws. Moses' commandments. Thoughts of
bulldozing the Vatican.

WEEK EIGHTEEN: Visitors and Imaginary Rabbits   144
Visitors' most frequently asked questions. A jet propelled
rabbit in physics.

WEEK NINETEEN: Munchkin Manners   153
Young boys kicking each other. Young girls destroying
Valentine cards.

WEEK TWENTY: No-TV Week   161
A week without TV in student and staff homes and why.

WEEK TWENTY-ONE: Collisions   169
Peer discussions. A success in reading. Collisions of oatmeal
and cannonballs in physics.

WEEK TWENTY-TWO: The Brain   177
The triune brain theory and its application in Fayette's
methods and philosophy.

WEEK TWENTY-THREE: Tests and Celebration 183
Book of Revelation. Pajama day. Bubble tests. Celebratory
lunches.

The Eleven Spring Weeks   191

WEEK TWENTY-FOUR: Parents Again   192
Thoughts on parenting skills by a grandfatherly gardener.

WEEK TWENTY-FIVE: Spring Training   197
Practice for baseball season. Exploring different number bases.
Creating flashcards.

WEEK TWENTY-SIX: More Flashcards and Freebies   204
Special rules of Fayette baseball. *The Iliad* in Greek. Secrets
in Latin.

WEEK TWENTY-SEVEN: New Latin Scholars   212
Analyzing the causes of Earth's seasons. Pressure in baseball.

WEEK TWENTY-EIGHT: Nerve Endings   219
Staff fatigue. Diagraming sentences in Latin. New swinging games in the Big Elm.

WEEK TWENTY-NINE: Parent Conferences and Spankings   226
Impromptu parent conferences. Spanking Fayette style.

WEEK THIRTY: Uncle Matt   233
Lessons learned on the baseball diamond. A guest art teacher.

WEEK THIRTY-ONE: Spring Climbing Week   240
Pushing limits and testing ropes in the Big Elm.

WEEK THIRTY-TWO: Los Alamos Fire and Pete   247
Concert preparation. Talks on fear.

WEEK THIRTY-THREE: Spring Concert and School Potluck   255
Our concert. Afternoons of baseball. School potluck. The growth of one girl.

WEEK THIRTY-FOUR: The Final Week   264
Final climbing days. A day at the water park. Graduation dinner. Farewell hugs and tears.

❦ Acknowledgments ❧

QUOTES OF WISDOM are posted in classrooms and on walled gardens of Fayette Street Academy. One by Bear Bryant, the legendary college football coach, has been my guiding principle at school. "If anything goes bad, I did it. If anything goes semi-good, we did it. If anything goes real good, you did it. That's all it takes to get people to win football games."

Bryant's sage advice holds for this book as well as for schools and football teams. I am the sole author of this book and the story is told through my eyes, but many have contributed to the project. All that is "bad" in these pages is mine – any lack of clarity, the inevitable typos, or essential information not included.

The "semi-good" qualities of the book are the product of a collective effort of myself, the staff, and especially the children.

All that is the "real good" should be credited to the following members of our school community:

The most important contributions are from the past and present students of Fayette. The school and this book are shaped by them. The rhythms, tenets, and styles of Fayette exist only because the needs of the children were and are the constant beacon for staff and curriculum. Returning alumni have always provided an important feedback loop for the direction of the school. Most chapters of this book have been emended by the present students and alumni.

During the school year 1999–2000, the members of the staff – Alison Bentley, Melanie Ranney, Tara Chandler, and Elege Simons – were constant consultants during the diarying of the year and through the rewriting process. For every scenario I documented in the text, for every student conversation I overheard, for every moment I was surrounded by a group of students, each other member of staff was equally involved in some way in the goings-on of the school – witnessing other vignettes, teaching other topics, directing other social situations. My testimony was but one of six adults' and three dozen children's views of a school year.

Teaching children is for me familiar territory – authoring a book is not. I have been blessed to have expert support on this project within our school community. Former Fayette parents Ken Richards and Eddie Lewis, authors in their own right, gave advice and encouragement throughout my journey of writing. Jackie Mathey, a professional photographer and parent during my chronicling, spent hours hanging around the school capturing the revealing photos used in the book. Another of our mothers, Barbara Doern Drew, is an editor by profession. Several red pencils gave their lives as she insightfully transformed my original manuscript into a more standard form of English. Eleanor Caponigro, book designer and good friend of both the school and myself, is responsible for the delightful appearance of the book.

Finally and most importantly, I wish to thank Marianne, my partner in life, school, and all things important. She proved ever patient through this journey, gave of her wisdom to help my words, listened when I needed to declaim my endless monologues, and sensed when I needed absolute silence.

✣ Foreword ✤

THIS BOOK is the story of thirty-six students, ages seven through fourteen, their six teachers, ages twenty-three to fifty-some, and their year together during the Fayette Street Academy's academic year 1999–2000. It's a great story. Fayette has been around for twenty years, and this is the first full account of its daily life and inner workings.

Over the years Fayette has taught hundreds of students, of diverse character and talent, from all different kinds of families, and sent them on to high schools and colleges, into careers, into life. It is ironic, then, that the students are not taught to "succeed," nor driven to any of the competitive ends of that ideal. Rather, these students are instructed in the fine art of their own humanity. Being human at Fayette includes having a conscience as well as a brain.

One might guess that with such cosmic purposes Fayette is a school that drifts with its students' impulses from day to day. However the opposite is true: this school overflows with rules, rituals, traditions, and exquisite organization. Everyone in their place and, more wonderfully, a place for everyone. One might also surmise that a school with its students' needs at its core would be academically lightweight. The reverse once again: Fayette students study algebra, physics, history, Latin, Greek, and Shakespeare. Also, and rigorously, soccer, baseball, handicrafts, choir, and climbing with ropes and harnesses. An amazing load in all, four days a week, thirty-four weeks a year, accomplished with great efficiency.

To put it bluntly, it turns out that within the known universe of contemporary educational strategies, many teachers are underchallenged and most students are definitely underestimated. The challenge for teachers – for all of us – is to refuse indulgence in pedagogy or programs, or to surrender to standardized testing and technologies – Fayette has none of the former and neither of the latter – but simply to do the work: the painstaking, daily observation of how students learn (each particular student) and in what contexts they learn. The end result of the teacher's learning at Fayette is that every single rule, ritual, tradition, and organizational flourish contains within it an evolved academic and human purpose, requiring every moment of each day to be successful in some way and making each child's learning another persistent step in preparation for the delights and work of this world. What students learn best at Fayette Street Academy is not to underestimate themselves.

This kind of teaching and learning depends on relationships, one to another: students to teachers, teachers to students, teachers to teachers, students to students, and parents to school. The meaning and values of these relationships and the teaching and learning they produce are, in fact, the vital content of this book – a story that brings us gently to the inescapable conclusion that teaching and learning are absolutely natural human gifts not dependent on textbooks and facilities or computers and legislation, but solely on respect for the craft of education and respect for those taught. Indeed, one unusual feature of the Fayette teaching staff is that none have been formally trained to be teachers.

I once asked John Chamberlain, Fayette's founder, headmaster, and author of this diary of the school, how he knew when his students were learning. "The eyes," he said. "I look in their eyes." That is a fair enough description of the Fayette Street "system": continuous learning by both teachers and students, continuous respectful interaction, continuous attention, each school day.

Turn the page, and here is Fayette Street Academy. Here is a safe, warm place. Here are some pencils and paper. Here are teachers who know something and young people who by their very human nature are given to learning. "What we need," say the poets, "is education in the obvious." What we need are more Fayette Street schools.

Additional note to the reader: Between the lines, this is a how-to book. If you want to start a school like Fayette, this account will remind you not how inadequate you are, but rather how much you already know. All you need is a DPA – a doctorate in paying attention – and most of us are born with that. The kids will show you how to do the rest.

Fayette's door is always open to visitors.

Ken Richards
Tesuque, New Mexico
December 2000

Ken Richards is a parent of two graduates of Fayette, a former political consultant, a writer of television documentaries, and the right-handed pitcher on our baseball team.

⌘ Preface ⌘

BEING A HEADMASTER and teacher at a small school is a relatively straightforward, if at times demanding, task: hold a positive emotional tone in all interactions, expound with enthusiasm on various academic topics, and act as host for visitors. This last job is one of my favorites as it is an opportunity to share the uniqueness of who we are with the community.

One evening a woman phoned asking if she could visit Fayette Street Academy the next day. She was considering new options for her second-grade daughter. After I had given her my standard directions for finding our street, she asked if she would recognize the buildings from their school-like appearance. I laughed and said that the buildings had a most unschoolish look but the large number of children in evidence would be a certain indication that she was at the correct address.

In the morning the children were informed to be on the lookout for a visitor. At 10:00, as a few boys and I bantered in one of our gardens, the cry came from one of the girls perched thirty feet above the ground in what we call the Big Elm, "Our visitor is parking across the street." I headed out to meet her and found her gaping at the half-dozen young climbers visible to all in the neighborhood.

"Hi, I am John," I introduced myself. "I told you it would be easy to find the school." Her eyes kept shifting from the tree to my attire, but no words came to her lips. "Oh, I only wear a kilt on the days of student birthdays," I informed her. She muttered her name and a few words of greeting. I escorted her through the gate to the courtyard dominated by our climbing tree.

Venturing to appear the responsible adult, I called up to one of the kids, "Are you clipped into a safety rope?" "Of course I am – I'm twenty feet off the ground." This dialogue didn't seem to immediately ease her discomfort at seeing children far overhead, but I could tell we had aroused her interest. I continued my tour by heading for our studio. A half-dozen kids were sitting on the floor manipulating small rows of colored wooden blocks. The children remained focused on their tasks, not our intrusion. Tara, one of our young teachers, said, "If that says 'gup' then show me 'bup.' Remember to tap your sounds." Hands moved to rearrange blocks. Our visitor whispered, "Those aren't real spelling words – and what is tapping?" Smiling, I explained, "They are not working on spelling, they are working on strengthening the neural pathways between their ears and brain. The kinesthetics of tapping fingers for each phoneme helps the process." More discomfort – and curiosity.

Desiring to lead our guest to more familiar ground, I suggested that we head to the main school building, where Alison was reading to the younger ones while the older students, my main charge, were taking a test. She objected, "Oh I don't want to take more of your time, if you should be monitoring a test." I smiled again, "They don't need me," I assured her. "No one cheats here. I can be your host until the tests are completed." As we approached the doorway to my room, she noted that, as promised, all the students were focused on paper and pencil, not their neighbors' answers.

We next peeked through the curtain of the doorway separating the two classrooms and observed Alison reading from C. S. Lewis's *Chronicles of Narnia* to kids sprawled around on floor pillows, some drawing, some staring at the ceiling, none distracting the reader or fellow students. I could sense that our guest had not seen a class so configured.

Having finished the tour, I took our guest out to a bench in one of our quiet gardens to ask a few questions and answer any queries. "How did you find out about us?" I asked.

"One of the children in my daughter's after-school clay class seemed so well mannered, so bright, so full of life that I asked where she went to school. That's how I learned of Fayette. My daughter is in second grade and seems less and less happy and inquisitive and more and more guarded every day. She told me she felt school was about following rules and not having fun." I pointed out that we had lots of rules but they were all directed to individual and group safety and comfort, so everyone could be at ease, socially and academically, in our environment.

She continued, "I think I am in shock from all that I am seeing here. This is nothing like I expected a school to be, but though everything seems so strange it all seems so right. I was surprised to find that you are not listed in the phone book. How can people find out about what you do here? I think many people would be interested."

"We always have full enrollment without advertising or being listed in the phone book," I said, "but as a matter of fact I am writing a book about the school right now." From her change of demeanor I sensed that talking about books was a more comfortable subject than viewing more of our nonstandard approaches to education.

"Who is your audience for this book?" she asked. "Are you writing in an attempt to change other teachers' methods?" "I don't have a specific interest group for whom I am writing, nor am I directly trying to change others," I told her. "I am giving the picture of one school that functions very well in times where there is much talk about what is wrong with our schools and many untested theories for change are being bandied about. I trust that any teacher reading the book could find a few tips and methods that might be added to their collection of classroom activities. I hope that others interested in education, including parents such as yourself, could use their interpretations of my pages to broaden their own thinking about the future of education."

"How do you even approach a description of Fayette?" she questioned. "I am overwhelmed just looking around. Everywhere I have seen flurries of activity that look absolutely random, but I sense there is a conscious pattern behind the surface. How can you set this down on paper?"

I thanked her for her frankness and interest in my writing and then elaborated, "I thought for some time about the way to structure the book and finally decided to let the activities of the children define the story. The book is a diary of the school year. At the end of every school day I take a few notes on the day's activities and each weekend write a first draft of the weekly chapter. I also weave in school philosophy and highlight different areas of curriculum in various chapters. The book is so structured that it can be read in chronological order or by serendipitous opening to any page."

"Do you have a title yet?" she wondered. "I understand that is often a difficult part of creating a book." "Interestingly, a title popped into my head early in this project and most around here liked it. One boy in my class, who can be a bit contrary and witty at the same time, suggested I call the book *Harry Potter – Book Five*. He felt that then marketing would take care of itself. My choice, *The Heart of the Matter*, seems to hint at many different aspects of teaching and our school's philosophy. On the first level, heart means 'the most important or essential point,' and that is what is needed in contemplation of education. The word can also signify the 'center,' or 'core,' and equally firmness of will, resolution, and fortitude, all of which are needed in teaching. Heart also stands for sympathy, generosity, and compassion, qualities critically important in instructing the young. And on yet another level heart represents the vital center of one's emotions and sensibilities. We work at Fayette not merely so our graduates will score well on standardized tests, but so they may know their own hearts.

"Matter is a similarly multifaceted word," I continued. "Of course we first think of physical matter, something that occupies space and is perceived by the senses. But it also denotes a subject of concern, feeling, and, hopefully, action – for example, 'a personal matter' or 'a matter of national policy.' I am particularly fond of its use in Aristotelian philosophy, where 'matter' is itself the undifferentiated and formless, which through development receives form and becomes substantial. At Fayette we are constantly focused on these two aspects: what the essence of each student is and what we can structure around them to assist their growth and the manifestation of that essence. So that's why I chose *The Heart of the Matter* as the title.

"Do you describe your personal fears and failures in the book?" she probed. For a breath or two I was silent as images of private angst and public blunders over the past twenty years flashed through my mind. "The book titled *John's Fears and Failures* would be much longer than the one I am now writing," I revealed. "The present book simply records what has happened during one school year. After twenty years of experimenting, adding, rejecting, and fine tuning every aspect of our school, we felt ready to document our small world. My personal journey is not important to that goal."

Kids burst from class and a glance at my watch revealed that my duties as host were over. Waving good-bye to our guest I headed over to chat with the children before classtime brought the topic of pronouns and their agreement with antecedents. After a review of the basics we would be considering the absence in English of a non–gender specific, third person, singular pronoun. Whereas in earlier times "he" and "him" were used universally to denote either males or females in nonspecific cases, current nonsexist usage included the, to my mind, cumbersome "he or she," "s(he)," "he/she," and "his or her" forms. I personally didn't like any of these options. For ease and naturalness of expression, I tended to use "they" and "their" knowing I was violating number agreement. I used this choice in my own writing.

I invite each of you to share with us our small but delightful world at Fayette. Turn the pages. Look at the shining young faces in the pictures. Read the words of their school experience.

Thank you.

John Chamberlain
Headmaster, Fayette Street Academy
Santa Fe, New Mexico
February 2001

ॐ Prologue ॐ
The End of Summer

Mighty things from small beginnings grow.

JOHN DRYDEN

WITH THE SCHOOL YEAR only a week away I assembled the staff. Calling our meeting to order, I informed them of a study reported in the morning newspaper. A committee of national experts had determined elementary education's four biggest problems: many school buildings were old, classrooms were overcrowded, some classes lacked textbooks, and teachers' salaries were low. The staff smiled. We were sitting in an eighty-year-old adobe building we called our school, in my classroom, which was less than thirteen feet by thirteen feet and soon would hold twenty students. We used no textbooks in our curriculum. Our salaries were among the lowest in the state. Yet we considered we were in an excellent position to begin the twentieth year of Fayette Street Academy, which was, interestingly, also the year of the millennium shift, 1999 to 2000.

Our small private school had a reputation for academic excellence and was known for innovative techniques and seeming total disregard for standard school practices. We had no endowments, used no government funds, were not listed in the phone book. We did not advertise and yet we had five applicants for each student opening. We held classes only four days a week, we did no academics for the seven weeks preceding the Christmas holidays, and in the month of May we played baseball all afternoon. Still, we covered more difficult academic subjects and in greater depth than most schools. We gave no grades, but the majority of our past students were on high school honor rolls and excelled in college and postgraduate studies. We had no desks; the students sprawled around on floor pillows. We had no computers in the school, but our eleven-year-olds studied Greek, Latin, and algebra.

Some of our students were from families wishing no part of public school; some were exceptionally bright children bored in other schools; some were learning disabled, falling ever farther behind before coming to Fayette; some were a combination of these. In times when many people were feeling elementary education served our children poorly and various theories for the improvement of our schools were being bandied about, we had for two decades implemented, tested, and refined a system whereby teachers, students, and parents were well served and satisfied.

Our staff of six had been together for years. Three of us, Marianne, Melanie, and myself, were in our mid-fifties. Marianne's education had been in the Catholic schools and colleges of Virginia, Melanie's in New England private schools and one of the Ivy League colleges. Their liberal arts educations were complemented by my mathematics and science studies in the California public schools and university system. Alison and Tara were in their early thirties; Ele had recently turned twenty-one. They were all New Mexico born and alumnae of Fayette. With Ele's help I held forth with the school's twenty older students, aged ten to fourteen. Alison, with Melanie as an assistant, taught the fourteen younger ones, those seven through ten. Marianne and Tara monitored our studio, with its unique approach to neurological development for which Fayette had become known.

Each staff member had duties and talents beyond their primary roles. I monitored all the swinging and the climbing of the ropes course in our giant elm tree, which we had fondly dubbed the Big Elm. Marianne taught our Latin classes. Melanie was our choir director and produced our two annual public concerts. Alison taught Greek to the older students and French to the younger. Tara, when not in the studio, served as secretary, nurse, and person who did all the little things that help a school function. I held the title of headmaster, but we all took equal part in decision making.

As we had worked and learned together for so many years, we executed our schedule and course planning smoothly and quickly.

After twenty minutes of discussion all curriculum and schedules were set, and we turned our attention to the more difficult task, the physical plant. Our school campus occupied two small city lots, a total area of less than a sixth acre, in a poor neighborhood of Santa Fe. Our four buildings were old and small. Marianne's and my home, built immediately after World War II, began as a three-hundred-square-foot, two-room house. Subsequent owners and finally ourselves had increased the number of rooms to six and the size to just under one thousand square feet. An eight-step commute delivered us to school.

The school building was even older than our home. Four adobe rooms, each under two hundred square feet, formed the main structure. One room had been partitioned to create a bathroom and an entry room. The entry contained the building's only heat source, a woodburning stove. In the first year of using the building for our school, we built a portal along the front. Some years later we enclosed it with wooden walls. This unheated, unlit front room held lunches, shoes, coats, and the occasional study group. Tara's home, similar in size to ours, and the studio, the smallest of our four buildings, completed the permanent structures.

With interior space so limited, we had over the years built several wooden storage sheds, useful to hold family and school materials, and handy as launching platforms for the several rope swings attached to the Big Elm. During school hours we used all the buildings, all the resources. Every space was used by children and staff. There were noisy and quiet zones, but all space, interior and exterior, was part of the school.

Our staff inspection of the empty rooms found walls painted and carpets cleaned. The previous four days had been the annual fix-up/clean-up, where with parent help we prepared the school for another year. The only items in the building were the several piles of our floor pillows, ready for student use. Satisfied with the interior, we moved outside to the brick entryway to survey our collection of school furniture. While no items in the school received abuse, all had to withstand heavy use. The six combination storage-box and seating platforms, one low elliptical table, and two sets of bookshelves had in common their construction of thick plywood and large-dimension lumber. They were freshly painted and ready to be returned to their classroom homes.

We removed a plastic tarp from a lumpy pile to reveal our school supplies. A stack of a hundred books for young readers and two sets of well-thumbed encyclopedias comprised our library. Three soccer balls, two jump ropes, six baseball bats, and a score of gloves constituted our sports equipment. After two hours of carrying furniture and books to their proper places for the next nine months, and a few minutes taping posters to the walls, staff and school were ready for another school year.

The campus had not always been so large and well equipped. The first year school was held in the only bedroom of our rented home. Six young girls, our daughter Tara one of them, comprised our first class; I did all the teaching. At the end of that year, the success and prospects for the future enabled us to purchase the city lot and its two buildings. Papers were signed eleven days before the beginning of the second school year. Marianne and I worked eighteen-hour days preparing the building for our enrollment of fifteen children. She would teach the younger and I the older. Within three years the school had more than twenty-five students, including Alison.

As we entered our second decade, Alison was a student at St. John's, a local college committed to classical studies, and an assistant to Marianne; Ele was one of my students. Marianne began to investigate techniques to help students overcome learning disabilities, which soon became a full-time job. Then in 1994 we purchased the adjoining property, doubling the campus size and number of buildings. Alison advanced to lead teacher for the young ones, and Melanie joined the school as her assistant. By 1997 Marianne's work with neurologic development had grown again and Tara became her assistant. At this time Ele became a student at the College of Santa Fe and was now my coteacher.

A last look confirmed that our humble but clean buildings, our dedicated and knowledgeable staff, and our uncommon practices and experimental methods were in place. The only missing ingredient was our group of thirty-six young children, who would bring with them enthusiasm, doubts, intelligence, inexperience, maturity, social problems, areas of brilliance, learning disabilities. We would be a small community for the next nine months. And it would all begin on Tuesday morning.

The children would not be merely entering the grounds, buildings, and awareness of the staff. They would be entering an unseen container designed to allow all to experience themselves, a protective zone where they could first *be* and only later *do*, a charged atmosphere where all would sense that they *were* OK. This was the invisible Fayette, permeating the gardens and buildings, shining through the teachers' eyes.

꙳ The First Ten Weeks ꙳

DURING THESE WEEKS new members of the school community settled in to our rhythms and rules, while returning students developed comfort with their new classes and roles in the school. Everyone, staff as well as students, was evaluated to determine their individual neural patterns and levels of development, so Marianne could create strategies and exercises for each person. The older students introduced the new ones to the Big Elm – its ropes and rules. Academically, we moved each child forward in their pursuit of the three Rs and with the older class also moved through as much algebra, Latin, and inorganic chemistry as possible in ten weeks.

ᴧ Week One ᴧ
Love

*And now abideth faith, hope, love, these three;
but the greatest of these is love.*

SAINT PAUL

As the morning parade of cars arrived after the three-month summer break, our twenty-eight returning students walked onto the entry bricks, glad to be back in their school community. All were inches taller and a step higher on the social totem pole than when they had left in May. The subtle difference between the total ease of those returning to their classroom of last year and the slight apprehension of those switching from Alison's class to mine was evident to the veteran school watchers. To those returning we were adding eight new members to our student body. Of these, the older girls were relieved to be spending their junior high years in our small, friendly environment. The new eight- and nine-year-old boys joining us came slightly twitchy and fearful. They were entering a strange new world not knowing what was in store for them, carrying memories of school dis-ease, and feeling the questions and concerns of their parents.

Fortunately the foundation of Fayette was acceptance of every person as they were at that moment. Our task was to help each child learn and grow from their current state. As we aided them, we applied heavy doses of love. I can honestly say the whole staff surrounded every child with love, but that word has many different meanings. For example, I loved the kids, but I also loved the vivid New Mexico sunsets. I loved Marianne as my life partner and soul mate, and also loved the smell of sun-dried laundry. At Fayette love meant embracing every child with an energy that signaled our wholehearted acceptance of who they were, as they were in the moment. It meant our constant willingness to pay the attention needed to assist them in their growth. At times we might not approve of some of their behaviors, but we saw, admired, and supported their essential selves. We adults of the school were friends to each child, every moment of every day. That was love at Fayette.

As the day began, each returning student was surveying the school and grounds, seeing what was the same and what had changed. They also hosted tours for the new students, explaining the rules, rhythms, and patterns of the school. They did this automatically because in the previous years this service had been provided to them. The staff wandered around greeting students, patting heads, and listening to their banter: "Late in the day this deck is shaded and a great place for afternoon break"; "The sunflowers bordering the path make a tunnel"; "Be careful when walking by the fish pond – the path narrows. John designs things like that on purpose."

The biggest change the students noticed was the replacement of the toolshed's ladder with climbing holds; we now had a mini-climbing wall as the way up and down to the platform topping the shed. Before 8:00 the veterans were already demonstrating to the new students the proper technique and safety tips for the "pendulum swing" from the tool shed roof. A rope with a foot loop was secured to a large branch of the Big Elm, making the arcing swing from the top of the shed a favorite activity. By 8:30 the braver of the new kids were enjoying the swing. I pointed out the newly constructed storage shed over the fence and behind Marianne's yurt. This shed had been designed as a distant landing platform, but I advised that for the first few days we each become proficient with the simple pendulum swing and save advanced flights for future weeks.

At 9:00 we gathered in our two classrooms – I with the older ones, known as the Bigs, and Alison with her younger ones, affectionately called Munchkins. Alison began by having each child talk about their summer. Young ones appreciated having their voices heard. Being heard was not a problem with adolescents, so with my class I jumped right into academia, passing out the papers we would be using during the first week. By lunchtime we had touched on Greek, Latin, algebra, and some of the other themes of the beginning of the year. I reminded my class that our first goal was for all the students, especially the new ones and young ones, to feel comfortable. Only when we were relaxed, not activating fight or flight impulses, could we learn effectively. Anyone could use fear to condition people. We believed that for effective education, both teachers and students must be at ease.

At Fayette the student social patterns were set and monitored not only by the staff but also by the "Boss," the oldest, most experienced student. This year fate had assigned this challenging role to Forest. He had been in the school six years, beginning as one of those eight-year-old hyperactive failures of other schools. I think he spent half of his first year sitting out in the gardens, the alternative to bouncing off the classroom walls. Even last year most Fayette watchers wondered how he would handle the role of Boss. However, he returned to school two inches taller and years more mature. At morning break he took me aside and asked for my tips on being Boss. I told him the first lesson was that I didn't know a thing about the role. I advised him to remember his impressions of the previous Bosses, call them on the phone when needed, and most importantly to trust his own instincts. The day ended with the return of the parade of cars and children greeting their parents with smiling faces. Not a single tear had been shed during this first day; usually we had a few. We were beginning a great year.

Wednesday brought everyone back to what seemed old rhythms: greeting friends and heading for the swing before class. In the Bigs' room, we began our reading of *A Midsummer Night's Dream*, the Shakespeare play for the year; discussed the third and fourth rules in algebra, the first two having been so well received on Tuesday; began our series of history lectures; worked on our weekly homework packets; discussed and clarified our rules of saftey; and wrote our first mini-essays. Mentally I raised the bar of what we would accomplish this year in the Bigs' class. Alison's Munchkins included six new students; the main themes of her class were the fundamentals of academics and social interaction.

As we taught, Marianne began calling older students to her studio. The new children wondered what this meant. In their previous schooling the only ones called out of class were those in trouble, being called to the principal's office, or the slow ones, headed for the resource room. As we continued our classes, Alison and I explained to the new students that everyone would be spending time in the studio and that during these first two weeks Marianne and Tara would be checking brain profiles and neural development of each of us. From the look on the faces of the new ones, it was hard to tell if they thought this better or worse than the principal's office and resource room!

The second day of school also brought our first birthday of the year: Lauren turned eleven. Everyone looked forward to birthdays at Fayette. There was none of the hazing I remembered in my early schooling, only good cheer. Every birthday I wore a kilt to honor the occasion. The children loved this ritual and the several messages it subliminally embodied: individual traits were OK, different cultures were comfortable with various conventions and styles, and their teacher had great legs. (To answer the often asked question, this honorary Scotsman wore spandex bike shorts under his kilt.)

At the end of the school day we gathered outside. Lauren stood in honored position on the Birthday Rock, while we sang "Happy Birthday." We then all enjoyed cupcakes provided by her mom. For years those with summer birthdays had felt left out of this ritual but the year before, our youngest student, Eliza, announced that we would celebrate her half birthday. One more small thread was woven into the fabric of our school traditions. Now no longer were children with summer birthdays slighted, and my kilts were seen on more school days.

Thursday morning Pete, our neighbor and climbing coach, came over to demonstrate the landing of the pendulum swing on the new storage shed. He was a mountain climber of the present generation; I of one past. Over several years we had trimmed branches, purchased ropes and harnesses, and built the sheds that comprised our climbing and swinging world. Mid-October would find us all in the tree for "Climbing Week," but this first week of school was devoted to the basic swing. Since Pete had been practicing swinging from shed to shed for two weeks, he made the flights and landings seem effortless. The kids would soon learn the difference between master and novice.

The afternoon ended with our second lecture on prehistory. Wednesday's talk had been a warm-up to the subject and had included a presentation of the creation myth of Genesis. Thursday's lecture, in seeming contrast, included the rudiments of the theory of evolution. In all of our subjects we preferred the examination of larger concepts over a parade of disconnected facts and figures. Both my topics of lecture and the kids' questions and discussion supported this larger view. We discussed the concept that a theory was but a plausible model of explanation of observed phenomena and never Absolute Truth. Since our lectures had already touched on two theories of human development that stood so far apart, we spoke of effective ways to interact with folks holding to theories different from our own cherished ones.

Returning to our main topic, I was interested to see that the class supported neither the literal biblical explanation nor the evolutionary mutational model – their discussion seemed headed toward a synthesis of the two. Jackson added the possibility of DNA from outer space, and James brought up the idea of an organism's consciousness being a factor in its own species change. We already were having a grand time musing and juggling the ideas and observations of prehistory.

Friday began with young Daniel trying to be the first to land on the storage shed. He approached the shed with too much speed, skidded across the roof, rolled over the side, and landed on the ground. Always an adventurous lad, he was unscathed.

Having a swinging and climbing environment as part of school demanded safeguards. In the weeks before school resumed, Pete and I had spent hours tying, testing, and checking every part of the system. Early on we had learned to rely on the natural primate reflex of our hands to hold tightly to a rope, especially when feet slipped. For example, on the simple pendulum swing, if the foot slipped out of the nylon webbing loop, the hands automatically gripped the rope more securely and the young Tarzan merely landed on the ground. Our ultimate pre-school testing was to invite some of Pete's rowdy young adult friends over on a weekend, give them each several margaritas, and have them go at the ropes. This was how I learned what would happen if a Daniel missed the landing on the storage shed.

The new young boys attentively watched my reaction to Daniel's crash. They were curious to see how this unfamiliar teacher would act as a disciplinarian. I was actually delighted that Daniel had demonstrated, especially to the newcomers, the consequence of exceeding one's abilities in activities around the Big Elm. Understanding that exercising caution and knowing our own limits are part of learning, I put my arm around him and joked about his flight. Out of the corner of my eye I saw the new boys relax. They saw that mistakes did not lead to trouble with the teachers. I knew that our messages of love, trust, and concern for each of them would pay dividends in future weeks and months.

The last two hours of Friday were devoted to art and music. One o'clock found the Munchkins in the studio singing with Melanie and the Bigs in the school sketching with Alison. At 2:00 the groups switched. Art with Alison was quiet, focused, and relaxed, an extension of her personality. Melanie's approach was based on her passion for music and how she felt everyone should behave in choir practice. Working with her, we all sat in silence, attentively focused on her directions.

Before class Melanie had said we would have no new songs the first week. She lied. Each old standard was followed by a song new to us all. Old songs were sung in unison; the new students would catch on after hearing the rest of us sing them a few times. We learned the new ones by echoing Melanie: she would sing a bar and we would repeat it. After several bars she would sing and we would echo a whole line, building toward the complete verse. Along with singing in unison we also sang in three-part rounds, which was confusing at first for our newest members, but provided great neural training. Art and music were a pleasure, especially since none of us was in top academic form after three months of summer.

The day ended, as was the tradition at the end of each week, with students and parents on the entry bricks gathered around a big bowl of popcorn – or I should say two. One of our new students had a dietary condition requiring the avoidance of fat and she had told me in the morning she was concerned about the butter on the popcorn. I said not to worry – things always work out. She left with one of those puzzled looks used by children when they couldn't quite tell what the adult meant. That afternoon, when Tara popped the corn she put some aside in a small bowl before adding butter to the main batch. Our young student was delighted to see what was now known as "Rebecca's Bowl" next to the big one. We really did try to fit the program to the child, not the child to the program.

∽ Week Two ∾
Safety

Salus populi suprema lex est.
(The people's safety is the highest law.)

CICERO

WE ASSEMBLED AGAIN on Tuesday morning following our standard three-day weekend. After a week where our foundation of love and comfort were the main themes, we brought our focus to the specific issues and rules of safety at the school. Safety at Fayette began with making the buildings and grounds safe for students. I was delighted that our summer fix-up had addressed almost every potential physical hazard. Wooden corners had been rounded, protruding nails or screws secured, cracked window panes repaired, the loose bricks of the school entryway and stones of the garden paths stabilized. I had since found two screws sticking through the back of one of the gates and during the weekend had covered them.

Though we wanted a safe environment for our students, we didn't want it to be cotton padded. Removing all potential dangers and excitement created timid and inattentive children. We had designed an environment where attention to the surroundings and observation of the rules of safety allowed for fun without injury. Directly opposite the school's front door was a cactus garden. *No bursting out of class at a sprint, please.* The path then narrowed going by the fish pond. *Maintain balance and no shoving here, thank you.* A few steps up large boulders, across a wooden deck, down the flagstones on the far side brought a pause at the gate – every time. *Someone is probably on the pendulum swing, and you must time your passage to avoid collision.* The ritual was to ascend the holds on the climbing wall to the top of the tool shed and stand quietly in line awaiting your turn on the swing. Place your foot securely in the green webbing loop, hold tightly to the purple strap, and then step off the shed for a high-speed ride. This was part of safety at Fayette.

In addition our school was a weapon-free zone. No guns, real or toy, were allowed; nor were knives, not even a pocket or paring knife in a lunch bag. Swinging sticks from the woodpile or throwing rocks from the garden paths was a violation of school rules. Members of the school community were there by choice and free will. We had agreed to practice the ethic of harmlessness toward others. Students were safe from criticism, taunting, or harassment by teachers and other students. Anyone feeling discomfort caused by the action of others had their concern immediately addressed. We had experienced that young children whose nervous systems were allowed to develop in such an environment grew into the strength and understanding needed to operate in the harsher world of later years. Students were safe to make mistakes, both academically and socially, as part of their learning process. One of the aphorisms posted on several garden walls was, "How can you learn from your mistakes if you don't make some?"

We had disciplined ways in which we each had to behave at school. No running, no screaming, no body stuff – that is, don't grab, poke, or hit the bodies of other students. We had lots of rules: rules for class, rules for walking to the park, rules for soccer, many rules for the Big Elm, rules for the art class. Everywhere we had rules – for individual and group safety. They were based on common sense and past experience. Any student at any time could ask for the commentary and history of a specific rule. We modified rules when someone suggested a valid reason for change. The rules were like the operating system of a computer, mostly operating invisibly in the background of comings and goings of school days. Within these rules, in our safe zone, we each were able to relax, develop, and learn more efficiently than if we were uptight, awaiting imminent harm and disaster.

Tuesday the Bigs' class began, as we would each of the next nine weeks, with two contrasting half hours. The first was spent on quizzes. This week tested knowledge of the Greek uppercase alphabet and the capitals and nicknames of the western states of the country, two of the topics highlighted the previous week. The silent focus of the test taking was in itself a marvelous unifying energy for the whole class.

The test scores were not entered in a grade book – at Fayette we gave no grades. The scores allowed each student to appreciate their own strengths or weaknesses and helped the teachers to judge the need for review or addition of new concepts to each subject. In the course of the year we would take over a hundred short tests. These were excellent practice for high school and college years, where teachers and professors would carve the scores in granite or at least save them on hard drives. In addition, many Munchkins and their parents spent a few minutes in the front room for final morning hugs and observed the commendable focus of the Bigs.

At 9:00 small chattering groups of Bigs, with Latin flash cards, conjugation charts, and vocabulary lists, spread through all corners of the school, save for the Munchkins' room. There, Alison began the day by reading to the students for half an hour. Over the course of the year a score of children's classics would be presented in this daily half hour. By 9:30 we all were warmed up for another productive four days of school.

The first week of classes was so smooth I found myself giving my much beloved "Boxes and Cannonball" algebra lecture earlier than in any previous year. We usually discussed the concept of balance and unknowns in algebra equations in the third week of school, but here we were on the first day of the second week! Even those who had heard this lecture several times before and were able to solve any equation thrown at them were required to be part of the class. This way we were all refreshed on our agreed languaging, allowing any member of the class to receive assistance from any other.

During the first half hour, the students new to algebra were on the spot as I asked them about simple equations and their representations by the balance beams, cannonballs, and opaque boxes of our mental model. The simplest problem had two cannonballs on the left side of the beam balancing a box hiding an unknown number of balls. After we set the rules that all balls had the same weight and the box was weightless, I asked the youngest, least confident student for the number of cannonballs in the box. As in past years the child sat silently until I told her the answer was simple and not a trick. When a "two" was heard we were launched into another year of solving algebra equations.

The next student was presented with two boxes balancing six cannonballs. "Three are in each box!" We were ready to take the first big step in algebraic thinking. I drew two boxes and one cannonball balancing five cannonballs. Those who had seen this in previous years were not allowed to speak. Cina was the first to see the path to the solution: "Begin by taking a cannonball from each side. The beam is still balanced and the steps to the solution are now easy!" The older students watched the new ones extend their logic and problem-solving skills and this teacher was again in the bliss of another group of young people excited by algebra.

The second half hour the novices relaxed and watched the veterans go through the same process but with bigger piles of balls and more boxes on each side of the balance beam. In the coming weeks, whenever anyone had trouble with the abstract nature of equations, we could refer to the cannonballs and balance beam. The early practice of team teaching and learning would pay large dividends to each of us throughout the whole school. The novices learned to recognize the boundary between their own knowledge and ignorance, and to ask the proper questions that would add more territory to their body of information. The older students learned to articulate to others the concepts they had internalized but had not verbally expressed. In this atmosphere no one felt the need to cover their ignorance. A class without grades has little competition, but considerable cooperation.

After lunch we walked, as we did most days, to the nearby city park for forty-five minutes of soccer. This year our first soccer game looked as though we had been playing together for weeks. The intensity of play and ball-handling skills were present from the first kick. The good habits of previous years were embodied in each year's returning players, so our play over the years continued to improve. Some of the great moves of kids now in college had been remembered, replicated, and passed down to the present players. At the end of the previous year I had been concerned because our young girls weren't bringing focus or intensity to the game. I had wondered what steps to take at the beginning of this year to overcome this attitude. Fortunately, many of the girls had watched the World Cup win by the U.S. women's team. This changed our young girls' image of the game, and they were filled with a renewed enthusiasm. Since we were not yet well conditioned, we played a short game and returned to school for some free time before afternoon class.

As we gathered under the Big Elm, Eliza had a few Oreos in a baggie. I reminded her that they were my favorite cookie. I received a wrinkled nose expression, which I took for a no. A couple of minutes later she wanted to climb the toolshed wall and asked me to hold the baggie now containing a single Oreo. I obliged and handed her an empty bag when she was safely atop the shed. She didn't believe the cookie was gone until I opened my mouth to show her the remains. A teacher's roles are many.

Wednesday we brought out the climbing harnesses and let the Bigs use them for the rest of the week. Now, instead of the simple pendulum in which the foot was secured in a loop of webbing, the harness and carabiners created a universal joint at the center of gravity. Inverted swinging and a range of tricks akin to those of skateboarders in half pipes were again being performed after a summer's respite. Harnesses allowed another favorite activity. We had several sections of climbing rope dangling from the tree and ending in loops six feet from the ground. Those in harnesses clipped onto these and hung in the air, bobbing off the trunk, talking to their friends hanging off the other ropes, eating from lunchbags clipped to their harnesses. Classes were conducted with half a dozen students wearing harnesses so at the next break they could immediately clip to the ropes with no loss of time. The swinging was closely watched by the Munchkins, for they knew that the following week it would be their turn to use the harnesses. As Eliza stood watching I handed her an Oreo.

As we settled into afternoon class, a group of educators passing through town stopped by to observe. They were amazed at how quiet everyone was as we began class, how interactive our lectures were, and how talkative study time was. They said they had never seen such a combination of relaxed and engaged students. The study time they observed was of two dozen ten- to thirteen-year-olds sprawled around the classroom on floor pillows helping each other solve algebra equations and translate Latin sentences.

When the children left class for afternoon break, I talked with these interested adults about Fayette's academic and social philosophies for a few minutes and then suggested they go out and observe the children at play. No one was ever prepared for a tree filled with ropes and swinging bodies. To the untrained eye it appeared that these seemingly uncontrolled flights would end in collision, disaster, and tears at any moment. The motions around the tree were a demonstration of complexity theory: conscious order disguised as random motion. After watching the action for a few minutes, one of our guests shook her head, smiled, and said, "We had heard that your school did things differently from most, but I must expand my definition of 'differently.' Thank you for sharing this marvelous world with us."

Thursday we brought out our graduated reading books, the Ladybird Books series and our favorite, the McGuffey Eclectic Readers. The Ladybirds, first published in England in the 1960s, were used with our young beginning readers and by those having extreme difficulty with the first steps of reading. The collection included thirty-six small books enabling young ones to feel, in a short amount of time, the accomplishment of completing a book. The strength of the series was the focus on "key words." In English, twelve words make up one quarter of those read and written by young children. One hundred words form half of those encountered by them. The Ladybird series gradually introduced new key words, frequently reinforced them, and, most importantly, carried them over from book to book. By the end of the series nearly two thousand words had been presented.

Though Ladybirds were a valuable tool in the teaching of our youngest readers, the McGuffeys were read by all and enjoyed by most. This series of six graded readers plus a primer were used in this country from 1836 until 1920. The copies we used were reprints available from the Smithsonian. Over the decades people's reactions to the McGuffeys had ranged from nostalgia to rejection. Our present parents had had no experience with the books so we could present them in an emotionally neutral environment. Those who had objected to the series had spoken of the outrages of Victorianism and the moralistic and didactic style of the writing. However, we used these characteristics to our advantage. While reading, we would discuss some of the hypocrisies of the nineteenth century captured in the texts. For example, temperance was the subject of more than one selection, but slavery was not mentioned. Also most of the stories addressed young male readers. We used this to discuss the stereotyped roles of women.

Personally, the staff had no objection to the many moral stories. Honesty, industry, courage, kindness, and courtesy did not seem overly represented in the hours of television watched by most children. These qualities were all found in the McGuffeys. The selections ranged from poetry to such varied topics as farming before agribusiness, history before the global savagery of the two world wars, and biographies of interesting people now forgotten. The works of Shakespeare, Dickens, Tennyson, Longfellow, Whittier, Poe, and Emerson, though sadly none of Twain or Whitman, were introduced to the young readers.

Several sessions a week, Munchkins, often with a Big at their side, would increase their reading skills through the use of our two series. At other times, the Bigs could be found enjoying the selections in the final books of the McGuffey series. Sharing favored stories with other students promoted both social bonds and academic strengths. Having a young reader experience the ease of reading when they dropped back one level or the challenge of opening a book one step above their present comfort level was a valuable use of these two graded series of books.

Friday morning brought another set of visitors to observe the school. Their words to describe our world were "safe and charged." Our reputation for academic excellence had preceded their visit, and they were expecting a competitive environment. They were surprised to see a cooperative one. Looking in on the Munchkins' room, they admired the way the children embraced and supported each other in their learning. Thinking that the closeness was explained by the children having been together as a group for several years, our visitors were quite amazed to find that six of the fourteen were new students in only their second week in our school. Two of these new boys had been diagnosed with strong hyperactive tendencies; they were both engaged and cooperative. A loving and safe atmosphere was an effective catalyst for rapid, strong bonding. A hundred pendulum rides, an hour of art, an hour of singing, and the gathering around the popcorn closed out the second week of school.

~ Week Three ~
No Textbooks

*I have always felt that the true textbook
for the pupil is his teacher.*

MOHANDAS GANDHI

ALISON AND I had our first colds of the year as the third week of school began. After two weeks of children coughing in our faces, various viruses had established beachheads in our sinuses. Now we both felt the school year had truly begun. I was most comfortable pushing against some adversity.

The Munchkins knew they would be using the climbing harnesses this week, so many of them arrived early on Tuesday morning. The Bigs helped them into the differently sized harnesses and showed them how to securely fasten the buckles, emphasizing the importance of doing so *every time*. I told them the story of the doctor who had been at a climbing class in the Grand Tetons the week before I attended. The instructors had harnessed him in the morning but he went behind a tree to pee and didn't properly resecure the buckle. No one caught the error, and he fell forty feet to his death. A sobering story. We taught the habit of constantly checking each others' harnesses.

The Munchkins enjoyed the freedom of swinging from the various ropes while secured by nylon leg and waist loops. Having learned from watching the Bigs, they clipped lunchbags to gear loops and ate while suspended from the Big Elm's massive branches. All of this was done less than four feet from the ground. We developed comfort with the equipment close to the ground before climbing to the higher branches during "Climbing Week," which was coming next month.

Rebecca noticed that one of the ropes was frayed. I had been watching this rope for the past week and praised her powers of observation. I used the occasion to demonstrate to the kids the anatomy of a climbing rope, where an outer sheath of colored nylon received the wear but inner strands of white nylon provided the strength. The rope was retired, and Rebecca took the frayed section home to hang in her bedroom.

Our classes were well launched by now, and since each student worked to some degree at their own pace, the classes began to break into various small groups. We used no textbooks, allowing the flexibility needed for individual pacing. Alison and I had an archive of thousands of master sheets, which were photocopied to create worksheets. We had used this system for years and could not imagine teaching without the flexibility. Some masters were from workbooks collected over the decades, but the best sheets were created using our computers and laser printer.

In Algebra the class had already broken into four groups. The advanced group, those who had had some Algebra the year before and enjoyed math, were racing through concepts at a furious pace so I often ran to the printer for more pages. The confident intermediates were solid in their understanding and moved forward at a predictable pace. The unconfident intermediates needed a few extra drills, which I created each evening and had ready for them the next day. The mathematically challenged, those not feeling comfortable with the letters found in algebra or numbers found in arithmetic, worked on straightforward exercise sheets and received Ele's undivided attention. The groups reminded me of bicycle racers: riding in a group was easier than riding alone. During our months of the "Tour de Algebra" various riders would sprint ahead to the next group or fall back to the one behind.

By not using textbooks we had opened up our curriculum to other ways of presenting material. The "weekly packet" was an excellent example. Every Tuesday each student turned in their packet from the previous week and received the one for the present week. Packets were a dozen stapled pages of various activities: an interesting cover to color, several puzzles, some poetry, some prose, a page of grammar, some geographical questions, and whatever else Alison or I wished to add that week. Again the flexibility of photocopied masters allowed the packets to fit the students. I had the easier job, as all Bigs received the same packet; the older students would give hints and assistance to the younger ones. Alison's job, on the other hand, at times approached a nightmare. Since her kids were younger and novices at most academic skills, she created individualized packets for each child, tracking their progress and changing the level of the material as they grew as students. Our graduates remembered packets with great fondness. I always had a few extras around so returning alumni could take one with them to again try their hand at the puzzles and analogy quizzes. Anyone who had been a Big at Fayette knew that when our cover was Escher's lithograph *Bishop and the Praying Mantis* the "Hard Nine Weeks," the period of our most intense study, were over. All knew that when we were coloring Hokusai's *Great Wave at Kanagawa* summer vacation was but a few days away.

Over the years I had tutored high school kids after school. I had found that faced with huge glossy textbooks, students could have trouble telling what was important information and what was just so much verbiage or fancy computer graphics. With the single pages handed out at the proper time to each student at Fayette, that kind of uncertainty was avoided. Every number and letter on the page was important. The algebra sheets I had created each dealt with a single concept and had incremental degrees of increased difficulty. Students knew when they are ready for the next sheet. The ritual of asking for and receiving each individual piece of paper seemed to have a power of its own. The flexibility of single pages also highlighted each student's improvement. The first time through the sheet "Inequalities One" was a slow journey. Two months later a student would fly through it. The paper was the same, so the change had to be in the student. Self-evident, undeniable progress.

Instead of teaching history and science from textbooks that limited both teacher and student to the author's and publisher's narrow presentation, I used several classic books on a particular subject as a basis for my lecture notes. For example, having the words and insights of Grahame Clark, professor of archaeology at the University of Cambridge, added a richness to my series of lectures on prehistory that could not be found in any standard school text. Using books from different decades gave a sense of the timing of discoveries in the various fields. A sequence of books was much like the layers of archaeology: digging deeper in the cave or village gave changing views of the past and the flow of that change. Including older books gave the partial models and limited information of previous decades, showing that present knowledge in any area was the result of a process of discovery and was itself only partial. Including the history of discovery as well as the information presently known added interest to the topic. As counterpoint to the use of "dated" books, our use of current magazines and the Internet allowed the latest information to be part of the lectures.

Also, class discussion was driven primarily by students' mental models, not a textbook presentation. Each person, even a young child, has a huge operating system of observations from life, facts from those around them, and explanations of the phenomena surrounding them. In our lectures we encouraged each student to articulate their beliefs, understandings, and questions. Our philosophy was to teach *to* each student, not *from* a book.

Another benefit of using photocopied sheets was lightening the weight of student backpacks. Textbooks had increased dramatically in size over the last decades and several of these on a youngster's back could lead to back problems. The cost of textbooks also continued to increase, a drain on a school's budget. With the rapid discovery in so many fields, textbooks were often outdated by the time of distribution, requiring the purchase of yet another series of books. We avoided all three of these burdens.

It was our strong feeling that reliance on textbooks tended to narrow and dull the minds of both teacher and student. One day Adele, our fine Boss of the previous year, came by to visit and report on her transition into high school. When I asked about algebra, she did not talk about the mathematical concepts but rather about her score on a recent test. One question had been to define the concept of equation. Using her own words and model she had done an excellent job. Unfortunately, she was marked down because she had not used the verbatim definition found in the textbook. If we at Fayette had been charged with teaching the fine art of regurgitation, I would have been at the forefront of textbook use. However, I viewed my charge as teacher as one where more complex thought and useful techniques were accented.

Replacing the textbook with the photocopy allowed for flexibility and the unexpected. On Tuesday, for example, we learned that our Scots friend and renowned Robert Burns scholar, Donnie O'Rourke, would be in town in a few days. We talked by phone and he suggested a half dozen poems by Burns best suited for children. That night we photocopied the poems and had them ready to distribute in class the next morning. The assignment was to read them at home that evening.

When Donnie arrived Thursday afternoon we were prepared for a most delightful hour. He sang airs, recited poems, and gave the background information on the life and genius of Burns. He eased us through the Scots dialect and shared with us some of Burns's immortal lines: "The best laid schemes o' *Mice* an' *Men* gang aft agley," "A man's a man for a' that." He finished by teaching us "Auld Lang Syne" with Burns's original tune. Melanie picked up the spirit and announced that our Winter Concert would end with this song.

On Wednesday a seven-year-old prospective student came to visit. He had been homeschooled and was looking for a larger academic world. At Fayette the parents were always asked to visit first and see if our school, program, and players fit into their image of possibility for their child. If we passed this test, then the child would visit for a day to see how they felt about our little community. After all they, not the parents, were the customers of this service industry. When children had been homeschooled we watched carefully to see if they were ready to go from a class of one to a school of several dozen, especially if they would be the youngest of the swarm. In this case the parents had liked the school and so we met young Walker. As with most young visitors he was initially reserved in the new setting. We went to the park for soccer, and after watching the boys' game for a few minutes he asked if he could join. Ele and I took this as a good indicator.

At afternoon break Walker said he would like to try the pendulum swing. We had him practice the proper techniques while on the ground, helped him mount the climbing holds on the shed, and had Forest coach him for his first flight. Often the novice's foot would slip out of the webbing loop and then the primate hand reflex would bring them safely to the ground with a skidding landing. The ultimate backup was that the ground in front of the shed had been spaded and covered with a thick layer of wood chips to soften any fall.

Walker's foot did indeed come out and then his hands let go. So much for my reliance on primal instincts. He landed with a thump. We picked him up, brushed him off, and sat him on a bench. All were most concerned and caring. I said crying was OK around here for it sometimes helped. He didn't feel the need. As he was recovering his breath I was getting ready to help him through the emotional shock, but he merely asked how to improve his form so the crash wouldn't happen again. This little guy could be on my team forever. Over the weekend his family would decide if he would join our world.

Thursday I was too ill to both teach my classes and watch the Munchkins around the Big Elm before school and during break, so I closed the tree for the last two days of the week. Not one of the Munchkins whined or complained. I promised them the harnesses on Tuesday of the next week. Young folks are most reasonable if given sufficient explanations and what they consider to be fair treatment.

As it turned out, the change in routine opened up new possibilities for fun and creativity. The school's hacky-sackers were happy to have the space around the Big Elm for their game. With the small size of the school grounds and its many gardens, they usually were forced to play in the few square feet of parking lot behind our vans. Also, Sylvan used the respite from harness swinging to invent a new game: Hold one of the ropes Tarzan style, jump from a large wooden stump, bounce onto our mini-trampoline, hang in the air, and land as far away as possible. This bouncing, suspended long jump became the latest addition to the many varied uses of the tree and ropes. As a result of my cold, the children got to see first hand how apparent adversity can be turned to benefit.

The end of the week brought us to the crux of *Midsummer Night's Dream*. We began each school year with the reading of a Shakespearean play. We would read a scene a day. At the end of each day's scene, new readers would be assigned for the following day and the lines would be practiced at home. We simply read Shakespeare's lines in class – recitation, not memorized performance was our goal. I would interrupt often to speak on the background of theater in Shakespeare's time, ask for modern paraphrasing of various speeches, and lead discussions on the psychology of the various characters, but every line was read by the students. This autumn the magic captured us all, as it did every year. We all were caught by the master, his language, and his development of character and plot. The slow pace allowed time to savor each speech and scene. The class discussions of reality, dreams, sexuality, changes in perception, and the possible realms of nonhuman consciousness were stimulating to all, regardless of their age or reading ability.

Our Shakespearean climax each year was the scene we staged in the Big Elm. *Romeo and Juliet*'s balcony scene had been performed in the tree, as had the ghost scene from *Hamlet*. The branch that anchored the pendulum swing had become known as the "Witches," since that scene from *Macbeth* had been staged there. In two weeks we would be staging the play within the play, *Pyramus and Thisbe*, high in the tree. Already the kids were working out who would play which role, which ropes and harnesses would be needed, and how the movements could be staged safely. After we finished reading the play and performing the scene in the tree, we would rent a video version and view it in class, the only time in the year video would be used in our room.

Friday we had art and singing in the morning instead of the afternoon so Melanie could leave early. The focus of the hour was learning a Bach cantata in several parts, which we would eventually perform in our Winter Concert. In art the assignment was "mirror drawing." Alison had sketched and photocopied line drawings in which she had created the right side of an object. The task was to draw the mirror image on the left. This was an excellent exercise in its own right, but we also did this early in the school year so Marianne would have another indicator of each student's eye-brain-hand functionality.

After students finished this exercise they were free to go out and sketch objects around the school. Dorothy and Rebecca both sketched the back of our van. Dorothy's was within reasonable proportion, but Rebecca's, though well detailed, was extra wide. Marianne later commented she was not surprised the van had been widened in her sketch because Rebecca's eyes didn't converge to a single point of focus, something that had shown up in the mirror drawing. Rebecca would be spending time in Marianne's studio and doing exercises at home to work on the condition.

Since we had sung and drawn in the morning we turned to academics Friday afternoon. By 2:30 none of us had the energy for any more work. I was delighted by our class accomplishments of three weeks. We had gone though the Greek alphabet, upper and lower-case; verbs, nouns, and adjectives for beginning Latin scholars; four acts of *Midsummer Night's Dream*; and prehistory from the earliest beginnings through simple tool making. We had each created a dozen short pieces of writing and learned the capitals and nicknames of half of the states. We had spent many hours swinging around the Big Elm and, most importantly, began forming a tightly knit, harmonious group of teachers and students.

Heather, one of the girls new to my class, asked an excellent question: "Do we work at this pace all year?" I praised her for her question and having the confidence to voice her fear. I drew a time line on the board and showed her the weeks of academic intensity and the weeks of relaxed change of pace. Our theory was that this combination was much better than grinding schoolwork at a constant pace.

I pointed out we had already completed three weeks of the first ten-week period of school. Following this academic block, we would have seven weeks with no academics. We could look forward to our first of two "Parents' Weeks," when parents took the role of the teachers for two hours at a time. This was followed by a week of vacation at Thanksgiving, three intense weeks of handicrafts and concert rehearsal, and then two more weeks of vacation. Forest, wanting to scare Heather and our other new students, reminded all of the dreaded Hard Nine Weeks of the winter months. I countered with the fact that we played long baseball games every afternoon the last month of school. With our new students somewhat relieved, we adjourned to the popcorn bowls. That evening Walker's mother called to say he would be joining our school.

∽ Week Four ∾
Marianne's Studio

*Nothing of fundamental value
can be accomplished through mass instruction,
but only through the careful study and
understanding of the difficulties, tendencies,
and capacities of each child.*

KRISHNAMURTI

TUESDAY MORNING I made my rounds before settling into the classroom: checking gardens, greeting the last few arrivals, touring the area around the Big Elm to see that everyone there was focused and observing all rules of safety. I then peeked into the studio. Six girls were dancing along a rope laid on the floor. Marianne was ordering, "This time walk backward on the left of the rope, even-numbered girls count the next number, odd-numbered girls say the next letter." This was followed by, "1A, 2B, 3C, 4D..." At some point the dance broke down into giggles. Marianne's studio was open for business.

At Fayette we embraced academic course work like most schools. We included art, music, and sports programs, sadly missing in more and more schools. But few schools devoted time, attention, and expertise to tracking each student's neurological development. We did. During the first two weeks of school each student was given a battery of tests to determine their "dominance profiles" – which eye, ear, hand, foot, and brain hemisphere was dominant in their particular configuration. We also tested each student's brain-eye coordination; their level of discerning and differentiating the different phonemes, the building blocks of speech and reading; and whether visual and auditory information was actually triggering mental imagery.

After gathering all this information Marianne created various studio groups. She, Alison, and I then juggled our weekly schedules to minimize conflicts between needed studio sessions and regular classroom curriculum. I didn't want any of my kids to miss the three weekly history lectures and Alison wanted her Munchkins for all French classes, so we scheduled these classes at alternate times, allowing some group to always be available for studio time with Marianne or Tara. Missing one of four math classes a week was fine, so various groups could be pulled from math. After about an hour of discussion and much erasing and rewriting on our three schedules, we arrived at a plan that had the right groups in the studio without anyone missing too much class time.

In the first years of school we had implemented the key concepts of love and safety, and these tenets produced improvement in our students. However, we also saw specific academic blockages in individual kids and did not have ways for direct intervention. Thus we began our study of the work done in this field. The discoveries and theories of the Swiss psychologist Jean Piaget were the foundation of all our work with children's development. He had created excellent maps of the stages of development and perception of childhood, and many of his suggested exercises were included, now in modified form, in Marianne's sessions. Over the years she had attended various workshops in different areas of child development assistance to expand her knowledge base and skills.

The first such class Marianne took was from Dr. Paul Dennison, the founder of educational kinesiology, often called Edu-K or EK. A pioneer in applied brain research, Dennison focused on the interdependence of physical development, language acquisition, and academic achievement. In his work he developed a series of simple and enjoyable body movements, called "Brain Gym™." The commonality of this set of movements was that they all assisted brain-body integration. Since fortunately the brain and body are linked, these movements lead to microadjustments in neurology, which in turn could dramatically accelerate academic progress. In studio and class we all used the exercises of Brain Gym everyday. Some exercises established better internal communication between the hemispheres of the brain, some between the front and back brain regions, and others between top and bottom. Integration of the brain and better connection with the body was the goal of all the work in Marianne's studio.

By the late 1990s different organizations had researched various aspects of human development and performance. Since so much of this work was recent, synthesis of the different theories, exercises, and diagnostics had not yet fully occurred. For example, Brain Gym was effective for brain integration but did not address specific aural or auditory deficiencies. Other disciplines had helpful research and practical information on these areas but had not linked the power of body movement to their exercises. Most of the techniques were designed for one-on-one sessions with a trained specialist and carried the corresponding large hourly fee. Marianne's time in the studio was an ongoing experiment to synthesize the available transforming techniques in sessions that could be done in groups within the structure of a school.

For some reason the human brain-body system gathers information more effectively if some of the internal signals cross the body's vertical midline. The "best" students are left-hemisphere dominant, with dominance in right hand, foot, eye, and ear. All the inputs dance across the midline, registering in the analytical hemisphere. These are the children who upset the grading curve for the rest of us, are often the teachers' pets, and whiz through most of their schoolwork. Many of us have only one or two inputs crossing the midline and we tend to overrely on these sources, too often not properly developing the ones that do not cross the midline. And then there are those termed "blocked dominant," where no dominant pathways cross the midline. This results in the right hand, foot, eye, ear, and hemisphere all trying their darnedest to help the child understand what those symbols on the board of their first-grade classroom really are supposed to mean. These children also spend time trying to figure out why it seems to adults a good idea to have kids sit motionless in a desk all day long. Six of Alison's fourteen Munchkins were blocked dominant.

Identifying children with learning challenges is not hard. Any experienced teacher can walk into a classroom and in less than five minutes identify the ones who will have no trouble in school and those who will never be on track. The challenge is how to help those who do not automatically pick up on the rhythm, symbols, and purpose of school. The communication of eyes and ears with the brain is of primary importance in schooling and educational development. We had created programs of intervention to assist each student in optimizing their own development of these important faculties. Early on we decided that any interventions had to be low tech: strings with colored beads, home-sewn bean bags, computer-generated and hand-lettered wall charts – no fancy machines with flashing lights and graphic readouts. Also the exercises used had to have easily discernible, instantaneous feedback for both teacher and student.

Many school difficulties center around reading. We identified whether the trouble was primarily ear, eye, or brain centered. Visual stress, from large amounts of TV and video gaming or from reading at an early age, can lead to eye strain and imbalanced development. Often very little information is passing through one of the eyes, leading to stress of the other eye. Various of our exercises either strengthened eye muscles or helped the brain to better use the optic signals received.

We also investigated ear-brain communication by tracking the receptivity of the basic components of our communication, the sound phonemes. The word *cat* is a single syllable of three phonemes. In English we use only twenty-six letters but have forty-four phonemes, thereby causing much grief in the young and those struggling with English as a second language. The standard, and for some unsuccessful, approach was to pound the twenty-six letters and their various attached sounds, in the hope that endless repetition by either phonics or sight-reading would bring literacy. A deeper investigation showed that the trouble was often in the retrieval, response, and differentiation of the basic phonemes. We observed that when specific difficulties were identified and repatterned, resistance and frustration in the student disappeared.

Some kids saw accurately and heard all the phonemes well, yet still didn't read for pleasure and when reading aloud used a flat monotone. Often these students recognized the words but were not generating internal visual images. Those having trouble with inner imagery needed sessions focused on creative visualization. Television had made many children passive to the creation of their own imagery; the bright moving images of TV could override natural abilities.

Throughout the school day, small groups were skipping to the studio for "PUBU," our phoneme classes; "VE," vision work; or "VV" the visualization classes. We all did Brain Gym as part of our daily routine. Unlike some schools where the troubled or slow few went to the resource room, at Fayette everyone spent time in one or more studio classes. The few who did not currently have sessions would be in advanced groups later in the year. There was no onus on studio work. We pointed out the difference between developmental blocks, which were quite common, and congenital stupidity, a much rarer occurrence. The students understood this and saw their studio time as an enhancement, not a criticism, of their skills and development.

While we were focusing on the first week of studio work, we were also settling into our school rhythms. By the fourth week our new students had dropped "good behavior in a new environment" and switched to "regular behavior in a familiar one." They had relaxed enough to begin breaking the rules. I never viewed these actions as personal challenges to my imperial edicts. I treated these young ones as junior social scientists who were testing whether school rules and their enforcement were substantive boundaries or chimeras. For example, Wednesday I saw pillows flying in the Munchkins' room before school. "Gentlemen, remember no throwing of pillows," I reminded them. "Go outside if you need to vent some energy before class." They learned that all rules of safety were consistently applied and that Fayette teachers used loving vibes and a calm tone both when students were being good citizens and when they were not. In every interaction we sought to speak positively and teach, not preach. Over time this manner built trusting relationships and an openness of ears and heart not achieved by increased decibels or threats. I saved my stern drill-sergeant voice for situations of possible imminent physical danger.

By now most were comfortable with the Big Elm and its ropes. I started watching for signs of complacency. We began the year with only seven climbing harnesses. This encouraged sharing and made sure we didn't overcrowd the flight paths around the tree. Some of the new Munchkin boys thought they would ignore an important rule: Only harnessed folks swing from the ropes. They attached their belt loops to the ropes with carabiners. This was not as original an idea as they had assumed; I had seen this in past years. Fortunately belt loops are amazingly strong – for a short time and for a body under sixty pounds. In my calmest tone, I decreed that all Munchkin boys were banished from the tree until further notice. I was glad when such scenarios inevitably occurred for they led to subsequent beneficial communications and teaching. The kids learned the useful discrimination between what was safe fun and what was potentially dangerous behavior. I began laying the groundwork toward winning their hearts and minds.

We were fine-tuning all the social aspects that made up the school community. I enjoyed this teaching even more than teaching the fine points of diagraming sentences or the proper procedure for handling messy fractions. An instance with Heather demonstrated our approach. We had a food rule: No candy. Heather asked me if a little bit of chocolate was candy. "In what form is this little bit of chocolate?" "A bag of M&Ms." I pointed out this was definitely over the candy line, but in honor of the way she had so openly asked I thought it would be a waste of good M&Ms to toss them in the compost and told her so. "But please don't bring them again." "Would you like a couple?" she offered. I thanked her but said that since I made the rules I had better follow them most closely.

Our best bonding and teaching went on during our morning and afternoon breaks. And on the soccer field. We had a sports rule: No swearing. Yet young Arlen was repeatedly saying, "Damn," all in self-commentary on his soccer abilities. I joined him in his wanderings around the soccer field and reminded him not to swear during the games. With a look of sincere amazement only a child could have he said, "I didn't know *damn* was a swear word." I pointed out that I was a bit old fashioned but in my book *darn* was the last non-swear word and *damn* the first on the list of "seven words we don't use." For the rest of the game he followed my desire.

By the end of the fourth week of classes, all school systems were up and running. Our task was now to maintain them with optimal intensity for six more weeks.

✺ Week Five ✺
Games and Animal Friends

A school should be the most beautiful place in every town and village – so beautiful that the punishment for undutiful children should be that they be debarred from going to school the following day.

OSCAR WILDE

IF OUR NATURAL WORLD were devoid of other species and our adult years were to be spent in windowless buildings, surrounded by asphalt, being told by our group leader the proper focus for every minute, I would have designed our school to model this sterile oppressive scenario. Fortunately some of us still have the possibility of inhabiting a richer, freer, more diverse reality.

Our school gardens and grounds were inhabited by many nonhuman citizens. During our twenty years as guardians of this small corner of the biosphere, we had used no pesticides or other toxins. The garden beds were home to unnumbered earthworms and a wide variety of insects living in a stable balance. Spiders were much admired and protected citizens in our corner of the world; several large golden orb weavers could be found every year under their favorite eaves. Each spring we all eagerly watched for egg sacks to burst, releasing thousands of little weavers. When we found the occasional black widow she was carefully transported to a nearby vacant field.

One day during history lecture, a wolf spider walking on the ceiling began a rappel directly over Lauren's head. Many in the room saw what was happening but not Lauren, who, looking for the source of distraction, scanned the room but not overhead. After a moment she caught on to the event and without an "eek" or twitch snagged the silken rappel rope on her pencil. She passed the strand over to Amani, who transferred it to her pencil and on to mine. I anchored the web on my bench and kept talking about tools of the Stone Age without missing a beat. In past years similar events had often emptied a quarter of the room. We had learned to admire, not fear, our spider friends.

Our dogs and cat were even more beloved. Max, our ancient, deaf, and nearly blind Airedale, had put in his years of active play and companionship, and now mostly slept in the sun and received an occasional pat on the head. He was the only male Airedale I had ever known who had never been in a fight nor bitten a person. In a few months or years he would be teaching us about death – with the same grace and dignity he had brought to life.

Annie, our seven-year-old fox terrier, had a quite different role at school. Her first responsibility was to remind everyone to close the gates leading to the outside world. She readily found any open gate and used the opportunity to escape toward nearby vacant fields and busy streets. Her second responsibility was to make everyone laugh and become infected with her constant joy of life. Her third job, lunch-box patrol, had been reinforced by Buddy, Alison's Boston bull terrier.

The previous school year Buddy had come into Alison's and the school's life after a puppyhood of abuse. He dragged a front paw but miraculously his valiant spirit had been unharmed. Any lunches not returned to the proper shelves were consumed by Annie and Buddy. They even teamed up to open zippers on the modern soft lunch boxes.

Xylo, our cat, had appeared in my wood yard the year before and immediately became a hardworking member of the staff. Many students looked to spend time before school or at break with one or another of the animals. These moments of quiet caring were excellent practice in sending loving-kindness toward all living beings, even toward that twitchy little boy often elbowing you during math hour.

Mice were also occasional citizens of our buildings and gardens. We didn't mind a few but did not encourage them to overpopulate. Xylo was a help with this task, but our best assistance came from the several large bull snakes living in the rock walls of the gardens. On quiet warm weekend days we would find them out sunning or hunting. Sightings on school days were rare, however, and brought great excitement. In addition we had many birds, local and migratory, who drank and bathed in our small pond and its waterfall. Sparrows enjoyed Friday popcorn as much as did the children. Any spilled by the kids was gone by 4:00. Pieces and crumbles of lunches left after the Annie and Buddy patrol were also consumed. We had very clean grounds.

At times we were surprised by a new guest. Tuesday at the end of school, Amelia asked if the turtle in the pond was real or a statue. Having no knowledge of either, several students and I investigated. It definitely was not a statue, since statues don't disappear under water at the approach of a crowd. We had several more sightings over the next few days. We were doubting that he could live through the winter there but thought we could have him hang around a couple more weeks. He had different ideas. Friday, as a group of kids headed to the studio for vision sessions, they found him walking across the yard. We took him to the local pet shop and found he was a twelve-year-old western painted water turtle, not native to this region and not suited to the environment. Amazingly, the shop had a ten-year-old female seeking a mate. As of this writing the couple could be visited during shop hours.

Our favorite mascot, soon to shed this status, was Coleman, Tara's five-year-old son. He joined the school four days after his birth. He was friend to all and our best ambassador-at-large. Every school should have young ones around. For some mysterious reason, acting like a jerk is harder when an innocent one is watching wide eyed. The following year Coleman would be a regular Munchkin holding to our regimented schedule, so we were all enjoying his last year as team mascot. By self-direction he roamed from Alison's room to my classes and through Marianne's studio. He often rolled in for my history lectures, listening intently and occasionally adding his views. This week we were talking about the early hominid's evolutionary split from the other primates and their various differences. He reminded us that gorillas had disposable thumbs.

In addition to having many animal friends, our school was also a place filled with games. This week, with the return of autumn weather, the jump ropes emerged from storage. Marianne led the jump roping, a job that required little encouragement. Hearing those decades-old jumping chants and the beat of the rope on the bricks brought satisfaction to veteran jumpers. Most of the new students had never jumped before, but after a few days they too were regulars. Card games and chessboards could be found at off times in corners of the rooms, on garden decks, and on the sidewalk in front of the school. I was master of cards, always kibitzing hands and giving tips on strategy for the various games. Finding someone alone before school gave me time to gain a new convert to one of several little-known versions of solitaire.

I held the belief that only the standard fifty-two card deck, ace through king, clubs through spades, was needed for any worthwhile card game. No gimmicks, please. However, this stance had been shot down with the invasion of the Japanese Pokémon card craze. Even Coleman now had his minideck in hand. Throughout the school day various groups were playing or admiring collections of cards. They were sharing, enjoying, reading character names, discussing the rules. I had no complaints. For those not petting animals, jumping rope, or hunkering down and dealing, there was always the Big Elm with its many ropes.

At Fayette students didn't talk much about TV shows or movies. Our world was rich and varied, containing sufficient activities to occupy us during our time together. Children greeted each other on the bricks in the morning with talk of which section in their Latin lessons they had finished the night before or what had happened in the chapter of *Harry Potter* they were reading as they fell asleep. This week roles, props, and staging for *Pyramus and Thisbe* were being discussed and finalized, for Thursday was the performance in the Big Elm.

Our classes were moving along more smoothly this year than in any previous years. Algebra and Latin were going especially well. When anyone needed help, another student was present with a clear explanation. I had observed that the more one knew about a subject the easier it was to add new information. The beginners were not yet in this fortunate position, so much help from Ele and the older students was needed for the novices to overcome the first hurdles of algebraic equations and Latin verb endings. In contrast, when the time arrived for a new concept for the most advanced group, only a few minutes and a few lines on the board were needed, and they headed off for intense problem solving. We made sure not to abandon the beginners in any subjects. After a few months they too would have a body of knowledge and the scholarly techniques needed for adding new bits to their own internal model and would no longer be rookies needing shepherding. In future years some of them would be the shepherds for a new flock.

With class going so well I spent much of the algebra hour wandering around the school observing everyone in their fine demonstration of team learning. I also sat at the computer in my office generating new pages of algebra word problems. These were one of my favorite parts of the curriculum because any student who could master such feared and at first inscrutable work could not doubt their abilities and accomplishments. You might be only eleven years old, not totally solid on all the multiplication tables and still a bit shaky on messy lowest common denominators, but you knew you could solve word problems in algebra. Later in the year we would call on this confidence when we faced those tables and denominators. In past years the first year students worked their way through about sixty word problems, but this year I tripled the number of word problems in our course.

For years everyone had battled a sheet called Number Problems: *There are three numbers such that the second is twice the first and the third is one less than three times the first. If the sum of the numbers is 71, find the largest number.* I loved the way these stopped a brain until approached step-by-step, word-by-word with the correct strategy. Through the magic of our computer and laser printer and a little of my time, we now had two more sheets: More Number Problems and Even More Number Problems. We would not merely be proficient but true masters by the time we had solved all of these. I also tripled the number of Perimeter Problem and Coin Problem sheets: *When Coleman counted the money in his piggy bank, he found that he had $3.75 in nickels, dimes, and quarters. There were three more dimes than quarters, and twice as many nickels as dimes. How many dimes did he have?*

I enjoyed teaching mathematics because as it was so purely intellectual – opinion and emotion had little or no place. I equally enjoyed teaching history because it was so embedded with human polarities. The week we began the school year and our history of early hominids, the Kansas Board of Education had voted to endorse creationism and remove support for the evolution theory. This week the New Mexico board voted the opposite way. What had happened to free exchange of thought? At Fayette we continued to discuss *all* possibilities. Jackson's alien theory, presented the first week of school, still was in the lead – I suspect because it was the most outrageous and adolescents enjoy the freedom of holding to the outrageous. As for God and creation, in our Winter Concert we would sing in Hebrew, verses from the first chapter of Genesis; in Latin class we would translate the first chapter from the Latin vulgate text; and during the Hard Nine Weeks our sacred text study was to be the Bible, beginning with Genesis. I was grateful no school board could interfere with our freedom of information.

Thursday afternoon arrived with good weather and enough of a breeze to make theater time in the branches of the tree exciting but not dangerous. Maggie was to be Bottom, the star of the play, but she was absent. Forest noted that this fit nicely with Bottom's absence in *Midsummer Night's Dream*. James quipped that he hoped she wouldn't show up with donkey ears the next day. Ah, Shakespeare-based humor in the age of Homer Simpson.

As the staff and all the Bigs not in the play gathered around the Big Elm, Jessica, Maggie's understudy, jumped, or rather harnessed, into the role. We were ready to begin the play. Jonah, Jessica's fraternal twin, was playing Moon, and we hauled him to the high pulley in the upper branches of the tree, tying the rope to our anchor post. He held a piece of styrofoam for the moon. Forest climbed to a high branch to deliver Thisbe's lines. Cina, new to the school and never having climbed, was Wall and found herself for the first time in her life having climbed twenty feet off the ground, a copy of Shakespeare tucked into her climbing harness. Matthew, our stage and safety director, had the overview from the high-traverse rope. He made sure Cina was double-clipped into protecting ropes and continuing to breathe. Others in the class were perched on the sheds and walls around the Big Elm. The play began.

James gave a flawless reading of the prologue, while Forest used a falsetto voice that set the perfect tone for Thisbe and the zaniness of the play. Cina was excellent as Wall, though the audience detected a small quaver in her voice. Jonah swung around effectively as Moon. Halfway through the play the Munchkins came out for their break, craning necks skyward. Since we had a four-year cycle of Shakespeare plays, four years in the future some of them would be Bigs and players in this same scene. Reese swung and roared as Lion; Pyramus and Thisbe died. It was a great play all around.

The drama over, one by one the cast descended. Cina breathed deeply for the first time in a half hour. Everyone headed off for snack and a recap of the funnier moments of the production. Jonah, sensing abandonment, called from the top of the tree for someone to let him down. Rachel, a new Munchkin, whose previous schooling had been most proper and sedate, was standing next to me as I unwrapped the rope from the anchor. I told her to carefully watch what was going to happen next. I let the rope run freely through my fingers; Jonah dropped like a rock. At the last moment I gripped the rope,

and he came to a stop a foot from the ground. Rachel's eyes were huge. She, being a young and innocent child, did not consider that next Thursday the Munchkins would be in the tree all day. We would begin their day by hauling each of them to the high pulley and giving each a gentle version of "the drop." We strongly felt that the experiences of school should be more than quietly sitting in desks and properly gripping a pencil.

Friday morning, with all the jump roping and Pokémon games, the Big Elm was empty, so Sophie and Nyssa took the opportunity to try something no Munchkins had yet attempted: the pendulum swing in tandem. I monitored their preparations for the first flight.

They each donned a climbing harness, double-checking their buckles, webbing, and carabiners. Nyssa climbed the shed first, then Sophie threw the rope up and joined her. They supported each other as they clipped into the pendulum loop. At the count of three both stepped off the shed. The thrill was not just double, but probably increased by the square, making the flight four times as exciting as a solo swing. The teamwork and shared trust were marvelous lessons. The two repeated the tandem swing at least twenty times during the day. When in the classroom, teachers defined what, when, and how the students would do their work. Before and after school and at breaktime, however, Fayette was the ultimate free school.

While Nyssa and Sophie completed their final swings of the day, we prepared for the celebration of Kyrie's birthday. I was kilted for the occasion; Kyrie had requested I wear my Gunn tartan, not my MacKay. Early in the day I had learned that Dorothy and Miranda were planning to surprise Kyrie with a puppy. As the secret was whispered around the school, I doubted the surprise could hold until the end of the day. Time would tell. When 3:00 came, I escorted Kyrie to the Birthday Rock, and on the count of three all sang "Happy Birthday." We lined up for cupcakes, oldest to youngest since Kyrie was in the Bigs' class. (We reversed the order when the birthday was in the Munchkins' room.) When the event appeared to be over, Dorothy and Miranda brought the puppy from around the corner. From the smile on Kyrie's face, I knew no one had revealed the secret. From the smile on my face, all could tell how pleased I was with all players and events of the week.

◈ Week Six ◈
Autumn Climbing Week

For climbing, two things are needed: enthusiasm and clear thinking. . . . the two qualities may appear contradictory, but are in fact complementary.

GASTON REBUFFAT

WE STRUCTURED the school schedule so we never fell into the monotony of unvaried routine. Sometimes the changes were subtle: switching from our regular singing hour to preparation for our two annual concerts or varying soccer by adding an extra ball or two to the game. Climbing Week, on the other hand, was a major break in our patterns, shattering any possible monotony. The Bigs had three days around the Big Elm and the Munchkins one. By Friday popcorn we were all ecstatic, exhausted, and filled with physical, mental, and emotional experiences we would remember decades from now.

Five years before, when we acquired the city lot and buildings adjoining the school, we added Tara's home, Marianne's studio, and the Big Elm to our domain. Pete and I removed many of the tree's branches, opening up the space for climbing and rappelling. Where we wished foot and handholds we hammered small wooden blocks to the trunk. We then tied to the larger branches lengths of differently colored climbing ropes with fixed loops for self-belaying protection and also strung rope traverses. In effect we sculpted a wood and nylon climbing environment.

In the past years our climbing program had been held on a rock six miles from school. We drove there only a few days a year, and only one person climbed at a time. That person was belayed by me. The other students waited on the ground for their turn on the rock. Having a tree on the school grounds changed our climbing routine. With the tree, we wished to design a self-belay system so more could climb at the same time, relying solely on themselves. After much talk of how to create a one hundred percent fail-safe system, Pete and I settled on each climber having attached to their climbing harness two loops of webbing, one red and another blue, each with a locking carabiner. "Where is your red clipped?" I would query, "Where are you going to clip blue?" "I have red clipped into the rainbow rope and after the next step I'm clipping blue into the orange rope," the student would call down. With up to ten climbers in the tree at a time, group communication and coordination developed naturally: "I need purple to get to the high traverse. Can you clip into the orange rope so I can get by?" Over this last weekend I had checked all the ropes, knots, harnesses, and routes in preparation for this year's Autumn Climbing Week.

The Bigs were divided into two groups: one climbed in the morning, while the other was in class. They switched at lunch. We began this Climbing Week, as always, with a lecture on the fundamentals: the terms, techniques, and principles of safety. We had rappels, numbered *uno* through *quatro*, rigged in the tree. We began with our more experienced climbers tying on to my belay and quickly executing *numero uno*. Their demonstration provided the others with a model of rappelling efficiency. After each of our experts had completed the first rappel, they donned a harness and headed to the upper reaches of the tree for self-protected climbing and rappelling. The others worked one by one on assembling the proper gear, then climbing up fifteen feet to "First Notch." They experienced the strange stability of leaning out into space, relying on their own balance, nylon, and high-tech alloy to descend to the ground in a controlled manner.

In an hour all ten members of the group had completed rappel *uno*, and we repeated the exercise from "Second Notch," ten feet higher in the tree. *Numero dos* required a more difficult climb and was more awkward than *uno*. After three hours all had completed both tasks, some several times, and many had spent some time free climbing.

A few, not yet comfortable with climbing, did not leave the ground, spending their time observing the struggles and successes of others.

Sessions in Marianne's studio would help their climbing skills in addition to their academic work. Invariably those not comfortable in the tree had poor integration of eyes and brain. They were not less brave than others but rather were responding most sanely to their level of neural development. After a half-hour lunch break the groups switched, and by the end of the day all participants had added to their climbing proficiency. During breaks the Munchkins gathered around watching the activities, knowing Thursday would be their day in the tree.

Wednesday's tasks were the rappels of *tres* and *quatro*, higher and highest. Though the climbs were more difficult and the ground much farther away, the rappels themselves were easier. After the step away from the tree, the rest of the descent was spent suspended in air. These were called free rappels. Heather had been absent Tuesday, and besides missing the introduction of the second declension in Latin she had missed the first two rappels. She boldly joined the group on the second day and became the first student to rappel *tres* and *quatro* without the practice on the lower ones. The few who were not yet comfortable with heights spent their time swinging around the lower reaches of the tree. This second day challenged each member of the group. On Tuesday we had blasted *Best of the Beach Boys* throughout the day to help pump up the energy, but on this second day the unanimous vote was to focus in silence.

Thursday brought Munchkin climbing, always a great day. Six hours with fourteen seven- to ten-year-olds up to thirty feet above the ground was a day of great neurological development for the kids and intense focus for Alison and me, their climbing guides. We began by having a couple of the Big girls secure each Munchkin in a climbing harness for their turn at the "hoist." One at a time the Munchkins were clipped to the rope passing through our highest belay pulley in the top branches of the tree. A team of Bigs hauled each to the pulley, forty feet above the ground. As each Munchkin ascended I took up the slack and anchored the rope passing through our belay system.

Every Munchkin spent a few minutes high above the neighborhood answering questions shouted up to them. "How's the mountain look?" "What's on the neighbor's roof?" "Is the neighbor's dog in the backyard?" Most answers were monosyllabic but a few whose whole brains were still engaged waxed poetic.

The descent was by the "spongy drop" witnessed the week before by Rachel. I would play out a couple feet of rope and then hold tight. The dynamic climbing rope gave a springy drop. As each Munchkin returned to the ground the next was clipped in for a trip to the top. Rachel went up and down, not truly enjoying the experience. Possibly by Spring Climbing Week she would have a different view.

After the Munchkins had had their free rides, the real climbing and further lessons began. Each practiced the tying of a bowline knot around the waist and through questions, answers, and demonstration established the confidence that whatever they did in the tree, the rope and I would hold them safely. A few minutes spent reviewing the gear and techniques required for climbing up and rappelling down, and they were ready for several hours of pushing against fears.

Alison was anchored in First Notch. Each Munchkin climbed up to her while I held them tightly on belay. With her quiet words of confidence they attached the carabiner and belay ring to the rappel rope and, against the advice of the voices in their brain, they leaned back and began descending the tree. I would never tire of watching such young ones begin a day in fear and after a rappel or two start to enjoy the activity. Each Munchkin watched friends go through this transformation. They cheered each other, adding to group unity and climbing proficiency.

After a rappel or two showing the proper technique to the others, the more accomplished climbers put on harnesses and spent the rest of the time free climbing high in the tree. Two messages were communicated: I trusted them to always be clipped into safety loops, and no one would be with them to hold their hand. For some ten-year-olds this was pushing the envelope of their self-reliance. However, every climbing day was different. This day had three ten-year-old boys ascend to the top branches and not come down for two hours. At lunchtime we sent their lunches up on ropes.

The great value of time in the Big Elm was that strengths and weaknesses quite different from those of our classroom personas manifested. Daniel had had a frustrating school life before coming to us. He had developed an adaptive conditioning of spacing out and appearing quite dull in the classroom. We had seen enough small signs to feel this to be a thin veneer covering many fine abilities. As we had suspected he had a completely different persona in the tree. Climbing, being a whole-body activity and one with no preconditioning in his previous schooling, didn't trigger any of his defensive patterns seen in the classroom. He demonstrated total understanding of the systems and routes, and embraced his classmates with a commander's energy. He helped others, shouted encouragement to timid climbers, and was relaxed hanging in his harness below the branches. One of these days, we knew, he would transfer this stance to the classroom and sail through the rest of his school years.

While some of the boys were isolated in the upper reaches, several of the girls were evolving their uses of the pendulums. Whereas the Big boys usually tried to crank the biggest swings possible, the Munchkin girls were exploring gentle swinging on several different ropes strung side by side. They moved in small arcs with much joining of hands. This was real swing dancing. We had a great day combining all the lessons of climbing technique and proper equipment use with creative spontaneous play. After a day of tracking the safety of these little ones, both Alison and I were filled with joy, tired in body, and mentally exhausted.

Somewhere in your reading the thought may have crossed your mind, "How much did insurance for such activities cost?" It didn't cost a penny! No one would issue a reasonably priced policy to cover the liability of such a unique school activity. So before I threw the first rope to the first student, now so many years ago, I sat in long solitary contemplation. I concluded that if I were not absolutely one hundred percent certain all injury beyond a few scrapes and bruises could be avoided, we should not consider any climbing. Having an insurance company hand a sizable check to a mother who had lost a child while under my care would not be an acceptable compensation.

How to assure this absolute safety? First, to rely on the innate heightened sanity of humans when high above the level ground. No child in our program had ever made a silly move while in tree or on rock – not one in more than ten years. They would act up in class, even occasionally while crossing the street, but never while roped. Second, to have a simple inviolate system where ropes, harnesses, and webbing protected the climber, never got them into trouble. Third, I would always be in the center of the activity with my full attention. So we had entered climbing and so we continued that year. The insurance was the thinking, feeling, and acting of everyone involved.

Friday brought our final day of Climbing Week with the Bigs again embraced by the Big Elm. Instead of having any defined schedule I instructed each group to harness up, free climb, and rappel for their two hours in the tree. Scanning a tree and seeing ten kids talking, hanging, swinging, totally relaxed together, many more than thirty feet off the ground, was a sublime experience.

For the final ninety minutes of Climbing Week, all the Bigs gathered around the tree. After the relatively tame nature of the past four days, the time had arrived to finish with wild action. Several years before while I was monitoring the kids climbing, a crazy idea popped into my head. One person would climb the tree with a rope secured to his harness that was passed through the highest pulley and then back to the ground, where it was tied to a lighter person standing in the doorway of the studio. When the climber jumped out of the tree, the one on the ground would rocket through the air ending with several pendulum swings. With knots correctly positioned, the two wouldn't collide but fly past each other. We named this activity "jungle ball." Experimenting showed that a twenty-pound weight difference gave a slow and uninteresting flight, while a forty-pound difference produced a fast, exciting, but safe ride. We tried a sixty-pound difference, but only once!

Michiah, our heaviest student, was absent on this day. Knowing we would call on him to be the "ball" and repeatedly leap from a stance fifteen feet off the ground, he chose to miss a day of school. Thus James, our second heaviest, became the first ball. Each of the lighter kids waited in line to clipped on and fly. Unlike the "static line" of paratroopers, this was a very "dynamic line"! The ball didn't merely fall out of the tree, but had to jump out about six feet to clear the path of the "flyer." This was one of the small details we had discovered when we tested our systems with Pete's drunken young adults.

The time came for the first launch. James leapt, Miranda flew. Fellow students ran to haul her back to the doorway and others helped James up the tree for a second launch. Switching flyers after each two flights we were able to launch many of the class. Eventually James became too tired to climb the tree again. Forest relieved him and we lost ten pounds of ball. Also, the flyers were becoming heavier so the flights were not as exciting. The half-dozen boys and girls combing and braiding each other's hair on the tool shed hardly turned to look at these flights.

But that was not the end of the afternoon's thrills. The energy around jungle ball always created a frenzy and people would think of things they'd never consider in their normal rest state. Amelia suggested she and Briana try a "dual ball." This was the same Amelia who the year before as a new student had never wanted to be in the tree, hated rappelling, and thought jungle ball quite insane. Oh, the difference of a year and a frenzied afternoon. She and Briana climbed together, clipped onto the rope, jumped, and launched classmates. Time after time.

Two o'clock brought an end to jungle ball and Climbing Week. We headed for the studio and an hour of singing. Though we were all exhausted, we sounded strong of voice – the adrenaline carried over. Personally, I found focusing on singing difficult. After four days of watching every student's movements in the tree, my mind wanted to relax and unwind. But the hour went by as hours do. As the relief at the end of another safe Climbing Week settled in, we each enjoyed a few handfuls of popcorn, our feet firmly on the ground.

Week Seven

Writing

*To me education is a leading out of
what is already there in the pupil's soul.*

MURIEL SPARK

WE HAD BEEN in school long enough by the seventh week that our regular rhythms were being reinforced by the repetitions of familiar tasks. Our writing exercises of the previous weeks were paying off. The foundation of our writing classes was the belief that each person had an Inner Voice, eager to dictate endless writing if only we would take time to establish a working relationship. We coached never to let fear become a choking editor. Most importantly, we wrote often.

At Fayette everyone wrote. Any new student looking around the room during writing time would see others intently applying pencil to paper. During writing sessions the teachers would help the creative flow with reminders to the class: "This is not a spelling test. Just sound out the word and keep going," followed by, "Don't worry about awkwardness – you can change words later." Only after each student was comfortable and convinced they too were a writer did we mention the links between writing hour, spelling tests, and grammar sessions. Especially for the Munchkins these different activities were not integrated until well into the school year.

Over the years we had established several specific writing exercises and assignments that we found helped each student become a better writer. The first was called "five-minute writing." We learned this years ago when Natalie Goldberg, a nationally known teacher of writing workshops, spent an hour with our class. We used this technique many times at the beginning of the year and occasionally throughout the remainder of the year. The rules were simple. A single "seed" word was written on the board, for example, "shoes," "closets," "sisters," "frogs." In silence, with the seed word held in mind, the students were to keep their pencils moving for five minutes no erasing, no asking questions, merely recording the words the Voice whispered. At the end of the writing time four to six students would read their papers. Some writings would be rather linear accounts close to the topic word. Poems would sometimes appear. Occasionally lists of words all beginning with the first letter of the seed word would fill the paper. Often the topic was mentioned in the first sentence and then the stream of words drifted far away. All these were excellent five-minute writings since the goal was to give as much freedom as possible to the mind-pencil link. Two or three cycles could be completed during a half-hour writing session. Through a mysterious process, these writing exercises both freed the creative energies and assisted in strengthening the more formal structure of standard writing.

Five-minute writing was analogous to calisthenics for a football team – they were useful exercises but should never be confused with the game itself. As with football, the next step was to work on the fundamentals of the game, in this case the fundamental unit of writing, the paragraph. For the Munchkins, we let their writing flow with only a casual mention of this specific structure. In contrast, the Bigs devoted the first ten weeks of each school year to a rigorous study of the paragraph. Every Tuesday each student chose one of three suggested topics. The thirty possible topics included, "How to Set the Dinner Table," "Why Curfew Is (or Is Not) Needed for Teenagers," "Five Thrilling Moments in the Big Elm." We rotated through narrative, descriptive, argumentative, and expository paragraphs. All topics touched interests in student lives and allowed for a range of style and focus, from serious description to comical parody.

The students thought about each topic a few minutes, then wrote quickly. At the following writing session each author reviewed their own work and applied more thought. We thought that writing was not a mere snapshot or quick sketch of a string of ideas; mature reasoned thought on a subject came in reaction to first drafts. Revision was the crucial skill. I demanded words be crossed out or added and for much scratching to appear on early drafts. Only then was the paragraph rewritten and turned in. Over the weekend Ele and I would read each, making as few red marks as possible to move the paragraph toward standard English, proper syntax, and overall strength. No grades were ever assigned, but we always wrote a few words of praise. The paragraph was then written a third and final time while a new paragraph was also in the works. As finished paragraphs were handed in, many were read aloud in class by Ele or me, never revealing the author. The class then spent a few minutes analyzing the strengths and weaknesses of each piece using the principles of unity, coherence, emphasis, variety, and adequate development as our standard. This sequence repeated for ten weeks created writers comfortable expressing desired thought in intelligible form.

During the coming winter months the Bigs would expand their writing skills through multiparagraph essays on opinions each writer held passionately. We looked forward to practicing the beginning of research report writing through note taking and writing the rough drafts of two short reports. During this same time the Munchkins would work on reports about small, cuddly animals, famous people, and occasionally the history of a state or country. Our mantra was, write lots, write freely, write from the heart, write listening to the Inner Voice.

Time not spent in the classroom with a teacher was spent outside with minimal direct supervision. We had three breaks from class during the day: a first break at midmorning, a lunchtime break before sports at the park, and an afternoon break. Time for some food, hanging out with friends, and occasionally testing the boundaries and rules of our small community. Two rules were no weapons, real or pretend, and no running.

Tuesday's morning break found a pack of young gentlemen leaping walls, racing around, using sticks from the woodyard as guns. On the positive side, the Big boys were relating to the Munchkin lads;

unfortunately, what they were modeling was not desired school behavior. This early in the school year I hadn't achieved a critical mass of trust and goodwill with the new young boys, so I sent them off for quiet snacking while I met with the older gentlemen.

The Big boys and I settled into a discussion. Matt brought up the excellent question of what was the difference between all the wild activities I encouraged around the Big Elm and a little stick pointing shoot 'em up? This seemed such a rich topic that I postponed our scheduled history lecture so could we devote the next hour of class to the subject, with boys' views, girls' views, and my view being exchanged, examined, questioned, restated, and better understood. Maggie pointed out the difference between the tree activities and shoot 'em up was that any fool could play cops and robbers, but to be in the tree required mental focus, physical control, and emotional discipline. I stressed the point that the activity of running around with toy guns was in itself not a bad activity, merely not part of our school program, just as bathing was a fine and at times recommended activity, but not part of most schools' curriculum. Since punishment and blame were not part of the agenda and understanding by all was the goal, such class sessions were time well spent, had long-term positive value, and allowed for the introduction of new behavioral models.

I had been musing on a future lecture concerning demeanor, and this seemed the perfect time to introduce a new concept. A. S. Neill of Summerhill School felt all boys needed to go through, as he called it, a "Gangster" phase on their path to healthy Freudian adulthood. Possibly in England of the 1920s this had been true; I didn't know. However, in America of the 1990s I had sought to encourage other pathways for our young gentlemen. My speech was titled "Gangster versus Warrior." Returning to the activities in the Big Elm, I showed how the steadiness of the Warrior archetype was needed to move safely and deal with fear. In my opinion, every climb in the tree added an energy that could be tapped as a source of strength through the rest of life. I posited that, by contrast, after a session of gunning and running, an expression of the Gangster archetype, one might feel a release but not an addition of energy or experience.

Labels are powerful, labels with substance behind them most powerful. A long lecture by a teacher on morals and ethics might soon be forgotten or at least filed in the deep recesses of the brain. Short catchy phrases, on the other hand, tended to remain active in a person's thoughts. By the end of the week I had heard discussions during several breaks about Warrior and Gangster behavior. I was most grateful those young gentlemen had jumped the wall with sticks in hand, thus creating the prologue for these new concepts.

Wednesday brought another Scots singer to the school. Deirdre MacMahon studied and preserved the Gaelic working songs of western Scotland. Quickly song sheets were produced in readiness for the afternoon. With Melanie we always sat or stood in stillness as we sang. With Deirdre, however, we were moving as we sang. Since the songs were communal working songs, we imitated shoveling, hoeing, stretching of fabric in time to her singing of verses and our joining in the choruses. We experienced the ancient union of song and work. After the work songs we sang for her several of the Gaelic songs we knew, ending with "Amazing Grace." She gathered a small group around her and taught them an old harmony to accompany the standard melody.

In *Vom Kreig*, Clausewitz reminded us that no plan survived the first moments of action. Though I was fortunate to be in a school and not on a battlefield, I still held to his maxim. I began each week with a detailed schedule of classes and assignments, but was always ready to bend to the unexpected or chance event. Tuesday's discussion and Wednesday's singing had not been part of the weekly schedule. As furthersome, to use an old Scots word, as our regular classes were, unplanned hours brought a spontaneity and were long remembered.

That evening I was rewriting my class schedule for the remainder of the week, trying to cover the topics missed due to our unscheduled events, when Melanie called and said another singer would be joining us Thursday. When it rains it pours, even in this high desert. John Cohen, American folk singer and music archivist, would be dropping in to share his stories and old vocal, banjo, and guitar tunes from Appalachia.

While Deirdre had sung with only the Bigs, as our Munchkins didn't know Gaelic, John wished to sing with all the children. So instead of using the studio, we assembled in our largest room, my classroom. To fit all teachers and students in the space the smallest Munchkins sat on the laps of Bigs. John had a packed and attentive audience. The day before, Deirdre had shared centuries-old Scottish songs. Now John shared songs from the descendants of those folks who had immigrated to this country. This was a powerfully demonstrated lesson in history and culture, done through song, linked by serendipity.

Three of the fathers in the school were banjo players and lovers of folk music. I was hoping one or two of them would be picking up their children after school. To my delight all three were there. As each parked I ran up and announced that John Cohen was in the school finishing an hour and a half with the kids. Each dad said the same thing, "*The* John Cohen?" and then rushed into the school to speak with an idol and legend they thought they would never meet. When four banjo pickers gathered and swapped stories a great time was guaranteed.

Friday did not bring any singers so we returned to academics, but the day did bring more Scots, a doctor and his family from the Isle of Skye. He had been studying our state's programs of rural medicine. They had heard of our school and its Scots connections and wished their two children to visit for a day. Our young guests had a marvelous time in class and enjoyed playing soccer at the park, but they were transfixed by the Big Elm. We were informed no tree on their island was as large as ours. Soon they were swinging fearlessly from the shed, the younger one using a harness for safety.

Walker was watching as he ate a snack, and I thought this a good time to get him back on the swing after his hard landing a few weeks before. With a harness for security, he swung several times. The young ones were still swinging as parents arrived. Though kids from various cultures may have noticed differences, both Walker's mom and our visiting mother had the same reaction of discomfort as they watched their wee ones fly through the air.

Noticing this, I came down from the shed to say a few good words about Walker's fortitude. His mother reciprocated by sharing with me a view of evenings at home. Every night Walker and his folks took a few minutes for their daily "Fayette meeting." The night before he had reported on various activities of the day and added his commentaries: "I don't always know what is happening, so many things happen every day. But the teachers are always nice. The kids are mostly nice; when they are not, it is very quick and then they are nice again." We bid a good weekend to all students and retired to our local pub with our Scots guests to hoist a few pints of microbrew inspired by the beers of their homeland.

ᴥ Week Eight ᴪ
Latin, Greek, and French

*I would make them all learn English:
and then I would let the clever ones learn Latin as
an honor, and Greek as a treat.*

WINSTON S. CHURCHILL

DAYS WHEN ILLNESS kept me from my classroom Marianne and Alison filled the time with extra hours of Latin and Greek. This week was to bring more hours of these noble languages than any other in the school's history. Sunday had been the annual walkathon for Santa Fe's private schools. I was completing a five-year term as overall coordinator. The most critical time was just before the opening ceremonies, when our safety monitors needed to be directed to their locations. I was racing around on my bicycle, thinking of many things having to do with the event and paying no attention to the fact I was on a bike at high speed. I never saw the unmarked speed bump in the shade. The bike stopped; I continued eighteen feet in the air, landing on my face and right hand.

Upon sitting up I popped my dislocated shoulder into the socket, levered my front teeth back into a reasonable position, walked, dripping blood, back to the center of activity, and collapsed in the men's bathroom, awaiting the inevitable shock and concussion. Soon a young man discovered me and sent for the doctor monitoring our event. I'd thought that with a bit of a wipe off and a day's rest, I'd be ready for school on Tuesday. However, the physician's learned opinion was that we were talking weeks and months, not hours and days. I saw hours of Latin and Greek in the Bigs' future.

Every year Marianne led the Bigs through a rigorous Latin course that included grammar, translation, reading, and writing of short stories in Latin – a program of depth demanding great scholarship. Over the years she had developed her own course and written hundreds of pages of Latin exercises. The foundation was the weekly *grammatica*. These sequentially structured grammar lessons each added another concept to the body of knowledge. Grammatica One introduced first-conjugation verbs beginning with the oft remembered "*amo, amas, amat.*" Somewhere between Grammatica Seven and Ten every student would hit the wall. Adding new declensions and such nasty concepts as the genitive and dative brought each student to a stop, indicating it was time to regroup by turning to the many review lessons.

The Bigs were divided into different levels depending on the number of years they had sat at the feet of Marianne. Alphas were first-year students, Betas second-year, followed by Gammas and the occasional small group of Deltas. Every year an Alpha would ask, after a few weeks of Latin and Greek, why we used Greek letters to designate Latin groups. A Gamma or Delta then informed them this was just an example of the quirky little things John and Marianne did to add to the interest and structure of school.

Along with the weekly *grammatica*, each week brought a translation. The first week's Alpha Latin text when translated into English began, "Britain is an island. London is in Britain. Europe is not an island." Betas were faced with a level of Latin having translations such as, "Marcus and two comrades brought timber from the woods and loaded the cart for their master." The Deltas renewed their pursuit of Latin with sentences of extreme complexity: "Do you hesitate to avoid the looks and the presence of those whose minds and senses you are wounding?" My contribution had been to write a Latin primer with ever increasing difficulty as the story developed. Several times a year each student wrote an original Latin story.

Every year we felt more strongly that the study of Latin was one of the more valuable parts of our curriculum. First, experience had revealed that after Latin at Fayette, students found that all language classes encountered in higher education were much easier to master.

Second, the study of Latin grammar was a great aid in mastering English grammar – Latin's use of endings on root words assisted in the study of cases and tenses. Third, the organization of thought and work required in the study of Latin was transferable to all subjects. Fourth, much of English was Latin based, and working with the source language removed some of the seeming randomness of words. Fifth, each student took pride in their progress in a difficult subject.

In the first year that we included Latin in the curriculum, one young girl was quite intelligent but most dyslexic. Her English writing was indecipherable. We were amazed to find that she was not dyslexic in Latin, and the patterning there helped her English; we later found the same with other students. Along with algebra, we believed the study of Latin to be the most effective training for the young mind. Also, when people asked about the rigor of our curriculum I could truthfully say, "We diagram Latin sentences." That set the tone for the rest of the discussion.

Alison was gentler with Greek than Marianne with Latin. We began each year with returning Bigs reviewing and new ones learning the Greek alphabet. Fourteen of Greek's twenty four letters have close correspondence to our familiar English, correctly named Latin, alphabet. Learning the symbols, their names, and the alphabetic order is an excellent warm-up for our Greek study. Alpha, A, and Beta, B, are a comfortable beginning. In the third position, instead of the troublesome C, with hard and soft sounds in English, is Gamma, Γ. The Z, Zeta, is the sixth letter, in Greek not relegated to the end of the list. The "th" sound of English makes more sense when seen as the substitute for the Greek Theta, Θ. Comfort with upper and lowercase symbols in Greek had proven to be helpful in high school and college science classes. When these symbols representing physical constants and quantities were encountered, they were old friends, not one more strange convention in an already difficult subject.

After several weeks of letters, the class was ready for the weekly word list. Over the year two hundred Greek words were learned. Each had a correspondence in English. Seemingly random English words appeared logically based with knowledge of their Greek origins. "Hormone," for example, was not just an arbitrarily selected word used to set teens apart from the rest of society, but came from the Greek word meaning "to excite." In her studio Marianne often spoke of increasing the dendritic connections in each of our brains. When we learned that *dendrite* was the Greek word for tree, we could more easily picture the many branches of our brains' networks. These words fit into our body of knowledge and were not merely added to a long list of random words.

Students with vocabulary in both Latin and Greek had a powerful perspective on the English language. For example, literature we had on brain physiology spoke of "neurons" and "nerve cells." Readers could be confused. Were two different structures being mentioned? Our students knew that *neuron* came from the Greek word meaning "sinew" and *nerve* from the Latin word with the same meaning. We often had been questioned for teaching two "dead" languages. We pointed out that after their study at Fayette, students could generally learn any "living" language with ease. Also we had picked the two deceased languages that have had the greatest impact on English.

While the Bigs battled with two deceased languages, the Munchkins enjoyed a living one, French. Since the younger ones were still struggling to write English, French classes were mostly conversational. Alison began with phrases of greeting and small banter. After the class had a level of comfort with friendly address, she moved on to building their vocabulary with families of nouns. By the end of the second month of school, cardinal numbers, days of the week, months of the year, many food items, objects around the school or home, and the names of anatomical features had been learned. To introduce verbs Alison wrote simple conjugations on the board and the class could be heard chanting these charts. Adding a few adjectives created the vocabulary needed to play a favorite French game, "telephone." Alison would make an imaginary call to one of the students. They would then converse in French while the others in the room listened. At the end of the dialogue another eager student received the next call.

Each week language flash cards were produced by every student. On one side they drew a picture representing the word and on the back wrote the word in French. By the end of the year each Munchkin had an extensive collection of cards. Reading and writing French and deciphering pronunciation were not rigorously pursued; enough of this was occurring in their study of English. Alison did include words, such as *cathedral*, that are spelled the same in the two languages and showed the different pronunciation in each. The Munchkins looked forward to the fun of French class.

All week as students enjoyed language and other classes, I could be found lying in our living room, enjoying a diet of pain-pills and liquids sipped through a straw. Tuesday morning the kids came over in small groups to see me and wish me well. My school persona had always been one full of energy, excited about most things, with an air of invulnerability. My temporary persona was the total opposite, with the added attraction of a face looking like a Halloween mask. I mumbled a few words to each group about how I so enjoyed seeing them and that I would soon be fine. Each visit ended with a viewing of my helmet and bike gloves. Children have one reaction when a parent nags about wearing a helmet and quite another holding a road-scarred, blood-covered one in their hands.

Throughout the week hand-decorated get-well cards were brought in by the kids. These were taped on the wall by my bed so I could spend my time focused on words of cheer from these young ones so close to me. My favorites were, "Even though you look different, you're still the same inside" and "Though you are hurt, your lessons still shine on." As word spread of my mishap alumni dropped by, our kitchen counter filled with flowers, parents delivered homemade soups and ice creams. I was surrounded by affection and prayers of healing. While mending I knew I was being transformed by the pain inside and the love of so many around me. As Dickens said, "It was the best of times and the worst of times."

Since Halloween fell on a Sunday in 1999, we celebrated the day at school on Friday. Most students arrived in costume, and swapping of capes and ghoulish masks dominated the day. Groups came in to visit me and check on my progress. Seeing them caused me to smile for the first time since my crash, which opened all the wounds of my lips. When our Halloween observance fell on a Wednesday or Friday, the days Alison taught Greek, all eagerly awaited the hour. Rarely in these modern times were young students taught Greek and only on these special days by a giant white rabbit. Years before Alison had found a whimsical bunny suit at a secondhand shop, and it was now part of our school tradition. She always got so involved in the Greek words and lists of English derivatives she would forget she had become a giant bunny.

The day was a highlight of the year for the Munchkins because they joined Melanie and her bunny friend for "Spirit Sing." While we had an open-door policy at Fayette and any parent or visitor could observe any school activity at any time, the sole exception was Spirit Sing. For this only the Munchkins and their teachers were allowed, our version of the Masonic orders and other such secret societies. The costumed Munchkins, Melanie, and the giant rabbit loaded drums and other instruments into vans and headed for the "spirit tunnel." The entrance road to St. John's College crossed a large, usually dry riverbed. The culvert under the road was eight feet high and forty feet long, a perfect setting for evoking the spirits of All Saint's Eve. To the beat of drums, spooky songs were sung, building the ritual energy.

The climax arrived when in a hushed voice Melanie passed out the "spirit bags" containing eyeballs, witches' fingers, bones, drops of dried blood, dragon scales and teeth, and other witchy articles. After a bit of nibbling while still holding to the energies evoked, the group returned to the vehicles and headed for school, reentering the mundane world. The Bigs, who in the recent past had been Munchkins, eagerly awaited the cars, hoping a few eyeballs and scales might be shared.

Though Melanie did much to set a haunting mood, there was no coercion to force a level of belief. Each individual and each year's group had the freedom to define how real and how deep the ritual went. Some years, when safely back in the cars, various kids pointed out to the others they knew the eyeballs were really grapes, the drops of blood actually dried cranberries, and the witches' fingers only green beans. This year all the Munchkins stayed in the suspension of reality with talk such as, "Oh, that was a tough bone to bite through," "These are the best bat droppings I have ever eaten," "Don't you find the dragon scales a bit salty?" Years before when Melanie had first suggested Spirit Sing, I had had reservations about adding an activity so foreign to our present culture. However, our litmus test for all school activities was the reaction of the students. I had learned over the years from observing and talking with the children that Spirit Sing was considered an essential part of our school.

The week had begun with many unknowns. Would I get better, or would nasty Greek- and Latin-based words like *hematoma* and *infection* become part of my reality? Could school function smoothly and instruction be sufficient with me supine? These, of course, were more the fears and demons of my psyche than probable realities. By Friday these fears had been set aside. My doctor was amazed by the rate of healing, especially for one in the grandfather category. Tara and Ele had been marvelous in taking up my work load and moving all subjects, save for my history lectures, forward. My wall was covered with cards, my counter filled with flowers, and the refrigerator held enough soups for the weekend. As the day ended Matt gave me a final card: "Please get well soon – all this Latin is overwhelming me."

~ Week Nine ~
Soccer and Court

There is no such thing as justice-in or out of court.

CLARENCE DARROW

TUESDAY FOUND ME standing on the bricks greeting parents and students as they arrived. Everyone was delighted to see that their worst fears had not actualized, but they also saw that my complete recovery was still far in the future. I stayed vertical long enough to hand out the Tuesday morning tests and then returned to my prone position next to my wall of get-well cards. I arose two hours later to check on the kids at morning break, seeking a few moments of quiet banter. I found a dozen children inside the classrooms.

We had a rule that stated, "Everyone outside at break time," so those students inside prepared to hear one of my lectures. However, I opened my mouth and not a thought entered my brain. Still too close to the concussion for spontaneous thinking, I said, "Go outside; I'll be right back." After I had sat quietly for a minute, a thought finally came through the fog: *The rest of the day we will have class outside and break inside.* I went out and shared my plan with the students. It felt good to be back in harness even if I could pull only a small load.

Since I was too weak to go to the park for sports hour and the staff rightly did not trust my ability to monitor the children while crossing the busy street, Alison and Tara took over my park duties. Every day except rainy days, a rare event in this high desert, one or two of the staff would take all the children to the park. In the autumn and winter we played soccer three days a week and had one free day. Free day had no planned activities, so some kids enjoyed a game of their choosing, some played on the jungle gym, some lay around talking with friends. During the spring we played baseball, our greatest passion, every day. Considering the small size of our school grounds, having a city park two blocks from the school was fortuitous. Other than its colony of prairie dogs, the park was vacant during the day and had for twenty years provided our playing area. We had playground equipment, a baseball diamond, room for two soccer fields, and even a small zoo. The family whose land bordered the park had horses, peacocks, chickens, ducks, big-horn sheep, and emus. The kids enjoyed hanging over the fence feeding and petting the animals.

At the park, our school's tradition of enjoyable soccer, good lessons in sportsmanship, and healthy use of the body unfolded. Most days we set out two pitches, with goals defined by piles of coats and the sidelines based on various prairie dog holes. There were alway several mounded holes in the middle of each pitch, but since they were stationary and quite visible, there was no need to sprain an ankle.

Each day brought a different type of game. One day an all boys game would be played on one pitch and an all girls on the other. The next day might find the division by age, and then the following based on soccer ability. Each type of game had a different rhythm and flavor. If a player felt uncomfortable one day, the next game was guaranteed to bring a more enjoyable style. One day best friends were teammates, and the next day opponents. The label of "us versus them" was not a part of our soccer time, nor was winning and losing. When one team gained a two-goal advantage, we switched a few players to even team strength and hopefully the score. Most games were played with two balls, creating more action. A coordinated two-ball attack on goal was a marvelous sight. Occasionally we played games with three balls, but the increased chance of being smacked by an unseen ball limited the number of such games. The perfect game in our minds ended with players tired, no one hurt, and the score tied.

Teams were usually equal strength, but occasionally we played "All-stars," where five superior players were matched against a dozen or more less skilled opponents. These games were our most intense. The best strategy for the "non–All-star" team was to use a swarming defense and keep the score close until late in the game when the legs of the quintet tired.

No arguing about calls or penalties occurred because years before a tone of good sportsmanship had been set that was passed on from class to class. We didn't shout to encourage greater effort. The only requirements were that all players remained in the bounds of the field during the game and sitting was not allowed. The spirit of the game and each individual's growing comfort level generated the intensity of play. Only one teacher was needed to monitor the student body during soccer time at the park. The group was self-regulated, and gentle peer guidance kept a unified harmony. During playing time, the teacher oversaw one game and the other was monitored by one of the older students.

For years local soccer coaches and some parents doubted our philosophy toward the game. It was thought that our noncompetitive approach might develop mild-mannered scholars but never an excellent soccer player. Now that so many of our students had played well in high school and on top city-league teams, this talk had stopped. Our players graduated with above-average skills, exemplary sportsmanship, and the rare abilities of being able to think while moving on the field and playing to maximize the whole team's performance, not merely their own. Marianne's studio work had no small part in creating these abilities.

The games with the Munchkin girls usually had the adult referee. Peevish interaction with peers seemed to be part of the development of these younger girls. We never scolded them but often reminded them that poking and nasty words never created an atmosphere of friendship. Though this theme also came up in class, the physical activity of the soccer field brought out more of these behaviors. We knew that by the time the young ladies had become Bigs they would have left these social patterns behind and would surround the new Munchkins with examples of harmonious interaction.

On Wednesday Alison related an incident to me from that day's game. Young Nyssa had dribbled the ball the length of the field when

Rebecca, a fellow Munchkin teammate, took the ball away and shot at the goal. Nyssa expressed her outrage. Alison suggested to Rebecca that a better tactic would be to position herself for passes from teammates. Five minutes later Nyssa again dribbled the length of the field, drawing out the goalie. This time Rebecca ran wide. Nyssa slipped a pass to her and she chipped the ball inside the far pile of coats for a score. They did a high-five celebration. Wellington was correct: much character is developed on playing fields.

Since I was still too weak to teach a full day, I asked our friend Ken to come in Wednesday afternoon and hold "court." Ken was known at the school as our right-handed baseball pitcher, but he also had been a parent of two students in the first years of the school. One year his Parents' Week project had been a mock trial, loved by the whole class. Over the years he had returned to be the presiding judge of various cases. All the Bigs readily filled the roles of an American court of law; they always enjoyed the sessions of psychodrama improv theater. Ken slipped in the rules of procedure and structure of our legal system with subtle skill.

We had not held court for three years, so only Forest and Matthew had actually participated previously. Through a somewhat mysterious transmission from the school's collective knowledge, by the time Ken called the court to order the whole class knew the various roles available and the verdicts of many past cases. This case was *John v. the College of Santa Fe*, on whose property I had crashed my bike.

Matthew and Reese represented me, and Forest and Zoe defended the college. The bailiff was Miranda, who used the weighty tome *501 Latin Verbs* in lieu of the Bible. With the studio as our courtroom the trial began, complete with jury, expert witnesses, and a TV reporter. In the opening arguments my lawyers stated that the speed bump I'd hit was ill marked, much too steep, and in the shade of trees. They asked for $1.5 million. The college's lawyers pointed to the sign warning of the bump and to the fact that I had been wearing dark sunglasses. They called on the president of the college, played by Ele, who testified that safety was her main concern and that, by the way, the walkathon I had been holding on their campus that day was governed by a general waiver holding the college blameless. My doctor, Heather, advised the jury that I might have permanent brain damage, would probably never play baseball again, and might possibly forget everything I had ever known about algebra. The doctor for the college, Jessica, insisted my injuries looked much worse than they actually were and, in her professional opinion, I'd be fit as a fiddle by Thanksgiving. For the college, the defense dragged out the actual bike I had ridden and called forth James, an expert on biking. He pointed to an underinflated tire and a possibly defective brake.

The class already knew many legal words and concepts, but new ones came up in this trial: liability, negligence, waiver, change of venue, medical costs, compensatory damages, expert witness, discovery (in the legal sense), and, of course, pain and suffering. At midpoint in the two-hour event, Jonah, the TV reporter, summed up the case and interviewed two of the lawyers. After deliberation a sympathetic jury awarded me $800,000 and through their foreperson, Maggie, admonished me to be more careful in the future.

As the court session ended, Marianne and Tara brought another group into the studio for neurologic exercises. After two months of school the rhythms of the studio were well established. The children needing phoneme sessions had broken into three groups, each receiving an hour-long session twice a week. Vision classes had a similar schedule. Small groups went to sessions with Tara or Marianne throughout the school day.

We knew we could demand the intensity of the classroom work only by supporting the students with studio time. We viewed this as analogous to weight training for athletes. The foundation of all studio sessions was the concept of brain-body integration. From this beginning different groups of students focused on different specific needs. For our phoneme awareness classes we based our sessions on the work of Patricia Lindamood, a leader in phoneme techniques.

One of Lindamood's brilliant insights was to link phoneme sounds to small wooden colored blocks. Each student in the session lined up six differently colored blocks in an arbitrary but agreed upon order; extras of each color were in a handy pile at the side. The agreed line might be red, blue, black, yellow, green, white. Marianne might then, for example, say "ip" and each child should position a red block followed by a blue one, the two different colors representing the two different phonemes *i* and *p* respectively. She next might say "pip" and they should all place a blue one in front of the two blocks, since in this drill the *p* phoneme was linked with the blue blocks. When the next word was "pup," the middle block, the red one, was removed and replaced by a black one, since the next block in the line was used for the new phoneme, *u*. A quick scan of the room revealed who had a blue-black-blue sequence and who did not.

Anyone who thinks these block-phoneme linkages were an easy task for all young people should try these exercises with a group of children. More than a few were not able to do this basic task, indicating extreme lack of phonemic awareness – they simply did not decode the auditory signals. For these children hours of sight word drills or standard phonics approaches to reading would only lead to frustration. The blocks were used both as an easy diagnostic test and a therapeutic tool. Tapping fingers while saying each sound, exploring the shape and feeling of the mouth and tongue for each phoneme, and finally linking the alphabetic symbols with the sounds were part of these sessions.

The phoneme classes were not conducted with children sitting motionless, moving block after block for an hour. Each session began with Brain Gym to awaken and integrate the mind-body system. After a few chains of phonemes and blocks everyone moved around the room before settling in to more blocks and words. When someone's row of blocks did not match those of the rest, they did not look at their neighbors and surreptitiously switch a few colors. Rather they would explain to Marianne or Tara and the rest of the group why they had placed the blocks in that particular order, the more proficient then commenting on similar moves they had made in the past and the better listening strategies they had developed over time.

Many sessions ended with the members of the group representing blocks themselves. Now when Marianne or Tara voiced a word, players would move around the room making chains of children representing phonemes. I came into the studio near the end of Thursday's session and found Avery standing in the corner. "Why aren't you part of the group activity?" "I am a red block in the extra pile and am waiting for Tara to say a *p*, then I will jump into line."

Friday was a free day at the park. This unstructured time allowed each child the choice of self-directed fun or embroilment in disharmony. Four Munchkin boys chose the latter path. Occasionally the sprinklers would come on during the noon hour, and getting soaking wet had been a favorite activity for many years. One rule handed down from the city staff was never to touch the sprinkler heads. Our four young gentlemen, being new to the school, did not know this and were blasting each other with these giant high-powered squirt guns. By the time older students had crossed the park and informed them of the rules they were already out of sorts with each other. Arlen was found muttering his desire to kill Walker. Forest, as Boss, pointed out that at Fayette we did not use lethal threats, even their offhanded verbalization. Sam and Avery, usually the best of friends, were also unhappy with each other.

The incident was reported to me on return from the park, after which Marianne and I took the water brigade into the studio for a short talk. Our approach was not to assign blame or attempt to determine who did what to whom, but to help each see how all of them had ignored early warning signals of potential disharmony. We told them that with a little practice they would soon be as facile as the older boys in finding ways to have fun without triggering discord. We adjourned to the Bricks, joining all the rest of the school in the celebration of Briana's twelfth birthday.

∽ Week Ten ∾

Cube Roots and Student Manners

*Teaching kids to count is fine,
but teaching them what counts is best.*

BOB TALBERT

As we gathered for the tenth week of school we had individual and collective feelings of accomplishment. In this short time we had molded into a smoothly operating group, moved through a large amount of academic work, and gained skills and strengths in brain-body integration in Marianne's studio. What in September had appeared to some an endless amount of work was now reduced to four days of academics in the calendar year or, for that matter, in the millennium. After such intense pencil pushing we looked forward to Parents' Week, a week of Thanksgiving vacation, three weeks of holiday crafts mixed with concert rehearsal and performance, and then two weeks of winter vacation – seven weeks without academic focus.

Our exploration of algebra had covered the scheduled topics so I used the week to present two of my favorite mathematical gems. Years ago someone had given me a pre–Civil War math text. The pages were filled with arcane languaging and methods no longer used in this age of hand-held calculators. One chapter gave algorithms for finding square and cube roots of numbers. The methods resembled the algorithm we used for long division but were much more complex. One step for the finding of square roots stated, "Double the first figure of the partial root for a trial divisor, and divide the remainder by it for the second figure of the root; annex the quotient to the root and also to the trial divisor." The rules for cube roots were even more difficult. One of the six steps stated, "Square the first figure of the root and multiply by 300 for a trial divisor and divide the remainder by it for the second figure of the root. Multiply the last figure of the root by the part which precedes it, and the result by 30. Square the last figure of the root, and add both of these results to the trial divisor." Whew!

Every four or five years I had presented this material sometime during the school year. Usually about half of the class had been able to eventually cipher a few square roots, and the two or three most mathematically proficient could find a few simple cube roots. Now that everyone was using both hemispheres of their brains, thanks to Marianne's studio work, and the Bigs were so practiced with team learning, I was eager to see how these exercises would be received this year.

Tuesday I demonstrated the square root technique on the board, gave the kids a half hour of group study time, and assigned some problems of varying difficulty for homework. Wednesday they returned with the majority of kids ready for cube roots and the ones who were stuck able to articulate their specific difficulty and ready to strengthen their models. Ele helped the ones working on square roots. I demonstrated a couple of cubes on the board, and soon several groups of students were penciling away at these nasty problems. Ariel noted that other eleven-year-olds in her neighborhood were still struggling with long division in their schools and was curious about the difference with Fayette. I pointed out that our advantage was not superior intelligence but a superior system of learning.

By the end of the hour we had collectively mastered more of this material than any previous class and we still had two days of school left in the week. Thinking quickly of what next to do I said, "How would you take a fourth root?" After a very short time Forest and Zoe together said, "Apply the square root method twice." With the help of my calculator new problems were written on the board. Answers appeared in a very few minutes. "How would you find a sixth root?" "Take the square root then the cube root." "Could you also take the cube root and then the square root?" I asked. "Yes, but that would be the more difficult path."

Thursday Ele showed her group the cube root method and soon they were using calculators to create problems for others: "I have a cube where the answer is a four-digit number with all the digits under five." "Here is a sixth root with a three-digit answer. Who is ready for it?" Since everyone was focused on gaining and sharing knowledge, not looking for test scores and grades, they moved at an amazing pace through difficult material. Whenever anyone sensed their brain had stopped and they had fallen into an unresourceful state, they would stop working, take a deep breath and possibly a drink of water, and spend a minute doing Brain Gym, then pick up their pencil and move forward. By Friday I had a few ninth roots ready, but these held no fear for the class.

Math was not the only class with superior achievement. In Greek, we usually studied a sheet for a few days and later in the week took a test on the new words. This week, however, Alison passed out a sheet, talked about it for a half hour, then passed out tests and graded them in class. Half of the kids scored 100 percent. After the volumes of Latin the previous two weeks, Marianne passed out a few papers that our Latin scholars were able to do without teacher assistance. Though Fayette long had been known for academic excellence and superior citizenship of the student body, we teachers were amazed at some of the leaps manifested in this year.

In singing class Melanie reintroduced a song that we last had sung several years before and rather poorly. In fact we had dropped it from the Winter Concert because we sounded so bad. Only five of the present class had been part of that previous dismal attempt. Now on our first attempt, after a few echoes with Melanie, it sounded great. Twenty years of ever improving tradition, teachers continuing to increase the amount of love and admiration beamed at the kids, and all the studio work and techniques Marianne had added to the school in the past five years were beginning to pay large dividends. Fortunately we always had the young Munchkins to bring us back to Earth.

Being a Munchkin was a phase of life, a difficult and delicate stage of growth where the hemispheres of the brain had developed but had not yet completely linked together. After years in relative fairyland, young ones now were spending time in a larger social setting with an importance placed on academics. They were asked to master new skills, such as decoding and verbalizing strange inky shapes on pages, memorizing apparently random charts of numbers called times tables, and interacting in harmony with other young ones who had been raised in families with different rules and customs. The staff and Bigs understood these challenges and supported the Munchkins in this phase of their journey through life. By the tenth week most Munchkins were showing signs of stress from the scholastic work load, and those who had had trouble socially with classmates were beginning to cast these patterns in bronze. This was one of the reasons we switched from a bicameral academic setting to unified craft and choral activities for a few weeks.

During one break I heard the particular tone that could only mean Munchkin group disharmony. I gathered the five boys and five girls who were involved and after listening to "He kicked her in class," "She kicked me first," "Yeah, but yesterday..." I called for silence and their good attention. Then I asked whether anyone could deny the statement "Each of you knows this will not lead to harmony." No denials. I was delighted that only ten weeks into this school year the young ones were beginning to truly listen to me. They were relaxing into the process of social education, not teetering between flight or fight. I knew the timing was right to begin actively helping them work through some of their issues.

Each member of the staff would have loved to have sat down the first day of each school year and said, "Everyone be nice to everyone else," and have had that be the end of the issue. The reality was that the Munchkins first had to experience enough of their collective disharmony in order to agree they needed help in learning the lessons we called Maturity 101. The staff was looking forward to some group discussions with Munchkins during the craft/concert weeks. The change of structure of these school days and the seasonal feelings of goodwill were an excellent catalyst for change.

Though healing well from my bike crash, I still needed to rest each afternoon, and since the Bigs had so enjoyed court, we asked Ken to return for another session. Instead of staging a new trial, however, we thought that studying the legal system in more depth was a better idea. He brought Eda, a professional jury consultant, to assist him. Ken began by raising the question of whether anybody could get a fair trial in a jurisdiction in which the jury were all personal friends of the plaintiff or, more specifically in this case, all students of mine. Eda explained that the lawyers for the college, Forest and Zoe, with consent from the judge, Ken, could have dismissed jurors who appeared to be biased, along with a set number of others, just on sheer instinct. Eda also explained that in federal cases jurors were picked only from the voters' list and in state cases from both the voters' list and the drivers' list. The class discussed the possible implications for federal jury trials, since statistics showed only half of the eligible population voted.

Returning to the specifics of our case, after she had questioned closely the six jurors on how they had reached their decision, Eda, our higher court judge, approved only one. The other five were dismissed out of hand, as five would be permitted to be dismissed out of hand in a civil case. Following this ruling Forest and Zoe demanded a change of venue. There was also cause for a mistrial, the class discovered. Ken, the lower court judge in the case, in trying to explain "risk management" had mentioned monetary damages to me would be paid by the college's liability insurance. It turned out, as Eda explained, that in a civil trial involving money the word *insurance* could not be uttered, and the utterance of it was direct cause for ending the case. New vocabulary included "dismissed for cause," "peremptory challenge," "contingency fee," "fair trial," and a meaningful revisiting of "change of venue." All in all, I lost $800,000 and my lawyers, who would have received a third of that, about $133,000 each. Easy come, easy go, and my teeth and shoulder still hurt.

As the players left the courtroom heading toward Ele's writing class, Tara had a group ready for their next vision session. In the studio, vision classes were not so much to improve vision but rather to correct bad habits of brain-eye communication. Overuse of one eye, poor signaling to the brain, and other such patterns can stand in the way of facile visual processing. Peeking in on vision class often meant seeing small groups of students with one eye patched playing pickup sticks, drawing on the chalkboard with both hands moving simultaneously, or playing jacks. Other times the patched ones were walking an obstacle course, which included balancing on beams and avoiding a swinging ball. All these drills were designed to integrate body-brain-eye activity. Thursday afternoon when I peeked in, the whole class was blindfolded. They were exploring movement, listening, and thinking without any reliance on vision. One never knew what would be seen in the studio as Marianne, Tara, and the kids continually created new activities.

I returned to my classroom and as always checked the configuration of the pillows and the students. Having a class sit on floor pillows revealed information not available to teachers faced by rows of desks. Who sat by whom and the amount of personal space occupied gave me data on group dynamics and individual feelings. Though the seating arrangement changed from day to day, the basic pattern found boys stage left, with the older ones facing me directly and the younger ones along the side wall with an oblique view. The girls were stage right in a similar age configuration.

Recently I had been tracking a shifting within this standard configuration. The week before, James had crossed the midline and his pillow was next to – more correctly, touching – Cina's. All this was fine and proper; at Fayette we prided ourselves on cross-gender respect and friendships. On Friday morning of this week, however, James and pillow had moved. They were now next to another female classmate, Reese. As I began a short drill of the capitals and nicknames of our northeastern states I made a mental note of the potential trouble revealed by the shifting pillows.

While Munchkins externalized their social conflicts with flares of drama, Bigs tended to internalize theirs. Situations could smolder for weeks and, if not addressed, burst into flames. I took James aside at the morning break. As I looked into his young, innocent eyes I thought of male-female conflicts and misunderstandings stretching back millennia. What to say to a young lad as his first surges of hormones led him into the territory of interaction with, and attraction to, the opposite sex? My strategy was to graduate students before they were in the full storm of pheromones and trust that their high school teachers would deal with the rocky ground. My tactics were to remind them to be consistently respectful to each other and to stay focused on larger social groups rather than couples.

I weighed my words carefully before speaking. "James, I am glad that you are so friendly and helpful in class not just with the boys but also the girls. But make sure in the deepest honesty of your heart that you never are playing off the attention of one young lady against another. William Congreve and his play *Love for Love*, written over three hundred years ago, are not remembered by many, but one of the play's couplets still rings in our language."

James responded that he had never heard mention of Congreve or the play. "Have you heard the quote 'Heaven has no rage like love to hatred turned, nor hell a fury like a woman scorned?' Believe it or not, when I saw your pillow touching Reese's this morning, I sensed you were on the boundary of scorn and did not know it."

Friday afternoon the Bigs went off on a field trip to the traditional "Deer Dance" at a nearby Indian pueblo. Citizens of Northern New Mexico pride themselves on the harmony of its three cultures: Native American, Spanish, and modern American. We enjoy our Spanish Fiesta, the oldest community celebration in the United States, and attend various sacred dances at the eight Native American pueblos within a short drive of Santa Fe. Cina's godfather, an elder of the Tesuque Pueblo, would be discussing ceremonial dancing, showing some of the costumes used, and speaking on his people's cosmology during Parents' Week. In preparation for this, the Bigs class attended the Deer Dance, where drumming, dancing, chanting, and costumes all were unified in a tradition older than our nation. We were fortunate to have this tricultural base as we extended toward comfort with the multiculturalism of the entire family of humankind.

The day ended with teachers and students alike enjoying our tenth bowls of popcorn. We could look back on an academic year well begun and forward to weeks of vacation and the neural cross-training of crafts projects and concert preparation. I noted that James had ridden to and from the pueblo in a van carrying only young gentlemen.

ಬ Seven Nonacademic Weeks ಬ

AFTER TEN WEEKS of academic intensity we did no standard school work for these seven weeks. Staff and students rested during three weeks of vacation, one at Thanksgiving and two at winter break. During the first of two Parents' Weeks, the staff rested while mothers and fathers viewed school from the inside and presented nonacademic topics to the classes. The weeks of December, staff and students were intently focused on various handicrafts and preparation for our Winter Concert.

～ Week Eleven ～
Parents' Week

*Parents are the bones on which children
sharpen their teeth.*

PETER USTINOV

ONE OF MY dearest friends, an octogenarian retired architect, once said to me, "Architecture is a marvelous profession except for the clients, and teaching is a marvelous profession except for the parents." Though I enjoyed all the activities with the children, many of the interactions with parents over the course of a school year tended to erode the pleasures of teaching. There were parents who were truly grateful and graciously expressed thanks, but many seemed preoccupied with their busy adult lives and saved their school interactions for times they perceived a problem in their child's life. Many of these interactions seemed oriented more toward complaint than toward process or solution. Such was the terrain of architecture and teaching.

We had an open door policy at school. Any parent, or any other interested person for that matter, could observe any school class or activity, Spirit Sing excepted. We were not looking for parents to coteach with us, but we had nothing to hide from them, and encouraged them to be part of the school and their children's education. In fact our annual schedule included two Parents' Weeks, where the parents were in charge of the school and all instruction.

Marianne had conceived this brilliant addition to our school schedule. After very few years of running the school we realized that to avoid teacher burnout, several breaks each year were needed for the staff. Marianne saw that if teachers could be freed of classes the week before both Thanksgiving and spring breaks, they would have two weeks away from school each time period. This would serve a dual purpose by allowing for both rest and class preparation. Her idea was to have the parents run the school for each of these weeks.

Parents' Week had thus become a valued part of our varied curriculum. Besides the importance of having a break for the teachers, after ten weeks the kids were tired of the class work and mannerisms of their instructors. The switch to other faces was a relief, and two weeks later they were again eager to see the staff. The parents also got an inside view of the school not possible from merely dropping off and picking up their young ones. This view included a short taste of the challenges teachers faced each day, how well-mannered and attentive the whole group of students was, and how the name oft mentioned in a complaining tone at the dinner table was actually attached to a child who really seemed little different from others. Parents' Week was valuable for the entire school community.

Here is how it worked: Each family was responsible for a two-hour time slot in their child's class. During this time they could engage the children in any desired activity. When parents asked for advice on possible projects, I would always tell them to pick something they were passionate about. We had a parent coordinator for each day; this role was filled by a parent who had been around the school for several years and knew the basic school rhythms and the expected student behavior. On smooth days the coordinator would sit by the woodstove reading a book. Other times they might assist a novice parent hold the beat in class or fill in with poetry or card tricks when we had the rare no-show. These four days gave a minimum of twenty-eight adults an inside view of Fayette.

In the first years of Parents' Week, when all on the staff were younger, they could be found, or more correctly couldn't be found, on a week-long backpacking trip in the Grand Canyon. Over the years however, as knees, backs, and simultaneously the collective parenting skills of the school's population weakened, we gave up the canyon adventures and now always had at least one member of the staff somewhere on the grounds during the school day. For years this was purely a psychological measure. On my assigned days

I played the role of humble gardener puttering about. No one ever needed me to solve any problems or hand out any wisdom, but the fact that expert backup was near gave the parents the confidence to do a fine job. As the years continued to roll by, however, the staff behind the scenes added the role of damage control for the occasional unwise actions of some of the parents.

These adjustments were befitting our philosophy. In the twenty-year history of the school most systems had gone through subtle changes. It was the role of the staff to continually meet the changing needs of the whole school community, not to force new members into the old ways in order to hold to a tradition. Since Fayette was an educational institution, if some of the effort of the staff needed to be directed at supporting parents when surrounded by a score of kids, it was hard to complain. The problems that Parents' Week revealed were always overshadowed by the interesting projects and interactions of the week.

Years ago many phone calls had been needed to schedule the various projects and convince folks that Parents' Week, though unique to our school, was a fine idea. Now the years of tradition had shown everyone that this was a week to enjoy, not dread. Scheduling couldn't have been simpler. Three weeks before the event we posted a large sheet on the bulletin wall, and parents filled in their names and project descriptions. In the first years we suggested possible activities to parents. This year they were coming to me asking which of several ideas would be the best. From the parental enthusiasm we sensed the week would be interest filled.

Marianne, Alison, and Tara had been doing extra duty in school since my bike crash. As a result, when Parents' Week arrived they took some time off and I was staff monitor for the week. This I could do – a simple job with no heavy lifting.

Tuesday morning the Bigs walked to the nearby Odd Fellows Hall for a session of swing dancing. At the beginning of the year the music and moves of swing had been brought to school by a few of the older students. After enduring years of heavy metal and rap, the staff was delighted to hear again the music of my parents' generation; Benny Goodman and Duke Ellington were now the preferred CDs.

Forest and Matthew had become excellent swing dancers, attending weekly classes and showing up at our local pub for Thursday night swing dances. To our and their amazement and delight, they now were hosting a weekly half-hour local radio show of swing music. With their assistance and the parent guides, the Bigs had a great time dancing.

During Tuesday's middle block of time, Cina's godfather explained the ceremonies the Bigs had seen on Friday. Holding the costumes and seeing the fine workmanship added a dimension of understanding to dances viewed from a respectful distance. The questions and answers touched on the radically different views of life, the world, and the cosmos held by various cultures and, more importantly, how these views had been fused together. Each pueblo had a Catholic church at its center, and the dances were performed in and around the church.

At the same time in the next room, the Munchkins were making beaded leather pouches. Avery's mom came totally prepared for this complex project. She had cut and prepunched leather pieces, had beads and sewing thong ready, and had even brought bone buttons for fasteners. At the end of two hours each Munchkin had completed a great looking pouch they would treasure for years.

The afternoon brought Walker's mom and a demonstration of print making for the Munchkins. Briana's mom and a French friend made crepes for the Bigs. The first day of Parents' Week ended with smiles all around and pouches at the waist of each Munchkin.

When we told the parents they had free range of activities and that many varied projects added to the interest in Parents' Week, we ended up with topics often not thought within the grasp of young children. Ariel's dad had worked in the medical profession for decades, so on Wednesday morning he spent his time with the Bigs on the topic of parasitology. Rebecca's dad was a stockbroker and had wondered if the Munchkins were too young to understand the workings of Wall Street, stocks, and bonds. My advice had been to never underestimate the sophistication of the mind of a Munchkin and that revealing the fascinating world of finance to them seemed a great idea. I pointed out that their questions would lead him to the correct explanation of the principles and models he was presenting. This was the strategy I had successfully used for years in my history and science lectures, and it worked for him as well.

In the afternoon another Munchkin parent had a craft project that lasted only an hour. Unbeknownst to me, she also had a personal agenda to share with the children. Her daughter was one of the three Munchkin girls struggling with the transition from only child at home to being a member of a larger group, a class of fourteen. In a school one does not always get their way, must learn to accommodate the needs of others, and finds that nastiness is often returned in kind. As a school community we were in the process of helping these young girls find better ways of social interchange. The mom thought she should use some of her Parents' Week time to address this situation.

With her daughter cuddled on her lap and the other Munchkin girls lined up on an outside bench, she told them that the only problem in their classroom was one girl and her behavior. The singled out girl was accused of poking and saying mean-spirited things to the other girls. There was no recognition that her own daughter was a player in this tit-for-tat minidrama This unfortunate and altogether inappropriate scene continued until the end of the school day. In the history of the school no parent had so overstepped the lines of propriety. The defamed young lady was Jewish, and one more time, this time in the postage-stamp–sized piece of the world I had been charged to protect, the Jewish scapegoat card had been played.

Damage control and repair began as the meeting ended. The little one, who had held her composure through this grilling, ran sobbing to her father when he arrived at school. Girls from the Bigs' class came back from a second dance lesson to find Munchkin girls muttering about how they wanted to hurt her. The Bigs gently reminded them this was not the way we at Fayette handled or learned about social interaction. They told the young ones that heartfelt love, open communication, and especially being honest about our own foibles were the principles we learned and applied at school. Marianne returned from her day away to have the mom pull her aside and expound on how well she had handled a school situation that in her opinion we did not have under control.

After such events at school I would be on the phone for hours. Calls to parents of the first party, those of the second party, those not even invited to the party. In my call to the young girl's dad I thanked him for his reasoned approach and measured response to this painful matter and assured him I viewed this as unconscionable behavior that would be aggressively and thoroughly dealt with by myself and the whole staff.

Thursday morning found me on the sidewalk greeting arriving students. I was reestablishing the proper school tone following our maverick parent action. The slandered child chose to spend the day at work with her dad and the rest of us settled into especially appropriate activities, given what had happened the previous day. Since the safe space of the school had been violated, I was delighted to find that the three activities in the Bigs' class involved music – four hours of singing and two of drumming. Perfect to cleanse the space and help reestablish the true feelings of Fayette.

Reese's mom arrived with a friend who was a renowned drummer. She brought a dozen Middle Eastern drums, and soon great rhythms were heard from the Bigs' room while the Munchkins made and painted masks. Forest turned out to be not only a fine swing dancer but an excellent drummer; he and our guest led the class through many complex rhythms.

The final block of the day found the Munchkins with Arlen's dad, a local contractor. He gave each child a tape measure and they spent the time measuring everything in sight. After school Coleman proudly showed me his tape. I pointed out it was really a very long retractable number line. (My inner math teacher rarely rests.)

Jackson's mom brought three friends to sing with the Bigs. I later found out they were members of a well-known a cappella group. These women had sung with children in several schools but had never before sung with a group trained by Melanie. No self-consciousness, everyone singing out, in tune, in three parts. I drifted in for the last few minutes, and Forest and I held the low part of a great African song. Thursday as the kids left for home, they felt much better than they had the day before.

Friday the Munchkins stuffed and sewed pillows in the morning and went bowling in the afternoon. Several years before when the previous year's Boss, Adele, had been a Munchkin her parents had taken the class bowling. This outing had been so well received that a tradition was established. Dorothy, Adele's sister, was now a Munchkin, so her class went off for another adventure at the bowling alley. Coleman returned excited that he had bowled a whole game and scored all zeros. Rebecca rolled the only strike of the day.

While the Munchkins were bowling, Miranda's dad had an interesting project for the Bigs. He was a theoretical mathematician whose hobby was studying the probabilities of gambling. I walked into my classroom and found my students gathered around a full-size roulette wheel eagerly placing bets. They had each started with twenty dollars in chips, and he showed that by the end of the session each player would on the average be reduced to seventeen dollars. The lesson was that over the long term, the odds favored the house. In the short term, however, Briana happily came away with a hundred and fourteen dollars in chips. In gambling, for every winner there is at least one loser. Forest complained that after only six spins of the wheel he had no chips left.

Bowls of popcorn brought another Parents' Week to conclusion. Parents and children had had a marvelous time together sharing many varied activities. Not in the plan was that one little girl would be deeply hurt. Now I had to find the way to use this incident as a positive learning lesson and to make sure the mother never acted in such an unwise manner again at Fayette.

Week Twelve

The Head Elf

At Christmas play and make good cheer,
for Christmas comes but once a year.

THOMAS TUSSER

WE RETURNED from our Thanksgiving Break looking forward to the next three weeks – time when we would be elves, not teachers and students. Our elf society was not egalitarian. We had a definite hierarchy, and I was the Head Elf. Years before, a parent had crocheted a whimsical hat that immediately became the Head Elf hat. When I wore this hat we did no academics but through the whole school day moved our hands on various projects, sang, or often both. In these three short weeks we had choral practice and then a concert to perform, a school to decorate, and hundreds of gifts to make. We prided our school on teaching children the joy of personally creating gifts, not merely buying them at the mall. Gifts were made for friends, parents, grandparents, and a surplus could be given to local retirement homes. Our elves were always busy and happy and hopefully a little silly.

The young elves looked forward to the Crafts Weeks for several reasons. Many referred to it as the most creative they would be during the whole year. Also it was the time we were most involved in our school "community." With no papers or pencils to focus on, we moved our hands over various materials and hung out with each other. When the children spoke to their friends about the school, they talked of the genuine sense of connectedness. The kids felt part of the "Fayette family" – in ways they understood but others didn't necessarily comprehend. The crafts and concert weeks were the apex of this bonding.

We had a traditional rhythm to the Crafts, beginning with the simpler ones and then adding the more complex and challenging. Tuesday we began with our customary paper chains, "God's eyes," and embroidery. Forest and Matthew cut thousands of strips of multi-colored paper, and the younger elves stapled these into enough paper chains to decorate the ceilings of the school's rooms. In past years the Head Elf had stapled the chains to the ceiling, but this year my dislocated shoulder meant one more task fell to Forest.

While the paper chains were being produced in the one room, God's eyes were being created in a corner of another. Two toothpicks, a ball of variegated yarn, and a bit of hand-eye coordination produced these beautiful hanging ornaments. We needed several hundred of these, so every elf lent a hand from time to time. Years before, someone had used three toothpicks to make hexagonal ones and we still had a few produced each year. Young elves soon found that holding three toothpicks was much harder than holding two. The crafts weeks were filled with innumerable small lessons of hand-eye coordination and manual dexterity.

The Munchkins' room became "embroidery land" for the Crafts Weeks. As with other activities at Fayette, the decades of collective consciousness and the passing on of knowledge had created an expertise in which beautiful stitching was produced from the first day. Alison and Ele spent hours threading needles, untying knots, showing new stitches, and generally admiring the work. Boys and girls were equally good with needle and thread. We did not believe most activities to be sex linked, and surely not handicrafts; the thematic expressions might be different but the ability the same. For example, embroidery with well-controlled stitches could create both a beautiful spray of flowers and a gory skull with dripping blood.

Young Arlen produced the bestever first embroidery, a fantastic Christmas tree. He then learned an important lesson of elving: we were into production. If you could do one, do six. In awed tones, word passed around the school that Walker could thread his own needle. "Geez, I was eleven before I could thread mine." "I still can't; that's why I sit close to Maggie when I stitch." Tara sewed a backing on each embroidery, after which the elves stuffed them with cotton balls and a pinch of potpourri, then sewed them closed, creating sachets.

Each year several hundred were made and found their way into drawers around America.

While the school was turned into an elfin workshop, Marianne's studio became Melanie's full-time music room. Everyone was introduced to their xylophone parts. In the 1920s Carl Orff designed xylophones used for teaching children. The bars were removable, so along with the ability to switch keys with the interchange of a few sharps and flats, most bars could be removed completely, leaving but a few well-spaced ones. The youngest Munchkins used only one mallet and by hitting a bar in time with the song, added to the sound of the performance. Older and more accomplished students faced more bars, wielded two or three mallets, and played more complex rhythmic and chord-changing patterns.

Each student had at least one xylophone part in the concert. We had five different instruments, ranging from a tiny soprano glockenspiel, small enough to hold in one hand, to a bass xylophone that required two people to move. Melanie wrote the parts for each instrument based on the intersection of music theory and student ability. The collective sound was marvelous and the neural development of the players tremendous. Four hours of Tuesday were required to introduce each student to their xylo part. The rest of the day small groups headed to the studio to learn songs.

Though most were comfortable in their elfish alter egos, we still had to deal with the Munchkin girl disharmony. While the rest of us were beginning our crafting and singing, Marianne held a meeting with the Munchkin girls. Her approach at such meetings was never to examine the details of the past or assign blame but rather to develop effective strategies and habits for the future. After some discussion all agreed on a common goal: to feel safe personally and also to get along with all others in the school community. They agreed that each poke or mean word by itself was not the problem, but they had linked dozens of these in tit for tat.

Marianne suggested the use of a hand sign and a word to help break their linking and escalation of negative interactions. Nyssa suggested a thumbs-up sign. Rebecca felt thumbs down would better express the feeling. Dorothy thought a thumb sideways would be an excellent and neutral signal. All agreed. After some discussion of words and their power, they agreed words like "stop" or "peace" were too loaded and a word having nothing to do with the situation would be best. Katherine said a picture of an umbrella had jumped into her head. And so the young girls joined the rest of the elves with the word *umbrella* and a sideways thumb as their defense against habituated patterns. By the end of the day students had been introduced to their xylophone parts and had spent hours elfing, and the young girls had used the thumb and umbrella to counter old behaviors. An excellent beginning to three weeks of creativity and learning.

Wednesday brought the return of the eager elves and also Cloud, a student from years past. Former students, as they sat in final exams in high school and college, fondly remembered the Crafts Weeks. Each year usually found one or two of them dropping by to watch and help for a little while; they were always welcome. This year Cloud was between life's tasks and available to help with crafts for two weeks. Since he added an extra pair of hands and all projects were going so smoothly, coil baskets could be started a day earlier than usual.

Coil baskets have been made from natural materials for millennia. The timeless nature of the repetitive motion of the wrapping of fibers around the core material was satisfying to mind and body. We used muted-toned variegated yarns around a core made from recycled cardboard. For years we used a thick coil, thinking this would be easier for small hands and would create large baskets more quickly. Then somewhere we acquired a roll of very small-diameter coil and let a few of the older, more experienced basket makers try their hand. Quickly a large number of beautiful miniature baskets were being produced. These became our standard, and only a few large coils were still used each year.

Matthew had become our best basket maker. For the past four years he had explored patterns more complex than our standard simple basket. As he created new patterns others followed his lead. Given the ways of Fayette, years from now his influence would still benefit this area of crafts. We now had baskets with lids, complex curves, and patterned changes of color. Michiah, who still had two years until high school, was learning from our young master and would undoubtedly add his style to our future baskets.

Cloud sat in the middle of the basket makers with a huge smile. He was remembering when he was only eight years old and I was helping him with needle and yarn. Now he was the teacher and other young ones were coming to him. The closing of such circles brings sublime satisfaction.

Zoe and Eliza each taught a small group of elves different patterns of finger weaving. Vast quantities of the God's eye yarn were soon wrapped around fingers, then looped over in repeated patterns, producing yards of multicolored cording. At the end of the day the sections were joined together and taken out for measurement on the sidewalk. One hundred fifty feet of finger weaving in a day must be some kind of Guinness record! This chain, all the God's eyes, strings of popcorn, and a mini–paper-chain would soon decorate our school tree.

Embroidery continued with good focus, fine stitches, and creative designs. Heather needled a beautiful cluster of grapes using six different purples. Briana stitched a piebald cow. Jessica made the face of a duck viewed head on. This looked like a Pokémon character to me, and overextending the metaphor I gave my encouragement to the finishing of the Poké-grapes, Poké-cow, and Poké-everything else. Silly word play was one of the main tasks of the Head Elf. Many excellent Poké-trees and Poké-menorahs were being stitched for our sachet contest.

With various Christmas CDs playing throughout the day elves worked in harmony. Marianne gathered the Munchkin girls for a short meeting to see how well they were getting along and how the sign and word were working. They were doing fine, especially since they were spread around the school surrounded by older elves who maintained a positive social tone. The only incident to recap was that Eliza, while stitching next to Katherine, kept repeating *umbrella* and would not stop when asked. Finally Katherine moved to another location, ending the incident.

In the studio each group of xylophone players ran through their parts. The Bigs played the instruments only twice a year, during the weeks before each concert. I was always amazed at the neurologic improvement in each student from year to year, especially the ones least proficient at the beginning. Last year for his first concert with us, Alexander had been given only three bars and the instruction to hit any one of them to the beat of the song. He came to us at age twelve after previous schooling had not been a great success. Kids not "on track" act out or withdraw, either of which effectively masks true talents. Alexander had chosen the withdrawn defense, making it hard to tell his real mental abilities.

In the third week of school, a group was playing cards and I saw him "shoot the moon" in hearts two hands in a row. I knew by this that he was bright and merely hiding. Marianne then worked with his dominance profile and helped him access and integrate his dormant abilities. This year his xylophone part had many bars and a chord pattern, one small but significant indicator of neural integration.

Thursday we settled into our now familiar rhythm of focusing on one craft, switching to another when tired of the first, helping younger ones when needed, heading to the studio to play the xylos or sing accompaniment while another group played. Everyone was so engaged with their projects they voted not to go to the park, but stayed at school for nonstop elfing from 8:30 until 3:00. Those who felt a little antsy would go outside, run up and down the sidewalk a time or two, and return to their projects.

This year's Winter Concert would have twenty-seven songs in eight different languages. We had five Latin chants in the concert, and since Munchkins didn't speak Latin, extra time and an extra person were needed to teach them the songs. James, our most trained singer, volunteered for this task. Melanie showed him a few pointers, and he gathered his flock of Munchkins for a teaching session. As much as I enjoyed teaching, I more enjoyed watching the children instruct each other. James did a marvelous job, and I was sure that in the concert we wouldn't have mumbling Munchkins during the Latin chants. Later in the day Marianne lectured on the meanings of the chants.

Our afternoon singing practice was well focused and had several surprises. We were doing so well that Melanie added a level of difficulty to the show: for our two Spanish songs the altos and "lows" were to sing "a third" down from the melody. Amelia had often expressed in algebra class that it seemed unfair that as soon as she grasped a concept, I would present her with a new and more difficult one. She said this was discouraging. I expressed a teacher's opinion that, on the contrary, this was challenging for the mind and possibly good for the soul.

Now just when the lows were finally singing on key, Melanie was having us sing off the key. Definitely unfair and discouraging. Whereas in algebra Amelia could turn to other students for help, in music we turned our ears toward James. He sang thirds and probably any other interval with great ease. Melanie was smiling, and Marianne thought we sounded good, but I was glad when the hour ended.

On Friday we opened the beading table. Running the beading table was a task trying for both eyes and nerves. Ele and Alison rotated every hour at the main chair, and one of the older elves was always at their side threading the tiny beading needles, untangling knots, and helping the younger ones pass the needle through the proper bead in the correct pattern. Though the first project for new Munchkins was to bead a single-strand necklace, most elves were found working on loop earrings, multistrand intricately patterned necklaces, peyote-stitched pendants, and more. We used the smallest of beads and the finest of materials. In fact, several graduates while in college had made spending money by using the techniques learned at Fayette to make earrings for fellow students.

When Cloud was a young student at the school he had desired to make a bracelet for his mother more complex than the single strand. Marianne gave him a beading booklet with drawings and instructions for various patterns and told him to pick one out, try it, and see what happened. In a short time he produced a beautiful bracelet and began teaching others the pattern. To his delight he found the present elves continuing to make these bracelets.

In music we had allowed some new traditions to become standards as well. The xylo parts scored by Melanie required no variation or improvisation except for those of one song. Several years before, I had told Melanie that the traditional Hanukkah and old English Christmas carols were fine but that the culture of my youth also had seasonal songs. A skeptical look had come over her face – for someone raised in Boston, Southern California surfers probably didn't have any culture and definitely couldn't have any Christmas songs. Having prepared for this moment, I had handed her the Beach Boys' Christmas CD and the sheet music to "Little Saint Nick." Three days later she had returned with the basic chording for the xylophones and vocal parts to fit our singers. This song was now one of the high points of our annual concert, and each year's players enjoyed working out their own variations for the xylophones.

Since this was the hardest song to play, the best were assigned the task. This year Forest, Zoe, Jonah, and Amelia had the honors. An hour of talking, experimenting, trial, and evolution, in the best spirit of Brian Wilson, created this year's instrumental version. When they were ready, the rest of the students joined them in the studio as we threw good vibrations back and forth between choir and xylos.

Next we practiced "Silent Night," sung in three parts. It became obvious that the sound from the lows had changed. Being a small school we knew each other well, both strengths and weaknesses. Until now Alexander had only mouthed words as we sang. As we finished singing, everyone looked at him in amazement: a beautiful voice had been added to the choir.

⌘ Week Thirteen ⌘

Tolerance and Sensitivity

*I have learned . . . toleration from the intolerant
and kindness from the unkind.*

KAHLIL GIBRAN

OUR SECOND of three weeks of crafts and music brought our focus to the festival of Hanukkah, the Islamic holy month of Ramadan, and ever increasing thoughts on the birth of Jesus. While the young elves were busy singing and crafting, we wove the theme of tolerance and sensitivity toward others through our banter and activities. Our local high schools and middle schools had recently realized that intolerance was a growing social problem on their campuses. At Fayette we started the teaching of tolerance and sensitivity the first day a student walked on the bricks.

Tuesday the arriving elves found the evergreen tree in the Munchkins' room, undecorated as yet, though as in all years past bearing a small candy cane for each elf. The candy canes, besides being a treat, were used as a demonstration of the different types of rules we encounter in life. Some rules, such as the law of gravity, are absolute. Others, like manners and etiquette, are at times useful but always optional. Our school policy of no candy was in a third category, arbitrary rules. New students learned that the Head Elf operated outside of the no-candy dictum. Not surprisingly, no one objected to the breaking of this rule. Nor did anyone use the presence of daily candy canes to assume other candy was permitted.

Rebecca, one of our Jewish students and new to the school, looked at the tree and came to me saying she was not comfortable with the idea of Christmas trees. I pointed out that sharing the customs of others was not a disloyalty to one's own beliefs – being a guest and a convert were two very different things. Working the theme that we all should know more about the traditions and ceremonies of others, I related how attending and participating in a bar mitzvah several years ago had been a great day in my life but had not made me Jewish. Playing my trump card last, I pointed out this was not a Christmas tree but rather a "pagan" tree: the use of the tree predated the Christian era in Europe and had been added to the collection of Christmas customs rather like the bunny had been added to Easter.

She thanked me, grabbed a candy cane, and headed off to practice her xylophone part for "Mah Tovu." This was a marvelous Hebrew song we sang in three parts with four Munchkins leading us on the xylos. Rebecca and other girls then decorated the tree with the yards of paper chains, finger weaving, popcorn strings, and hundreds of God's eyes.

The week also featured the annual return of Dylan Thomas's "A Child's Christmas in Wales." We began each day by listening to the Head Elf read from this enchanting short story. Forest and Matthew were lamenting that they were hearing it read for a sixth and final time. Ariel and Michiah were in the more comfortable position of having the images in their heads from previous years and knowing they still had several more years of listening to the story. The new students fell into a synchronous resonance with all the veterans. Staff, alumni, and an occasional parent gathered to once more be touched by the magic of Dylan Thomas and his Welsh roots. As I ended the first sentence, "I can never remember whether it snowed for six days and six nights when I was twelve or whether it snowed for twelve days and twelve nights when I was six," out of the corner of my eye, I saw Forest and Matthew mouthing the words. This was one of the special moments in the life of this teacher. The rest of the day was spent with baskets, beads, and embroidery as small groups skipped to the studio to practice their xylophone parts.

Wednesday Kyrie brought the first book of the popular Harry Potter series on cassette tape. Most of us had by now read or listened to at least one of the three books so far published, and the young girls gathered in the stove room to hear the tapes. While hands still moved on projects, ears were cocked toward Kyrie's small cassette player, trying to hear the story over the sounds of Bing Crosby's "White Christmas." Over the years we had assembled a large and eclectic collection of Christmas tapes and CDs: performers from the forties and fifties; many different instrumentals, including harps, dulcimers, and string ensembles; various choirs; and styles from different cultures – Spanish, Celtic, Hawaiian, and such. Different years brought different favorites. The least favorite never changed however – a collection from the forties of country-western Christmas songs.

Years and years and years ago, when I was a boy, when music was only on the radio, before Garth Brooks, before music videos, "country" *did* sound hokey. I was now allowed to play this tape only once a year. This year the CDs most requested were Bing's and Nat King Cole's. There was a comfort in their voices that seemed to fill a void in the psyche of our modern kids raised with computer mouse in hand. The favorite single cut was "Santa Baby" by Eartha Kitt. Kyrie began a movement to have this steamy parody added to our concert the following year.

This day added tie-dyeing to our already busy schedule. While many elves focused on one of the "three BS" – beading, baskets, 'broidery – different groups were scurrying to the studio for xylophone practice and individuals were called to the tying table in the front room or later to the dyeing table out on the bricks. Whereas beads are beautiful bits of glass and basket and embroidery yarns are brightly colored fibers, tie-dyeing is liquid, chemical, and messy. Any elfin prissiness was quickly revealed.

After finishing the dyeing of her collections of shirts and socks, young Rachel approached me with gloves covered in dye and hands held out like a surgeon headed to the operating table. The messiness was about to overwhelm her. "How do I clean these?" "You could stick them in the pond." Her look of disgust showed me further talk was needed. "I know you think the pond is full of foul, stinky swamp water, but you haven't looked. I cleaned the pond over the weekend and the water is clear." I headed into the school, leaving her alone to mull over my suggestion. Through the window I watched her dip her gloves into the pond. This went on much longer than it takes to rinse off dye.

By late morning the heat from the stove room had worked its way into the Munchkins' room. On one of my circuits through the school checking on elfin productivity, I saw eight pairs of legs sticking out from under the tree. Upon investigation I found that Kyrie and her *Harry Potter* group had their heads under the tree listening to the tapes. "Which of the three bs can you be working on lying under the tree?" "We have added a fourth b – books," was the reply. Hard for a teacher to object to books or a Head Elf to want to change such a tableau. In twenty minutes we would be singing together for the rest of the day and many fine items already had been produced, so Harry Potter continued.

Our concert was now only seven days away, and we were beginning to both feel the pressure of the performance and become more comfortable with the material. We worked mostly on the more difficult songs, those sung in three parts. Melanie repeatedly cued us until we knew the timing of our own parts and also could hear those sung by others. She had thought of a surprise accompaniment to the last song in the show. Zoe and Sam's dad, who played many musical instruments, joined us. He played, we sang; the combination worked. We swore the choir to secrecy. The day ended with happy elves singing and carrying boxes of wet tie-dyed articles to their cars. After the last elf drove away the Head Elf restocked the tree with candy canes. This time not only a cane for each but three extras. A temptation test for young elves.

Several copies of the daily newspaper came to school on Thursday. Heather's mom was an artist and one of her paintings was on the front page. She had donated the piece to our community college, and several groups had taken exception to seeing a gorilla crucified on a cross. Interestingly, Lauren's mom was the college's administrator dealing with the issue. This was an excellent example on the subject of sensitivity. Discussion around the beading table was filled with talk of artist's freedom and the use of symbols disturbing to people holding different beliefs, all done as hands moved without ceasing.

Someone suggested Ken should come in and hold a trial on the matter of the painting and the college. Alison pointed out our schedule did not have room for a lengthy trial at this busiest time of year but said they could continue our roundtable discussion as they beaded. After Heather and Lauren had shared what each had heard from her mother and others gathered around the table had added their thoughts, consensus was that the theme of human harm to the animal kingdom was noble but the message could have been expressed with symbols that did not offend major religious groups. I so enjoyed when real situations were presented in order to teach the lessons of tolerance and sensitivity. They always took better hold in young minds than abstract platitudes.

In the afternoon Rebecca's mom came with a menorah, several dreidels, and a large bag of peanuts. After relating the story of Hanukkah and the lighting of candles, she explained the rules used in the spinning of the dreidel. Soon small groups were spread around the school. Peanuts passed back and forth according to the fall of the dreidel. Everyone enjoyed the hour. At the end of the day the Head Elf found three candy canes still on the tree. A more honorable group of elves could not be desired.

Friday was the beginning of Islam's holy month of Ramadan. Christmas at Fayette meant making presents and the reading of the birth of Jesus in the Bible. Hanukkah brought the lighting of the menorah. Honoring Ramadan was not so easy, however. Going the school day without food or water did not seem appropriate as we knew that the real goal of the fasting was not weight loss but rather to break unconscious habits and thereby turn attention to the Deity. Several years previous we had begun our own ritual for Ramadan. The morning after I saw the new moon I would announce the beginning of the holy month at Fayette. We would leave one floor pillow for each student in the school and the rest were moved into storage by a procession of the Big boys. For the month no one could touch more than one pillow at a time. Why pillows? Because they were a huge symbol at Fayette. The students sat or reclined on them during lecture and study; graduates later lamented the return to the rows of hard desks of other schools. Having only one pillow was a reminder that this month was different.

We crafted through the morning. Our new elves had mastered each of the skills and embraced the idea of production. As soon as one project was finished, hands turned to another. Small groups around the school were exchanging pointers on the various crafts. "How did you make that French knot on your basket lid?" "Wind five times around the needle and then pull the yarn through." In beading, the designs were becoming exceptionally complex. Beaders combined different techniques and patterns. Each completed project generated new ideas for the next: "I wove through every fourth bead for two rows and then through every third." "Five purples and then a red helps me remember the pattern and looks cool." Our most difficult technique was the "peyote stitch." Word passed through the school that Miranda had shown young Eliza the stitch and she was actually doing it. Through the day we all watched in amazement as her pendant continued to grow. She had shattered the age record by several years.

All beaders were in one of three classifications: Kitten, Fox, Tiger. "Kitten" beaders were the beginners and worked seated on a denim floor cover. They inevitably spilled their beads and this way the beads did not disappear into the carpet and eventually the vacuum. "Fox" beaders sat where they wished. "Tiger" beaders helped others, added clasps, solved others' problems, and untangled the hopeless knots of Kitten beaders; they were also the only ones allowed to sit behind the bead table with Alison and Ele. Matthew, an indifferent beader though our best basket maker, commented that advancing beyond beading was silly because you then had extra work helping others. Miranda countered by saying the increased status offset the added burden. Dorothy spilled her plate of beads and declared herself a Kitten beader for the rest of the day.

Before our first complete run-through of the concert program in the afternoon, we went outside for a few minutes of sunshine and fresh air. As I was setting up the xylos in the classroom, Amelia came in to say Sylvan had just sung an anti-Semitic parody of one of the Hebrew songs to a group of girls. Briana, who was Jewish, was upset, and Amelia was upset because Briana was upset. Word spread through the student body and everyone waited to see what the Head Elf would do.

Instead of the usual strategy of asking Sylvan and the two girls to be the center of a discussion, I told Briana and Amelia, "Shake it off. Get ready to sing. This is one reason we sing – to push back such words of poor taste. Remember what Arlo Guthrie said, 'If you want to end war and stuff, you gotta sing loud.' *Stuff* includes what Sylvan said." I went back to finish setting up xylos and music sheets.

The rehearsal was fine; we were smooth on most songs and found the few spots needing increased focus. Everyone, save Sylvan, felt confident and united. Throughout the rehearsal he stood back in the corner singing with small voice. Waiting for attention from the Head Elf can be worse than the discussion itself.

After Melanie dismissed us we went out on the bricks to await the arrival of the parent cars. Still I said nothing to Sylvan. Kids were looking at each other, wondering why the change of pattern from dealing directly with an incident as soon as it happened. After a few minutes Sylvan's dad arrived, and as father and son came together I quietly said, "Sing to your dad what you sang to Briana." In a small, dry, eggshell voice, with others around, he sang the song again. Father and son had a heartfelt meeting on one of the benches, a talk on the boundary between humor and insensitivity.

∽ Week Fourteen ∾
Winter Concert

*All creatures of our God and King
lift up your voice and with us sing.*

SAINT FRANCIS OF ASSISI

SEVERAL PARENTS unable to attend the concert on Wednesday came to our final rehearsal Tuesday morning. Amelia's mom could stay only a short time and asked if we might perform "Little Saint Nick" before she needed to depart. The xylo play of Amelia and the three others had been the main talk at home. Most concerts have encores, so why not a pre-core? The song was well played and our mother happy. We also practiced our three most challenging numbers, then ran through the whole show. By 11:30 we had done everything individually and collectively to prepare for the concert. We relaxed and began gathering strength, each in our own way, for the performance.

Some headed for the bead table, several card games developed in various corners, sachets were finished. Melanie quietly embroidered, showing Rachel several new stitches. Forest lay on the pile of coats in the stove room, reading Steinbeck's *Of Mice and Men*. Seeing he had but a few pages left I whispered to those in the room to watch his reaction in the next few minutes. Right on cue he jumped and yelled, "He killed her! He broke her neck!" Ele commented she had had the same reaction when she read this classic novella several years ago. Marianne seconded her statement, saying only to change *years* to *decades* in her case.

Every teacher is happy when a student enjoys literature. This moment was extra sweet as reading had not come easily to Forest. His own perseverance, his parents' patient years of reading to him, Marianne's studio work, and the absence of a TV in his home had combined to add a member to the Readers for Pleasure Club.

For the past two weeks Melanie's every thought had been about musical keys, xylophones, timings, and chord progressions. Now she was resting. Kyrie seized the moment to pitch her desire to add "Santa Baby" to next year's show. She put on the CD. Eartha Kitt began to sing, six girls joined her, Forest and I sang the bass line. Melanie, poker faced, listened intently. The song ended. Kyrie waited for the edict. Would Melanie think the words inappropriate for young children? Would she find something in the musical structure outside of our abilities? After a long pause where we knew she was listening to the voices inside her head, she said, "I can hear the xylo parts." Kyrie whooped in triumph. The day ended with reminders to get a good night's sleep, eat a real breakfast, and be dropped off at the chapel, not school, in the morning.

The Loretto Chapel was the first Gothic church built west of the Mississippi and was located on a narrow street in Santa Fe's historic center. Its small size and vaulted ceiling were perfect for our voices. The chapel had been deconsecrated and was now a tourist attraction. I greeted each student as they were dropped off on Wednesday morning and sent them inside to join Marianne and their schoolmates. The veterans showed the new ones around. Inside the chapel we were surrounded by the visual richness of nineteenth-century Catholicism: statues of the Twelve Stations of the Cross and the Virgin, stained-glass scenes from the Bible – religious images were everywhere. I whispered a prayer and opened the gate to the altar platform; the xylos were brought in. Melanie assigned final positions on the altar steps to each group and individual.

At 9:15 we began our warm-up. Melanie called for the first verses of several songs. As we sang she walked to the back of the chapel, returned, adjusted the volumes of the different sections, changed a few vowel sounds. We repeated these warm-ups and soundings for half an hour. The few early tourists were delighted. Our collective voices sounded crisper and bouncier with the rows of empty pews than they would in the concert with seats filled and aisles packed with people. Zoe and Sam's dad played a few bars, we joined our voices, Melanie smiled. Our surprise should work. Rehearsal finished, we left the altar and chapel single file, walking slowly in silence as we headed for drinking fountains and bathrooms. The kids were excited. We teachers kept them calm, saving energy for the performance.

When we were finished with the facilities, I gathered the choir for our pregame pep talk. "'Why are we singing this concert?" I asked. "To have fun." "To show our skill." Fine answers, but nothing to get the blood boiling. Briana spoke next. "I'm tired of everyone looking at my friends and me like we are criminals and gang members just because we are teenagers." Now I had a theme to work with: "In the next two hours, if we focus on Melanie's direction, remember our breathing, and do what we have practiced, we can blow away any of those thoughts from three hundred parents and friends. They might not think you quite angels, but surely not gangsters. By the way, Pete is videotaping and we will be on the evening news statewide." With my last statement in mind we all retraced our steps to the chapel.

The empty pews we had left half an hour before were now packed with people buzzing with excited small talk. At the gateway to the altar, I handed each choir member a songbook; most touched my gold tiepin for good luck. Years before in Scotland I had been given this pin which originally had been presented by Queen Victoria to a grand-nephew. The royal touch had now for years been part of our concert tradition. Once we were seated Marianne led us in a few minutes of Brain Gym. She left; Melanie came forward; we stood. Show time.

Our opening selections were two chants, one Islamic and one Hindu. We warmed our voices, quieted the audience, proclaimed the oneness of God, and prayed for world peace. A good start to any concert. We also gave a hint of how our different sections sounded in the chapel. The "middles" were a fine blend of the voices of all Munchkins, some Big girls, and Alison and Tara. Their sound was our anchor and filled the chapel with the melody of each song. On the second verse of the Hindu chant we few "lows" broke from them and held a long-sustained "om," which rolled slowly out over the audience. For the third verse, also leaving the main melody, the "highs" bounced their descant off the vaulted ceiling. The three sounds mixed, separated, and danced in the Gothic acoustics.

Our next few selections were three-part rounds embracing Yuletide themes. The Munchkins played our first song with xylo accompaniment. Like our voices the various instruments filled different parts of the space. We sang "Deck the Hall" in unison, the closest we would come to popular holiday songs in our concert.

Our largest challenge, the Bach cantata, arrived next, followed by another choral piece from the same era. This was where we each would increase our own confidence and integrate with the others to build a unified sound, or we each would withdraw into our own fears, close our ears, and mumble the rest of the show. A subtle courage moved through the young choir. We united, we strength-

ened each other, we held together; our different sections blended chords, melodies, and countermelodies with growing confidence. The highs blasted a few "Alleluias" off the rosette window at the back of the chapel; Pete's camera rolled; the audience staggered. We were in the Zone.

From the staid majesty of Protestantism's choral music we switched to our Hebrew selections with their mix of lively melodies and minor keys. Melanie had created marvelous xylo parts for these songs. The Hebrew phonemes were easy and a joy to sing after the attention needed to enunciate the English phrases of the previous hymns. Marianne returned for a short Brain Gym session. We each remembered to breathe, took a moment to integrate, and gathered our energy for the final three songs before intermission.

"Pat-a-Pan," a French carol sung in three parts, and our two Spanish carols with challenging xylo parts and singing in the dreaded thirds harmony brought us to the end of the first half. We had sung fourteen songs in six languages, enchanted the crowd, and left our fears behind. We sat for a few minutes. Tara and Alison passed around bottles of water. Melanie distributed slippery elm lozenges. I looked in the eyes of the singers to make sure each was comfortable. Many small fingers reached to touch Victoria's tiepin.

After ten minutes, Forest blew our train whistle to announce the start of the second half. The Munchkins began by leading us in the old spiritual "Mary Had a Baby." These young ones stood on the lowest step of the altar with nothing between them and the audience except Melanie and her music stand. They looked adorable. This year Coleman and Walker were front and center – one with a red sweater and one with green – angelic choirboys.

While the audience was still enamored with the sight and sound of the wee ones, we began "Dancing Day," an old English choral that featured a beautiful descant by the highs. While the middles singing the melody held the attention, the lows added a richness with a countermelody. The highs delayed and then from an impossibly high note sang down the scale. As the chapel filled with intersecting sounds, we again felt the audience reel, saw parents weep, heard the applause explode. Two fine wassail songs, one English and one American, brought us to our Latin section. "Adeste Fideles," two Gregorian chants, and "Hodie Christus Natus Est" from Benjamin Britten's *Ceremony of Carols* were well pronounced and sung, showing our ease with the language and our ability to sing long phrases without sneaking breaths.

Melanie always used the selection and order of songs as well as the different combinations of our voices to bring variety to the program. We employed a device learned from the funeral of Princess Diana for our most extreme change of pace: Elton John had opened up the audience with rock 'n' roll and then the Earl of Spencer had pierced their souls with his message. Our technique was to open the crowd with the Beach Boys' "Little Saint Nick" and then thrust with "Silent Night." So far through the concert the audience had applauded graciously, alternating between dry and teary eyes, but sat still. For "Saint Nick" they all rocked – Easterners a little, Californians more. The crowd was happy and open; it was time for the coup de grace. We sang the first verse of "Silent Night" in English in two parts – sacred, solid, familiar. This was the setup. Archimedes said he could move the whole world given the right fulcrum and lever. The second verse, sung in German, was our fulcrum, the highs our lever. As the rest of us continued our two parts from the first verse, the highs blasted a descant that moved the audience, me, Melanie, and possibly the world. At the end there was no applause, only stunned silence.

As the Munchkins quietly set xylo bars for the penultimate song, half a dozen teenagers left the pews and joined the choir. Our alumni had returned. During this move Zoe and Sam's dad slipped behind the altar screen into the sacristy. With five Munchkins on the xylos we sang "Christmas is Coming" in a three-part round: "God bless you, everyone, God bless you."

In past years this song had ended our concert. Now, however, a sound hard to identify came from the sacristy and grew as it came into the chapel. We began singing "Auld Lang Syne" to the accompaniment of bagpipes. With each chorus, more and more of the audience joined in the singing. Following the Scots tradition we joined hands on the final verse, pumped them up and down on the final chorus, and finished the concert with hands in the air waving to a standing ovation.

Our job done, the force that had held us in unified focus and as one voice was gone. We broke our formation at the altar. Each child headed toward their parents to be greeted by hugs and kisses. As Melanie and I packed the instruments and music stands, many people came forward with congratulations. Those who were attending for the first time expressed amazement at the difficulty of material and the quality of the kids' singing and playing. They noted that even the youngest sang eight different languages with comfort. I pointed out that no one was selected or excluded for their vocal talents, that everyone in the school sang, and that each child played on the xylophones. I added that though we had been working on the harder numbers longer, we had had only two weeks of rehearsal for the majority of the concert. The children and families headed toward various restaurants for celebratory lunches, and then we gathered at school for a quiet afternoon, enjoying the relief following a performance well sung.

Thursday we assembled still mentally and emotionally spent but happy the concert had been so well given and received. Melanie congratulated us and told of the phone calls she had received from some of those in the audience. We finished projects, played games, listened to Christmas CDs, and awaited the final school day of the week, year, century, and millennium.

Friday was filled with once-a-year activities. We began by preparing each craft for storage. Basket yarn was wound into tight balls, embroidery thread sorted, beads bagged and labeled. We played a tape of Dylan Thomas reading "A Child's Christmas in Wales." As in previous years all were enchanted.

Throughout the day I announced my upcoming reading from the Bible. The veterans and I played a gentle game on the new ones. "I will be reading every word in the Bible concerning the birth of Jesus," I informed all. The older ones grumbled how this took hours. The young ones knew this was to be the final activity before the opening of presents and were duly concerned. Fortunately the birth is covered in only fifty verses read in less than ten minutes: Matthew 1:18–2:21 and Luke 2:1–20. When I was finished, our new students breathed audible sighs of relief.

Before my final duty as Head Elf, monitoring the exchanging of presents, I had the kids "practice their lines." Ariel gave the line for a present really desired: "Thank you very much." Then Forest delivered the line used after opening a present impossible to relate to: "Thank you very much." So reminded everyone enjoyed the giving and receiving of gifts.

The previous week the names of each student had been placed in the Head Elf Hat and drawn for the exchange. Cina had pulled Matthew's name and used the occasion to employ the "multiple box" trick adding a new twist. When I handed him his present, Matthew tore his way through seven beautifully wrapped boxes within boxes to find not a present but a scrap of paper saying the CD he had wished for was with Ele at the bead table. Arlen opened the best present, a box full of various magnets complete with instructions for little engineers. I later saw in the newspaper these were being recalled for having lead paint. I trusted Arlen hadn't eaten any. Alison received the most presents, a heart warming response to her semester of love and care of her young charges.

We finished the day singing those popular Christmas songs we didn't sing in our concert: songs about Rudolph, Frosty, Jingle Bells, and Santa's imminent arrival in town. When 3:00 arrived we exchanged holiday cheer with parents and said good-byes as each student left for a two-week break. That night, like the boy in Dylan Thomas's story, "I got into bed, I said some words to the close and holy darkness, and then I slept."

∽ Hard Nine Weeks ∾

FOR NINE WEEKS, uninterrupted by holidays, spring fever, or year end fatigue, all worked at maximum intensity. Subjects were explored to deeper levels, homework loads increased. Each person, staff and student alike, pushed beyond previous limits of scholarship.

∽ Week Fifteen ∾
Hard Nine Weeks

The most important motive for work in the school and life is the pleasure in work. . . . I have known children who preferred school time to vacation.

ALBERT EINSTEIN

TEACHERS AND STUDENTS returned to school glad to be together again after two weeks of vacation. Everyone had a touch of anxiety, for the Hard Nine Weeks (HNW) were beginning. In many schools peak efforts and final exams occur near Christmas and at the end of a long year. However the holiday excitement and the year-end fatigue do not optimize performance. Years before, we had realized that the winter months were the best time for our maximum academic effort. Students and staff knew we would work harder than ever before and the scope of the subjects would also be greater. The Bigs faced the Bible, the Constitution, the prehistory of Scotland, and physics in addition to our standard courses in Latin, Greek, mathematics, and writing. The Munchkins would push their three Rs, speak more French, and write a weekly research report. The staff worked hard during class hours to help each student maintain the intensity. Both staff and students spent many extra evening and weekend hours on classwork during these demanding weeks.

The studio sessions were also gearing up again. We had held no studio sessions during the craft and music weeks. We felt that singing and listening were the best stimulation possible for ear-brain connections, while threading needles, embroidering, and beading were excellent for hand-eye coordination. Both the crafts and singing used and strengthened uncountable pathways for whole body-brain integration. Added to this were the social and emotional development of working outside the usual class groups and curriculum, plus partnering with schoolmates of different ages and teaming with familiar friends on new activities. The studio work of the first months of school had laid the foundation for neural development during the crafts and singing weeks. The activities of these weeks then set the stage for the intense studio work of the Hard Nine Weeks.

Most schools in Santa Fe scheduled an extra week of vacation in the winter of 1999–2000 to avoid the potential disruptions of Y2K. We instead ordered a Port-a-Potty. However, since Y2K turned out to be a nonevent and our electrical and water systems were functioning, the Port-a-Potty became a playroom for the Munchkin boys. They locked each other inside, packing in a half dozen at a time. They lifted the tank lid to explore the workings of the system. I was sure they would be more comfortable the next time they were confronted with one and its standard use!

Walking on the ice on the pond was the other favorite activity of the Munchkin gentlemen. Winter temperatures had finally arrived, freezing the pond. After a time of gentle walking, the boys enjoyed stomping through the ice. I asked only that they not damage the beautiful ice sculpture created each night by the waterfall.

Wednesday night had not been as cold as the previous two nights, so on Thursday morning when young Robby, our leading icebreaker, gave his biggest jump, he found himself through the ice, standing on the bottom of the pond, shoes and pant legs soaked. The girls took this as more evidence that males come from another planet or at least as another demonstration that living with only one *x* chromosome was a severe handicap. The Big boys just shook their heads. I reminded them of the time several years before when I was hanging their shoes and sox above the wood stove after similar breakthroughs. Though by Friday the Port-a-Potty was gone and our mini–Ice Age disappeared with warmer temperatures, for three days the Munchkin boys had a marvelous time with our hands-on learning systems.

The Fayette philosophy was that Munchkins, being young, should have fun every day, even during the HNW, but for the Bigs the burdens began at 8:00. Before lunch on Tuesday we had surveyed all the work for the next months, exploring factoring and primes in number theory, reading excerpts from the Declaration of Independence as a prelude to our study of the Constitution, and beginning the use of the metric system in preparation for our physics studies. The afternoon brought an hour of Latin with Marianne and an hour of writing with Ele. Munchkins could be found in small groups with McGuffey Readers or surrounded by encyclopedias and Zoobooks, a series of animal booklets published by the San Diego Zoological Society, as they started researching the facts related to various admired mammals, avians, reptiles, and the occasional marsupial.

While Tuesday was a day of transition from the weeks of crafts and vacation, on Wednesday we returned to school operating at full speed. In the Bigs' class during each HNW we studied a sacred text. We had a four-year cycle: Buddhism's *Dhamapada*, Islam's *Koran*, Hinduism's *Bhagavad Gita*, and this year the Bible of the Judæo-Christian faiths. Though I gave historical commentary and answered questions using the belief system of each year's religion, most of the time was spent with the class reading aloud and discussing the actual text. Each of these texts has a powerful captivating literary style and deals with the deepest questions of human experience. Wednesday brought the book of Genesis and the creation of the world. Thursday introduced us to Adam, Eve, the Garden of Eden, and the serpent. On Friday we read of Noah and his ark.

Wednesday's text with the two versions of the creation of woman, Gen. 1:27 and Gen. 2:21, brought excellent discussion. Our goal was for each student to become knowledgeable with the material and spend time creating their own beliefs and opinions about the texts, and then by extension the world around them. Forest thought God unfair for putting the forbidden trees in the middle of Eden; most agreed with him. Amelia felt that the curse laid on women of painful childbirth just for eating a piece of fruit was way too harsh. I pointed out that this was not just any piece of fruit and also this was an account from a people living over three thousand years ago, creating a story to explain the phenomena experienced in their daily lives. Weaving this with our lectures on prehistory, I reminded them that for humans to be bipedal required a small pelvis but to have large brains required a big head. The pain of childbirth and the years spent obeying parents impatiently awaiting maturity were the prices paid for these two incompatible traits. The week's Bible stories had an uplifting ending with the rainbow, the symbol of God's promise never to destroy the world again, at least not by flood. We were off to a great beginning with our sacred-text study.

We read the Bible every four years and the Constitution every two. We purposely timed this to coincide with the years of presidential elections. The combination of the two texts, background lectures, class discussion, and the evening political news made for a powerful civics course. I pointed out that when I was their age we were tested on the Constitution – we had to write out the Preamble from memory and a score of at least 72 was required for a passing grade. I observed that the goal of my classmates had been generally to pass the test rather than embody the material. I assured my class we would have no written test but hoped each would strive to grasp as much of the text, its spirit, and its impact on our history and lives as possible. I wanted them to muse on what was meant by such phrases as "Blessing of Liberty" and to know and aggressively exercise their rights proclaimed in this document.

Article 1, section 2 brought the first gasps and some sadness. Maggie read the formula for the apportionment of the House of Representatives: "whole Number of free Persons . . . excluding Indians not taxed, three fifths of all other Persons." I spoke a few minutes about the compromises needed to create consensus in the new nation. Forest said, "Basically they are saying Whites count one, Native Americans zero, and Blacks three-fifths."

In these discussions I always led toward the big picture and the silver lining. In this case I pointed out that the authors of this document were not perfect people living in an ideal world and neither were we. I explained how over our weeks of study we would see amendments to the original document that headed toward the self-evident "truths" noted in the Declaration of Independence. I observed that we ourselves did not fully live these ideals but that knowledge and effort by each of us would add to the forward movement of our nation and world. James asked if the opposite was equally true – whether ignorance and inaction would lead to backward motion. I pointed out that life and history dance between these two poles.

After the large ethical considerations brought to mind by both the Constitution and the Bible most felt comfortable with the mathematical certainties of the Pythagorean theorem and scientific notation. In both of these, after a finite number of steps one arrived at an answer where all must agree. Say no more; move on to another problem. (This was never the case with the Bible and the Constitution.) After a few minutes with Pythagoras, students were finding the unknown side of the triangle by squaring the other sides and applying the square-root technique we had learned in our last academic week, now so long ago.

We spent some time studying scientific notation every year. Our numerical thinking was usually linear – one, two, three; with each counting number, one more object was added to the pile. Now, with the exponents of scientific notation, one meant ten times bigger, two meant a hundred times, and six meant a million. Thinking in orders of magnitude and its notation system required lecturing, much practice, and many examples. The lectures were easy for me. I could drone on forever about powers of ten, orders of magnitude, and the simplicity of sliding the decimal point to the left or right. The practice came by completing the many work sheets our laser printer had generated over the years. The examples were the most fun.

For a numbering system that can seem at first so abstract and arbitrary, we had created what were known as our "various sheets." Each contained a large range of measured properties expressed in scientific notation. Various areas, volumes, velocities, energies, and pressures were sheets for future weeks. "Various Distances," expressed in meters, was our first. The diameter of an atomic nucleus was the smallest listed quantity, having an exponent of negative fourteen, a hundred billionth of a meter. The largest number, the distance to the farthest galaxy, had an exponent of twenty-four, a trillion trillion meters.

These quantities at the extremes of our ability to measure might make us comfortable with the notation system, but to capture their everyday significance was difficult. Comparing the objects and numbers between these extremes was more useful. We found that eighty round-trips from Santa Fe to Albuquerque and a single one-way trip to London were about the same distance. We calculated that walking to and from our park three times a day for a thousand years would equal the distance to the moon. Over the weeks, such examples of equivalencies would expand into a comfort with the metric system and scientific notation.

Since colleges had longer breaks than elementary schools, we often had alumni visitors these first weeks of each new year. Friday brought two returning graduates accompanied by college friends. Nina, our Boss several years ago, came with two friends, arriving during our Bible discussion. She joined right in, read some verses, added her comments – still one of the gang. Her friends watched: the kids sprawled on floor pillows, the reading from the photocopied text, the student discussion, and my commentary.

When the class left for break I stayed with our guests, talking about the previous half hour. They were amazed at the level of discussion and felt the thoughts and comments were at the same level as most of their college classes. I pointed out our staff never underestimated the potential of young people. Over the years we had found models and phrases that better resonated with our students and learned that children expressed ideas in ways fitting with their experience, but realized that their grasp of concepts was not inferior to that of older folks. As I waved good-bye to Nina and friends, another alumna and friends drove up.

Hallie, while a student at Fayette, never attended school on days it snowed – the view from her bedroom window was too beautiful. Neither did I teach her during the month of May – by then she had had enough school and was ready for summer. She never fielded her position in the baseball outfield – she preferred weaving dandelions into necklaces and tiaras. She never was interested in math and seldom completed assignments. Yet Hallie was one of our many successful graduates. I told them all, "Explore different techniques and make mistakes here; this will help you prepare for life and other schooling." Much of the lecturing and work found its way into her body of knowledge, if not back onto paper. She was an excellent college student and well on the way to having a long, sane, and happy life.

Now she was returning to show her friends the little school where her academic journey had begun. Once again first impressions were powerful. While Nina's friends left with the view that we were similar to a Talmudic university – Hallie's saw us at break time. The kids were in their own rhythm – eating, playing on the pond ice, sitting atop the garden walls – all at ease with each other. This did not fit with our visitors' model of school, but did fit with their ideal of the environment children should grow up in. Visitors who saw the relaxed nature of the students often thought the curriculum must be light. This was one reason we posted the Bigs' course work on the outside bulletin board: Latin, Greek, physics, Bible, Constitution, essay writing, et cetera. Our attitude about learning was to be relaxed and focused, the best of both worlds.

As with all visitors who were rethinking their definitions of school, children, and learning, we waited until we sensed the critical moment and then directed Hallie's group to the Big Elm. Forest was the host of the tour and later told me of their reaction. Looking up at the high pulley, one asked how old kids had to be to go that high. "Two or three years old," they were informed. "Of course, that is with a body harness, and we haul them up. Nine or ten to climb there yourself." Another internal shuffling of definitions and models.

The week ended with each Hard Nine Weeks subject introduced, students braced for the demands of the next weeks, the staff happy to be passing out papers and not endlessly threading needles, and myself delighted to see former students doing so well. Popcorn and my kilt and donuts for James's birthday closed out our week. For the staff, this had been one more week in that huge bundle of weeks when we were surrounded by young kids learning about themselves and their world, and when at any moment a graduate might return to see that this little world had not been just a dream of their childhood, but was a continuing reality.

~ Week Sixteen ~
Gravity and Patriarchs

The test of a good teacher is not how many questions he can ask his pupils that they will answer readily, but how many questions he inspires them to ask him which he finds it hard to answer.

ALICE WELLINGTON ROLLINS

Each day of the previous week students had asked if Ramadan were over. "When I see the crescent of the new moon, Ramadan ends at Fayette," was my standard answer. Friday night had brought the crescent so on this Tuesday morning the stored pillows returned to the school. Amelia used this event and the removal of the one-pillow limit to arrange four into a soft bed, where she proceeded to get very comfortable and doze off. I reminded her that this was school, to limit herself to two pillows, and to have her head higher than the rest of her anatomy. I passed out math and Greek quizzes, and we began another school week.

Whereas the previous week we had been resuming school after two weeks of vacation, this week we were returning from a weekend of homework with all subjects at least begun. Three half hours – one for the two quizzes, one of prehistory, and one for the study of the Constitution – brought us to an hour of math and another of physics. All this before lunch. Such was the pace of the Hard Nine Weeks.

Math for this time period surmounted three hurdles. Our first goal was increased comfort with the four operations – addition through division – applied to whole, fractional, and decimal numbers. This was followed by the exploration of percentages and their equivalencies with fractions and decimals. Finally, each young mathematician tackled our packet entitled "One Hundred Word Problems."

This journey began as each student pulled sheets from folders of the different operations – whole-number multiplication, fractional division, decimal subtraction and worked at their own pace on operations they knew they needed to strengthen. Ele and I cruised around giving tips and encouragement.

When a student felt they had mastered a specific area they took a short standardized test, scored it themselves, analyzed their errors, and decided if they needed more review or were ready to advance to another topic. The Tuesday-morning quizzes of a dozen varied arithmetic problems were the ultimate reality check. For some of the older or more mathematically proficient students these three hurdles were completed in a short time. These students then pitted their skills against problems found on SAT tests and reviewed areas of algebra.

While we in the Bigs' class were moving through our subjects, the Munchkins focused on their weekly research reports. Animals were the topic of the first three reports. *Zoobooks* and encyclopedias covered the Munchkins' room and the study. The oldest Munchkins wrote extensive reports including the most common facts about various animals. Though the younger Munchkins couldn't yet read beyond basic primers or write more than simple words, they still wrote a report a week. The reports of the youngest had many pictures and a little writing, those of the older ones several pages of text and a few pictures. All worked at their own level and received appropriate help. For those few still working on the basics of reading and writing, Alison, Melanie, or a Big was always available to read the text aloud to them and then take dictation from the young report writer. The students then copied this in their own handwriting.

Everyone was acquiring information, organizing thought, asking for the help they needed, and developing new levels of independence when ready. They also enjoyed becoming experts on their subjects. Rachel's first report was on kangaroos. I had thought the wallaby was their closest relative. With a look of disdain for having to deal with the hopelessly ignorant, she informed me that the kangaroo's closest relative was the *wallaroo*. I also was instructed by others on the eyelids of eagles and the unique features of parrot beaks.

Coleman did picture reports. One of the Bigs read to him from a *Zoobook*, then he picked out facts of interest and drew pictures to relate the information. Others helped him with written labels for each page. His first report was on gorillas. Tara and Marianne fought over who got to keep it; Granny won. The first page was a five-year-old's drawing of a gorilla in a dense jungle; another was of the gorilla's favorite foods; a third looked like an abstract drawing, but Zoe's label explained that this was a map of Africa with the range of the gorilla indicated in yellow. I knew that the next year, by the time he was reading and writing, he would already be a pro at organizing the material for reports.

Years before we had focused on research reports with the Bigs as well during the HNW. However over the years we had come to spend more and more of this time period on the structure of writing and tapping inner creativity. On Tuesdays Ele's writing hour concentrated on drawing from one's inner creativity, while Thursday's hours dealt with thoughts expressed through more formal structure and syntax.

The first few Tuesdays were spent on one of our favorite exercises. I had searched on-line for silly, short Associated Press wire stories: run away chickens, teachers taping kids to desks, folks trapped in elevators. Two of these then were copied to a single sheet. In class they were read silently by all, then aloud by one student. This accessed both eyes and ears as input systems. The writing assignment was to use the characters and incidents in the AP news items to write a fanciful story. The lightness of material and the zany combinations led to marvelous creative writing.

By contrast, on Thursdays more thought was applied. Ele assigned topics about which young folks could express strong feelings, for example, parents' rules, curfews, TV. These stories were then written in the classic five-paragraph essay form. A week was given to polishing each essay. Ele read them and wrote a few comments for possible improvement. All were rewritten; many were read and discussed in class.

The story of Abraham and his clan was our Bible study for the week. Before we began I asked if Sodom and Gomorrah or the pillar of salt had meaning for anyone in the room. No hands were raised. I pointed out that in my view the historical European basis of our culture could be divided into four eras. The first was ancient Neolithic and Celtic, so long ago only echoes were still felt. The second was a time when the myths and teachings of the Greco-Roman and Judaeo-Christian traditions were found in an agrarian society. I marked the transition to the third era with James Watt's steam engine, when the power of technology was added to the world but people still held to the lessons and images of the much revered past, especially as a moral guide. We seemed now to be entering a fourth phase, where the technology continued to unfold ever more powerful tools, but the morals and stories of the past had been discarded by many. The belief seemed to be that technology itself was a sufficient guide to meet our needs, even our emotional, spiritual, and moral ones. I expressed my extreme reservations regarding this last change.

By the end of the week we had followed Abraham into Egypt and back; enjoyed his bartering with God over the possible saving of Sodom; seen the survival of Lot and his daughters; rejoiced at the birth of Abraham's two sons by Hagar and Sarah; and held our breath at the climax of the saga, the near sacrifice of Isaac. This epic drama led to many points of discussion. When I was a child in Sunday school we read only short expurgated sections of these stories; here we read the complete chapters. Sunday school never revealed that Pharaoh possibly slept with Sarah, thinking her Abraham's sister, not his wife. As a youth I never read the verses where Lot wished to substitute his daughters for his houseguests when the fine citizens of Sodom wanted to abuse them, nor that these same young women went on to sleep with their father. The more complete stories added dimensions to the class discussion. For example after we read about

God's covenant with Abraham, Amelia raised her hand and asked, "What is a foreskin?" This brought much cringing from the boys.

I answered every such question asked. I avoided the easy path when faced with a tough or delicate issue, of giving a terse answer, switching the subject, and by subtle hints reminding the class to avoid such queries in the future. Rather, I started talking far away from the subject, encircling as much ground as possible, and approaching from an oblique angle. "You know people are not like algae, which simply divide to create new beings." That statement was light years away from foreskins. When on delicate ground I wandered through etymology and didn't get caught in explaining details of the question. "The egg and sperm come together and need to be in a protected area for the months of growth. This secure location is named *womb* in Old English, *uterus* in Latin, and *kalpos* in Greek. How are we going to deliver the sperm safely?"

When talking of subjects such as these, I danced around using alliteration and then switched to mundane images. "Possibly distinct delicate delivery devices need their own protection. A foreskin might be considered similar to this cap on my marking pen. Some folks might for sanitary reasons remove that pen cap so it doesn't trap dirt and such. Some people might leave it as is. Any more questions about foreskins?" Everyone seemed ready for the next Bible verses.

Physics on the other hand, never brought up such questions. I enjoyed our Bible times but knew that in physics we could meet each question head on. After the talk of measuring systems in the previous week we began the actual journey, the world as viewed through the lens of physics. We started with free-falling bodies, the tower of Pisa, observed phenomena, and their explanations in the language and models of physics. For instance, Aristotelian common sense held that a heavy cannonball fell faster than a light one; we knew feathers did in fact fall more slowly than rocks. As we spent the week's physics times exploring the falsehoods, truths, veiled insights, and mysteries related to falling bodies, we learned that Aristotle had been wrong: that gravity affected masses equally, that the invisible drag of air explained the difference, and that no one knew what gravity really was.

Adding to each student's current operating models and body of knowledge through personal observations and the ability to visualize was the most effective way to help better embody scientific theory and languaging. Before building a tower of physics facts, models, and vocabulary, two steps were necessary to prevent the tower becoming a house of cards. First, to establish the importance of understanding different physical properties and their respective units – for example, length and volume, meters and cubic meters, were quite different. Second, to highlight the difference between the mental ideal models and the realities of physical evidence. When these disciplines were established, much progress could be made in building a strong structure of science.

We used our mental ideal of a box to represent volume and its three dimensions; a sheet of paper as an example of area and its two dimensions; and a piece of string as length and one dimension. We began our analysis of physical units with distance, before adding time, mass, and all the messy combinations then possible. After we established the habit of never confusing meters, square meters, and cubic meters, I used the same objects to demonstrate the differences between our mental models and the real-world objects. After everyone thought of two dimensions when visualizing a piece of paper, I pointed out that a real piece of paper had volume. In fact, a piece of notebook paper had a volume of about 500 cubic millimeters. Though we might idealize a single sheet as representing two dimensions, a pack of 500 sheets surely had volume and mass. After a rather short time of learning to watch the units and to always separate the ideal mental model from the real-world manifestation, we were ready to start building the edifice of kinematic physics.

Examples of physical-world phenomena added greatly to the abstractions of the standard lectures on theory and equations. We turned our attention to falling bodies. Near the Earth's surface, bodies would fall at the same rate if not affected by the drag of air. The equations we used neglected air resistance, making them simple enough for our level of math. We did discuss the real-life observations that led to the topic of terminal velocity. I had some data ready. Since terminal velocity decreased with the size of the object, a mouse thrown from an airplane had a reasonable chance of walking away after impact since its velocity never exceeded 30 miles per hour. Humans, whose terminal velocities were around 120 mph, were encouraged to use parachutes to increase drag and consequently slow the descent to below 20 mph. I mentioned that without air drag raindrops would be deadly. We began to separate the different factors influencing both observed and idealized phenomena.

As a general practice, I performed very few experiments or demonstrations in class, relying rather on *gedanken experimente*, thought experiments. But Friday I did a short magic show. I dropped a piece of notebook paper and a penny, and we observed that the penny hit the carpet first. Amani then asked if I would drop the paper edgewise, not as I did the first time holding it flat. I asked for them to predict the result. All thought the paper would drop more quickly when held in this position. I bent a corner before releasing it. The sheet knifed through the air and did a couple of loops before landing. I revealed my sleight-of-hand trick, stating that aerodynamics was now involved.

Forest then asked to see the drop with the bent end trailing, not leading. Different flight path. We were all thinking in physics models. I returned to my basic experiment by crushing the sheet of paper into a tight ball. Same mass, different area exposed to drag. Amazingly, the paper and the penny hit the floor at the same time. The students learned that physics was not found only in a textbook or a distant laboratory; it was all around us, all the time. Physics was a way of thinking and seeing.

This week also brought the end to a construction project. For years the Big girls had used a small courtyard for their breaks. But recently the old wall had been removed; the neighborhood sauna had been moved from across the street to its new home on the back of our school, and a new wall had been built. This wooden wall now enclosed much more space and, more importantly, was constructed to support climbers. The crosspieces were designed as footholds, the top plates were six inches wide, the upright posts were massive and secured by lots of cement. Form and function. At break ten girls were traversing section to section or quietly sitting atop the wall. One more whole-body activity and multifunctional structure had been added to the school's terrain.

While the girls were lounging quietly on new and old walls, the young boys were swinging again. Winter lasted only one week in the year 2000. After a few days of freezing temperatures we had afternoons of sixty degrees and a return to the pendulum swing. Cloud dropped by to play soccer and stayed the afternoon. When he was a student here we didn't have our climbing world, and when he was assisting with crafts no one had been swinging. Now the boys showed him the pendulum. He was most impressed by the sensation of the flight and the ease the young gentlemen had with the ropes.

The ropes and platforms had been created to be areas where calm mind and controlled body would always be exercised. However, the difference between a teacher's mental model and its real-world manifestation at times appeared in places other than physics class, especially when ten-year-old-boys were involved. Alison found six Munchkin boys sword fighting with sticks on the toolshed roof. She ordered everyone off the structure and reminded them of several rules they were at the moment ignoring.

When she and I talked later we agreed it was commendable how they could sword fight without hurting each other, without anyone falling off the shed, or without any mean spirits. Still their actions were too close to these possibilities. I gave a version of my "Gangster versus Warrior" lecture to the young gentlemen, noting we were exploring free-falling bodies in physics but didn't want any actual demonstrations with animate beings.

∽ Week Seventeen ∾
Newton and Moses

Nature and Nature's laws lay hid in night:
God said, Let Newton be, and all was light.

ALEXANDER POPE

THE SEVENTEENTH WEEK brought Newton's three laws, the Decalogue of Moses, and the birthdays of Martin Luther King, Robert E. Lee, and Stonewall Jackson to the Bigs' classroom. Alison's Munchkins were researching and writing their third report in as many weeks and had enough hours of French behind them that they were having math class in French and addressing the rest of us in the language. Marianne's studio was operating at full pace with many old drills and some newly invented ones. While football teams peaked for the Superbowl, we peaked for the Hard Nine Weeks. We now had the intensity; the task of the staff was to hold this level for another seven weeks.

By this time the four levels of Marianne's Latin classes had split into sublevels based on individual student needs. For example, the Betas, the second-year students, had divided into two groups. Half continued with a new grammar lesson a week; the other half needed time to assimilate the material of the past before again moving forward. Our computers stored hundreds of supplemental sheets created over the years. These pages helped the young scholars who needed a few weeks of review before again advancing. The object was not to arrive at a predetermined level of Latin at a scheduled time but rather to exercise the brain and hone the study skills. The journey rather than the destination was the most important part of our Latin study. This flexible pace produced uniformly competent Latin scholars. Our alumnorum university professors were always amazed at the depth of Latin study that they had recieved in their elementary education.

The Munchkins had settled into report writing and now were comfortable finding the information in the *Zoobooks* and encyclopedias. Many had a Big at their side; everyone could benefit from a pedagogue from time to time. The older Munchkins had switched to reports on famous people while the young ones were still researching favored animals. Time not spent on grammar or packets seemed to be spent in French. At one break Dorothy said something to me *en français*. When I asked for a translation she said, "You are a stupid potato." Everything does sound better in a romance language.

In our Bible study the story of Moses was much enjoyed. Unlike the story of Abraham and his clan, which only two students had remembered hearing, many of the kids were contributing facts about the life of Moses. After a few minutes of hearing their versions, I noted that these thoughts didn't fit with the biblical account. An insight flashed in my mind: "Is this Moses according to Disney?" Sure enough, many students had gone to see the new movie over the holidays! That was the reason for the difference. After an appropriate amount of scholarly grumbling I suggested we read the source material and use that version as our model.

The story of Moses, his talks with God, and his struggles with Pharaoh never failed to excite the class. I photocopied the first two and last two plagues, skipping over the six in the middle. Zoe and Reese went home, read from their family Bibles, and related to the class the stories of lice, locust, and boils. Class discussions pierced to the ultimate questions of religion and philosophy. Forest asked why, if God were all powerful, did he create Pharaoh to be hard hearted? With much give and take, we talked of divine power, free will, and the best ways to learn life's lessons. I reminded them we would not come to definite conclusions but would posit many questions to consider for the remainder of their lives.

The week ended with the Ten Commandments. We read them slowly, one at a time, with paraphrasing, definitions of terms, and discussion of their meanings in our lives. I did not demand each of us live by them, but I asked what would it be like if each of us obeyed them. Only one hour of class time every four years was devoted to the Decalogue. We made the most of this time. Following the reading they were posted on our classroom wall. I pointed out many classrooms were prohibited from displaying the Commandments because of the current interpretation of the First Amendment of the Constitution. In two weeks we would be studying the Bill of Rights. These would then be posted along side the Ten Commandments.

In these times of polarized opinion of religion and science, we enjoyed putting away the Bible and immediately turning to physics. The class had been thinking in the models of physics for two weeks. We had turned the inertia of ignorance into the momentum of knowledge. The eager anticipation of each student for daily class and their desire for new sheets of information made class time a joy. This week's various sheet dealt with areas. Two weeks before, the numbers in scientific notation and their comparisons had been foreign; now everyone wanted to volunteer a comparison for work on the board. From Lauren's suggestion we found the number of straight pins needed to fill a parking place. This seemingly difficult problem was trivial when approached with scientific notation. Since the area of a pin head and that of a parking place differed by seven orders of magnitude, ten million pins pushed in the ground would be needed to fill a parking place.

I never knew which relationships would come up in class, but I always tried to bring a sense of reality to the numbers and objects. Amani asked to compare the area of a soccer field and that of Vatican City, two of the facts on our various sheet. Since we knew kids needed more soccer fields, I suggested we bulldoze the Vatican, demolish the Basilica of St. Peter, move his tomb and those of the popes to some quiet cemetery, dismantle the Sistine Chapel and reconstruct it at Disney World, run the gardens through a chipper, and compost the heap. Several of the class had been to Rome and most were familiar with Michelangelo's frescoes and their recent restoration.

The mental image of such destruction was so out of the realm of possibility we laughed. Our calculations revealed that the whole Vatican would yield only sixty soccer fields so we decided we might as well leave the Vatican intact and look for another location.

Jonah suggested using Asia, whose area was also listed on the sheet. Instead of the factor of six and the difference of a single order of magnitude for the Vatican, Asia compared to a soccer field was a factor of six and nine orders of magnitude. We figured out that Asia could be turned into six billion fields. I pointed out that this number was the same as that of the present world population; therefore every person on the planet could move to Asia with each of us having a whole field for personal space. Europe, the Americas, Africa, Antarctica and the 70 percent of the planet covered with water would be void of humans. Is this a crowded planet?

I knew that because of the rigor of this kind of work, when these young students had science classes in high school and college they would not be struggling, as would many of their classmates, when scientific notation, orders of magnitude, significant digits, and the like were presented. Yet as instructive and entertaining as the various sheets were, they were not the main thrust of our physics. Newton's laws were the pillars of kinematics, the area of physics devoted to the study of motion.

Again, the contrast of this work with our sacred-text studies was interesting. For example, the Ten Commandments given to Moses were optional in our lives – obey them or not. Newton's laws were mandatory; they were woven in the very fabric of the universe. Like Galileo and his insights about the commonality of falling bodies, Newton's genius pierced through the veil of shallow daily observations to reveal immutable principles. The average person would not think that "an object continues uniform motion in a straight line unless acted upon by other forces" – things didn't seem to behave this way. Newton saw that air resistance and gravity were not universal but rather localized phenomena. Just because humans had never operated outside of gravitational force or atmospheric drag did not mean the effects of these were part of the most fundamental principles of physics. After a genius published such insights, rather average teachers could spend classtime discussing them with students. When we began to look at our world and our experiences with Newton's three laws, we shifted our points of view. In the coming weeks we would examine distance, speed, acceleration, force, energy, and power, and work from this stance on the shoulders of a genius.

Though in the HNW most of our time was spent in the classroom or studio, we fortunately took a few short breaks outside and birthdays still rolled around. One break I saw young Arlen seated by the pond holding a bag of Oreos, and staring at the waterfall. "Arlen what is the waterfall telling you?" "Nothing." "Isn't it saying to give your teacher a cookie?" "Nope." I continued my rounds. When we were headed for class, he came to me with a big smile on his face. I noticed other Munchkins watching and I sensed something was up. "The waterfall said to give you this cookie." "Thank you, Arlen. Hey, there's no white stuff – only the two brown wafers." "The waterfall said to scrape off and eat the frosting before giving you the cookie." All the Munchkins burst into laughter.

Thursday we celebrated Sam's birthday. His mom and dad brought the making for root beer floats. Sam was a Munchkin, so we lined up youngest to oldest for the treat. Through miscalculation the root beer and ice cream ran out with four Bigs still in line. They said that was OK and didn't complain. I was proud of their citizenship.

Then we heard a cry. Looking around the corner we saw Eliza on the ground with a skinned elbow and her root beer float running down the sidewalk. She headed to a bench, where she sat and sobbed. I asked Amelia, the nearest Big, if she thought Eliza could use a bit of attention. After a moment of assessment she headed for the bench and I turned to other matters. When I cycled back to the scene, not only was Amelia comforting Eliza but she had given her younger schoolmate her own float.

By Friday afternoon so many phoneme blocks had been moved, so many eye patches worn, so many Latin verbs conjugated and nouns declined that the studio itself seemed ready for a change. The Munchkins and then the Bigs each had a welcome hour of music with Melanie. The Munchkins began by forming a circle around the xylos. Every week in the HNW they learned a different Rondo, each created by Melanie. The playing, as the name Rondo suggested, continued around and around. The first one was titled the "January Rondo," played in the key of C. For this all xylos' B and F bars were removed; the remaining ones formed a pentatonic scale. Eight beats were played holding to Melanie's rules for this particular rondo, and then eight counts were improvised by each player, hopefully in rhythm with the other xylophones. The next eight beats were counted out by Melanie as everyone moved one space clockwise around the circle of xylos. This was sustained until all had completed a full circle of the xylophones. The rondos were superb foundation work in music theory, rhythm, beat, cooperation, attention, and other fine points of neural integration. After putting away the xylophones and passing out songbooks, the Munchkins sang for a half hour before heading to art class with Alison.

The final hour of the week found the Bigs with Melanie, but with no xylos. The first part of the hour was spent singing many two- and three-part rounds. One of the rounds was so constructed it could be sung in up to eight parts. We divided into seven groups and sang twice through without anyone getting lost. The last portion of the hour was devoted to patriotic songs, including "America the Beautiful" and "The Star Spangled Banner." We sang three verses of each: "Till all success be nobleness and ev'ry gain divine," "Praise the Power that hath made and preserved us a nation." Since this was Stonewall Jackson's birthday we also sang a few southern Civil War songs. The studio was well used during the HNW. As we left it Sam's mom had root beer floats for Amelia and the others who had gone without. Eliza got to lick the ice cream scoop.

~ Week Eighteen ~
Visitors and a Bunny

Students do not need to labeled or measured....
What they need from us is common sense, dedication,
and bright energetic teachers who believe that all children
are achievers and who take personally
the failure of any one child.

MARVA COLLINS

NEW FAMILIES interested in our school were calling on the phone. For prospective families we requested that the parents visit and observe first before bringing their children. Should the parents like our staff, students, and curriculum, we asked that the child spend a half day with us. Interestingly, the kids were always easy and fit right into the school rhythm; the adults were the ones who needed individual attention. We had visiting adults come the third week of January, February, or March. This way at least three weeks each month the staff could devote full-time attention to the present students. During visiting weeks we arranged our schedule so Marianne, Tara, or I were available to answer questions, speak on school philosophy, and give tours of the buildings and grounds. Anyone with a child aged five through thirteen could visit and receive some of our attention. Our goal was to have the next year's enrollment completed by the first week of April.

We spent hours of time with dozens of adults during these visiting weeks. In the Bigs' class only three students would be graduating, and the next September five Munchkins would become Bigs. Therefore the chances of adding an older student from outside the school were slim. The Munchkins' room could easily be filled with learning-disabled nine- and ten-year-old boys, but this would not lead to a balanced mix of students, and Alison would probably run away screaming. So we were looking for only a few six- through eight-year-olds to fill out that class. Years before, we had realized that parent visits were not so much about our sieving for new students but rather for holding an open house aimed at educating adults in the broader possibilities of childhood education. We would see many of these people only on the days of their visits. Hopefully they left with a changed view of what could be added to and what should be subtracted from the standard model of education. We enjoyed telling others of our history, philosophy, and time-tested but seemingly unusual techniques and ways. We endeavored to answer all their questions even if it meant missing a few break-time cappuccinos. Following are several of the most-asked questions from the winter of 2000 and a composite of our responses.

How did you start this school?

Over twenty years ago Marianne and I were homeschooling our two daughters in the years before this was commonplace or legal. A call from a neighbor brought the truant officer and led to the enrolling of the girls in the local elementary school. Tara was placed in a fifth-grade class with a teacher in her twenty-fifth and final year of teaching, a woman with nothing left to give to children and merely counting the days to the end of the year and the beginning of retirement. Madigan was placed in a first-grade class with a bright young teacher who informed us she had a class of thirty kids, all less literate and numerate than our daughter, including many with behavioral problems, and therefore Madigan would get very little of her attention. Though not thrilled about either classroom's status, we were willing to give this a try.

Two months later Tara came home from school saying a nice policeman had given a drug-education talk. She told us how to cook heroin in a spoon, how to prepare and snort cocaine, and other fascinating facts from the drug world. I called my attorney friend who happened to specialize in school law and asked him to find a way to "make me a school." I enjoyed my final visit with the school's principal, informing him he would never see my daughters again and that the school district had better cancel their present drug program immediately or face several interested attorneys. Two days later papers were filed with the state, and Fayette Street Academy was born.

How many kids are in that room?

My classroom, thirteen by thirteen feet, has twenty-two kids. All are focused and engaged during lectures and help each other during study time. Thirty floor pillows and three plywood storage boxes, each designed to seat two students, allow for comfort and daily shifting of seating and neighbors. Each student has their backpack beside them and notebook on their lap. Switching from subject to subject happens with the flip of a divider. (Visitors were not only amazed by the room's small size, number of students, and scholarly focus, but also by how they all packed into several tight groups and how much of the carpet remained visible. I pointed out that we could actually fit thirty six-kids in the room but no one could move to go to the bathroom, sharpen a pencil, or get a drink of water. Of course, during study times they could move to the study, on warm days work in the gardens, and even use our house if they desired.)

The two classes seem so different. Why?

Though only a few years separate the students of each room, these are years of rapid growth. The needs and comforts of the two groups are quite different. Each room has evolved to meet the personal-space requirements of each age group. In the Bigs' room we pack together and grapple with large concepts. I often use a booming voice and frequently wave my arms while talking. In the Munchkins' room, most are working on the first building blocks of academia and the beginnings of peer socialization, often for the first time or after a disastrous start in another school. Alison is quiet and patient with them.

Her room, which is the same size as mine, holds only fourteen children. They are just beginning to develop their own personal space and seem to need a bit more of it for these formative years. In two of the corners of the room are lofts, each designed to seat two students at a time. The spaces under the lofts are also prized seating, with a

good view of Alison and the whiteboard. The high ground of the lofts and the cavelike nature under them make for good defensive positions. Others sit around the low elliptical table in the middle of the room. They rotate day to day through the various locations.

What happens when after two or three years the students go to a school with desks and grades?

After a period of adjustment all do very well. Depending on the individual this can take from a few days to several months. Since they have learned study skills and how to acquire knowledge, they are in an excellent position to quickly move ahead. Since they have learned the different between studying for knowledge and merely studying for better test scores, but also have taken hundreds of "practice tests," they do well both in classes and on tests. Since they have experienced the "love of learning" they stand out as eager, engaged students. At Fayette they have learned to interact in harmony with every member of the staff and student body, and therefore they have the tools and experience to successfully engage in larger social settings. As they sit in rows awaiting report cards, they miss their time at Fayette but know they have been well prepared for further academics and life beyond.

Why don't you have them call you Mr. and Mrs. and Miss? How will they respect you?

Their respect for us is reciprocal with our respect for them. If I demanded they address me as Mr. Chamberlain, I would also address them by their surnames. Communication would take considerably longer, especially with the current trend to include the mother's surname. "What is the answer to question fourteen, Miss Melander-Dayton?" "Master Carter-Goldberg, would you please remain silent?" Class goes more quickly when we address each other with given names. "Dorothy, next answer, please." "Forest, be quiet." Also the use of the surname evokes family history and accompanying baggage. First names call to the individual. As Kahlil Gibran expressed so eloquently in *The Prophet*, "Your children are not your children. They are the sons and daughters of Life's longing for itself."

Do you teach manners and say please *and* thank you *to each other?*

We do not have a class titled manners nor times when we demonstrate which fork to use for which course. We teach manners by using good manners with staff, students, and parents. All members of the staff use *please* and *thank you* at every appropriate opportunity. When students are heard using any of the "seven forbidden words" they are reminded of alternative phrases to better express their point. We stress the use of loving-kindness in all interactions.

What do you use to discipline behavior?

Behavior is generated by the collective peer pressure. Since the older and more veteran students have found interacting with mutual respect feels good in both mind and body, this practice and its emotional tone are transmitted to the newer and younger students. Whenever anyone feels uncomfortable because of the actions or words of another, we set aside time for a discussion with all involved and interested students.

How do you make sure they don't run out into the street when you are waiting to cross?

We screen each student and family before accepting them into our school community. While learning-disabled children have always been part of our community, children who exhibit self-destructive behaviors or violence toward others are not admitted to our school. Those waiting to cross the road have manifest sanity and practice self-preservation. We always use the same pattern for assembly and the same words of command. Therefore problems never develop in this area.

This is not just a school but a way of life. I think we would need help to know how to be part of this community.

School should model a way of life. Parents don't need lessons on how to be here because this is not a school for them. It is a school for their children. Children very quickly pick up from the older students and staff the atmosphere of considerate interactions with others and the joy of learning. The parents' task is to get their children to school on time with proper clothing and food, and to create a time and place in the home for homework. The parents of our more successful students also limit television and engage with the child's studies.

How will I know if my kid is in the right grade and is caught up?

People thinking in terms of "grade" or "caught up" are imposing a rigid bureaucratic template on children. At Fayette we meet the emotional needs and academic skill level of each child where they happen to be that day. This method of meeting the child and not dragging the child to an imposed standard is the most efficient way for faster, saner, and more integrated personal and academic development.

What do you think of single-sex schools?

Single-sex schools have their place in the diverse range of school choices hopefully found in every community. Here at Fayette we enjoy the skills acquired from relating to peers of both the same and the opposite gender. All classes and most sports days are coed, though we play enough single-gender soccer games each year so all can learn from the varied natures of the different games. At times meetings of either boys or girls are called to bring harmony to intragender social interactions. During breaks and lunchtime, students have a choice of coed or single-sex areas. Various days find various combinations. The school time and space are structured so at times diversity of age or gender are part of the social experience and at other times similarity is the operating principle. The many courtyards, benches, wooden decks, and gardens of the school grounds make this a natural pattern.

Why do you go only four days a week?

Most schools don't operate five full days; many have a shortened day in the week. Holidays and in-service days also bring the average down from a true five days a week. Here we go four days every week from the beginning of September until the end of May. The only exceptions are the vacation weeks of Thanksgiving and winter and spring breaks. Four days of school means three days in the family rhythm. The ratio of four to three is much more balanced than five to two. This allows for more family time and nonacademic activities – dance classes, horseback riding, team sports, violin lessons, and such – without overburdening young children. At school every moment is fully used; we do not have dull down times. By attending four days a week neither staff nor students experience burnout. We are all fresh through the end of the school year.

VISITORS CAME and visitors went, but the Hard Nine Weeks rolled on. Wednesday morning we received a call reporting Amelia would be missing school that day. She had spent three hours Tuesday night in the emergency room with suspected appendicitis. Between various medical tests, while in pain, she did her homework. She worked on her essay, translated Latin, solved math and physics problems. Her mother related that the doctor found this commendable but outside of his experience with most patients. Amelia's reply was, "Normally I wouldn't do this, but this is the Hard Nine Weeks." I related this to the class.

Thursday Amelia returned to school to a spontaneous ovation. We learned that the pain wasn't from her appendix but possibly her ovaries, active for the first time. At a quiet moment I asked her how she was doing and if she had thought about Eve and the curse in the

Garden of Eden. She said when we had read Genesis she had thought God was a bit harsh, but now she felt He was being extremely harsh. I mentioned she had missed some of our Bible reading and advised that if she wanted to see harsh she should read Deuteronomy 20: 10–17, where the text speaks of how to deal with the survivors of a conquered town.

Physics for the week explored the interrelationships of distance, velocity, and acceleration. Though we used and constantly relied on the classic equations we reified them with vibrant examples. This was the week Coleman's imaginary bunny made his eagerly anticipated appearance. We each conjured our own images of this little rabbit and began our *gedanken experimente* by visualizing him munching grass at different distances from his hole. We then imaged him hopping along at a steady rate; physics would call this velocity or speed.

Tuesday's homework included a few quiet minutes at home visualizing the bunny hopping along a number of times – short journeys, longer ones, slow ones, quicker ones. I reminded them that as simple as this exercise seemed, it was an important foundation for future, more complicated physics. Over the weeks we would be analyzing more complex properties of the bunny and several other silly scenarios. Returning the next day all agreed that greater speed, longer time of journey, or both would always increase the bunny's distance from his hole. The equation $s = v \times t$ (distance equals velocity multiplied by time) was now linked to personalized mental models in each student, not just noted on a piece of paper.

With everyone comfortable with constant velocity and able to solve the equations, we strapped a jet pack on the little rabbit (in our inner vision anything was possible!) and explored the concept of acceleration. Wednesday night's physics assignment was to visualize Coleman's pet moving faster and faster, and hence farther and farther away from the hole, as the rocket continued to fire.

The next day the class was prepared for the specific equations of constant acceleration. We began with the little guy sitting stationary as Coleman fired the jet pack. Soon the whole class was finding the bunny's speed and distance from his hole for different accelerations and durations of rocket blast. The night at home working on a few problems had resulted in two groups in the class. Those who had easily solved the problems became the class tutors. Those who returned confused or stuck knew exactly where their mental-model and equation-solving skills needed assistance. After a half hour of brainstorming in small groups, we tackled the more difficult problems where the little rabbit was hopping along at a constant rate before Coleman remotely fired the jet pack.

This had been a great week of physics not only because of the topics we had covered, but also because we were well aligned to continue adding more properties to these first three of distance, velocity, and acceleration. Coleman's little bunny had many more journeys in his future.

～ Week Nineteen ～
Munchkin Manners

*Good teaching is one-fourth preparation
and three-fourths theater.*

GAIL GODWIN

IN THE PREVIOUS week several visiting parents had asked if we ever handled the social conflicts of our students. In a week such as this one it seemed that was the only thing we did.

Rain had fallen throughout Monday night, so the combination of wet grass and the light sports shoes the kids generally wore precluded soccer games on Tuesday. Instead Ele took the kids to the park for free time. On return she informed me that the Munchkin boys needed a discussion session. She said that *mud* and *wire* would be the key words. Ariel added I should ask about one boy kicking another.

Arlen, who had voiced the complaints, stood on the Birthday Rock. The other Munchkin boys sat on the nearby bench. Girls gathered as combination audience and Greek chorus. I opened, "Remember, our primary goal is for each student to feel safe at school at all times. Arlen, did you feel safe at the park?" "No, I got splattered with mud when Daniel threw rocks in the mud puddle." I gave them my Spencer-Tracy–Clarence-Darrow look of silent deep thinking. "I'm going to throw that out of our discussion because mud doesn't hurt, and one day last week you boys came back covered with mud and I remember Arlen calling it the best day of his life. Fair enough if we throw the mud scene out?" All agreed. I always looked to establish rapport and a sense of ease at the beginning of these behavioral discussions.

I asked Arlen to proceed to the next point. "Avery tripped me with a wire." This time I conjured my Leo-McKern–Horace-Rumpole persona and proceeded with my examination. "Avery, did you place a wire to trip Arlen?" "No, I actually tripped over it myself." "Did you alert Arlen to the danger?" "No." "Maybe to avoid a negative accusation you should be positive with safety tips for others. Are we all happy with our discussion so far?" "Yes," by all a second time. I sensed there was more to the incident than was being revealed, but one of my principles of these teaching lessons was to allow the saving of face. I had found this paid dividends when months later I needed to apply moral force to further situations.

Taking the lead, I turned to the issue we would face directly today. "Sam, while walking back from the park did you kick Arlen?" Head down, cap pulled low, no eye contact, "Yes." "What was your reason?" In very small voice, "He laughed at my hair and I kicked him." I pointed out that Arlen had been verbal and the response had been stepped up to the physical. Referring to our Bible reading that very morning I said, "Deuteronomy, chapter 19, verse 21; 'eye for eye, tooth for tooth, foot for foot.' I don't believe it said 'foot for word.'"

Removing Sam's cap, I asked him to look me in the eye. I ran my fingers through my hair, which stands somewhere between Einstein's and Bozo the Clown's. "Sam, if I kicked everyone who over the years laughed at my hair, I'd have a permanently sprained ankle." He smiled. "Are we clearer on behavior and seeing each others views?" "Yes," again.

"OK," I said, "one of you restate the beginning principle." Several students spoke out at once, talking about not splashing, not tripping, not kicking. "Nope, I don't want statements of the negative; I want the original positive goal." Silence from the boys. Turning to our Greek chorus, "Girls help us out here." Eliza stepped forward and said, "For us to feel safe at school all the time." As the Munchkins headed for class I overheard Eliza said to Nyssa, "John's hair looks regular to me. Of course, it took a year and a half for me to think that."

Wednesday was clear and cold. Park time went well with an excellent soccer game, but on our return to school we found the Munchkins' room was very cold. Someone had opened the windows before the class left for the park. A brief investigation by Alison revealed that Daniel, Arlen, and Robby were responsible. To me again fell the task of handling the teaching lesson. Coming so soon after our previous incident I turned to an ancient effective device. "Write thirty times, 'I won't leave windows open at school during the winter.' I want this done at home tonight. If not finished you will complete the writing outside first thing in the morning, on a bench in the shade."

Throughout the afternoon the three boys discussed strategies and options of bravado. As Daniel and Robby were leaving school at the end of the day, they formed a pact to leave the writing until morning. This I overheard. "Fine, but in the morning it will be sixty sentences." Robby was amazed. "That's not fair." I smiled. "The number can always go up." I turned to see Robby's dad, with whom I had a scheduled conference.

Robby was nine years old with academic skills a bit behind and soccer skills years ahead of his age. He played on select soccer teams that required hours of daily practice and many weekends devoted to games. He had developed the habit of using his classroom time as his down time. Since everyone else in the class was working and focused, he had begun to act the class clown. This role, along with others such as class bully or class tattle, were not listed in the Munchkin "table of organization." One devoted teacher, one caring assistant, fourteen eager students. No other roles to be filled.

Robby's dad and I had a fine talk. He agreed that classroom behavior and academic effort came before soccer and said he would talk with Robby and work more with him at home. I was glad to see that while we were talking Robby had completed twenty-five of his sentences. As the last car left I, too, turned to my homework: correcting piles of papers; studying for my history, physics, Bible, and Constitution lectures; and wheeling several loads of firewood to the school.

Thursday, as the Bigs and I were deep in physics, we heard through the curtain voices and commotion that couldn't come from French class or report writing. Since it didn't escalate to the sounds associated with imminent death or dismemberment, we continued with our own business. At the end of the day Alison recapped the events of the disruption. Rachel had discovered in her lunch box an early Valentine addressed to Nyssa. The misplaced card had gotten smeared with a bit of apple sauce.

Now, to you or me this may have seemed small and not worth the expenditure of much energy. However, one of our rules was to stay out of other's lunches, and to Rachel this was reason enough to cut loose. She returned into class, interrupted Alison's lecture, and, read aloud the valentine, looking to embarrass the author. In a trice Rebecca sprang across the room and grabbed the card. Struggle and a bit of tug-of-war left the class interrupted, several girls upset, and a fine valentine reduced to scraps littering the floor. Marianne, who had been looking for a quiet hour of correcting Latin papers, took time to counsel Rachel. Alison spent class time with the other Munchkins on the subject of behavior. To me fell the long-term handling of the incident.

Friday morning I asked Alison to continue her Greek class with the Bigs past 9:00 so I could hold forth with the Munchkins. I picked this time to maximize the effect. The half hour from 9:00 to 9:30 was when Alison read to them. Over the years *The Hobbit*, *Treasure Island*, The Chronicles of Narnia, most writings of Roald Dahl, and scores of other classics of children's literature had come alive in story time. The Munchkins knew they were missing this special period so I could handle the previous day's incident.

Two of our constant messages were that actions had consequences and that every time we reacted unconsciously to a situation we were missing optional responses that might better have served our desired intent. Another embedded message was that straying from standard behavior caused John to think of more interesting lessons and tasks than children might like to see! Tuesday the girls had been the Greek chorus as the boys were at center stage; today the roles were reversed. This parallax allowed the Munchkins to see I used a calm tone in these discussions and I endeavored to bring fairness to each situation.

We reviewed the facts in the present drama, agreeing on the basic story line. Katherine, ever reasonable, pointed out that Rachel's and

Nyssa's lunch boxes looked similar and an honest mistake might have started this chain of events. I explained I was not so concerned with the valentine slipped into the lunch box, though this was counter to the school rules. I was concerned by the linking of improper actions by several people, creating a growing chain of ill will.

I reminded them that they never saw the Bigs get into such situations because when something untoward happened in their interactions, the next person was usually more resourceful than to merely react. This way harmony was soon restored, and life and school moved on. I pointed out the Bigs had not been born with this ability but had learned valuable lessons from incidents such as this one when they were Munchkins. Throughout this drama the boys delivered the lines of the Greek chorus as well as the girls had on Tuesday. Dorothy, our oldest Munchkin, pointed out that not all Bigs had been Munchkins at Fayette – some had joined the school when they were older. I thanked her for bringing up this excellent point and explained that the good behavior of our long-time students set a tone for the new ones of any age.

Returning to our main discussion, I decreed valentines would not be exchanged by the Munchkin girls this year. From the class reaction no one had thought I would say this. I continued: If the person who placed the card in the lunch revealed herself, only she would be excluded from the card giving and receiving.

As I returned to my classroom I was delighted. I had their attention. They had a better sense of the consequence of actions. Each had more incentive to remain within the bounds of proper deportment. The possibility existed that no one would come forward and the girls would be without valentines. I made a mental note to think of some day near the end of the month when we could make nonvalentine cards for each other. Possibly we could exchange goodwill cards on the Century Leap Day, a rare occurrence, happening only once every four hundred years.

When parents would come to me saying their child had related a mean-spirited incident at school, I would remind them that for

each of these inharmonious events uncounted positive interactions filled the school day. I encouraged parents and students to include gratitude for the many positive moments when examining the few negative ones. I didn't tell parents that if their little one didn't take an occasional shot at others they wouldn't have shots directed at them. One lesson at a time.

During yeasty weeks like this I remembered to listen to my own advice. In reality, though it felt emotionally like much more, I had spent less than an hour of the school week with my attention focused on behavior issues. The rest was spent on the academic topics of percents in math, momentum and energy in physics, and the Psalms in the Bible. Most of Alison's class time had been devoted to reading from finished reports, helping research new ones, advancing the French language, and solidifying the fundamentals of mathematics and grammar.

Break times were as active as the classroom hours. Daniel, who in the first week of school had demonstrated how not to swing from tool shed to storage shed, applied the adage that "if you can't bring Mohammed to the mountain, bring the mountain to Mohammed." This time he started from the storage shed. His past experience led him to ask me for a few pointers before the first test flights. I said, "Make sure you use too little force as you learn the correct amount needed. Don't ever use too much force."

Forest, who was watching this, asked me what happened with overforce. He remembered my tests with the margarita filled young adults whom the kids now referred to as the "drunken crash-test dummies." "With overforce," I explained, "your momentum takes you off the shed, you bounce along the top of the rattan-covered chain-link fencing, hit both gate posts, and land in the little evergreen by Marianne's yurt. Don't overshoot the shed."

Forest climbed atop the tool shed to be spotter for Daniel. In a short time Daniel had perfected the landing. He then gave pointers to Robby, who quickly duplicated the feat. Daniel next focused on the more difficult tool shed-to-storage-shed flight and soon was going both directions with flair and ease. As the week progressed other Munchkin boys joined the "lander's club." I noted none of the Bigs felt the need to match the proficiency of the younger lads. Maybe soon we could coax a few to swing.

While the Munchkin boys were extending their abilities on the swing, the Big girls were becoming comfortable in their new improved courtyard. By now all had worked out the moves to climb and sit atop the walls, and they turned their attention to the sauna. I had said they could go inside if they wished. For the first week no one had ventured in. This week, however, when I looked for them the courtyard was empty – ten of them were in the sauna. The sauna was only six feet by eight feet with one very small window, yet it seemed none of the girls was claustrophobic. They had found that their body heat caused the temperature inside to rise one degree per minute. The small size, the good insulation, and the body heat of a thousand pounds of flesh combined to create this effect. Miranda said this was like a temperature velocity. I smiled and said temperature was part of thermal physics and it was now time for class and our study of kinematic physics.

Secure with Coleman's bunny and the related equations of motion, we explored momentum, force, work, kinetic energy, and power. Though we would now be tracking many different units and equations, the beauty of physics was its interrelationships. After gaining comfort with acceleration and its units of meters per second squared, properties such as kinetic energy measured in joules or in the fundamental units, kilogram meters squared per second squared, could be considered and mentally filed in an orderly way.

Of course, attaching the properties to a little rabbit helped tremendously. By the end of the week we were calculating the values of the different properties affecting the bunny at each second of one of his rocket journeys. Given just the mass of the rabbit and the force of the rocket, eight other quantities could be derived. Pages of charted numbers were being produced by the class. Calculating eight different properties using as many different equations over a ten-second rocket blast not only gave practice through solving eighty equations, but, more importantly, the patterns in the numbers for each property were easily discerned. Two weeks with Coleman's little friend had quickly gotten us far into physics and ready for the next step, the laws of conservation.

After class on Friday, while most were gathered around the popcorn bowls and a box of fortune cookies in honor of Chinese New Year, Robby showed his dad the shed landing. When his dad asked how he had learned this he said, "Daniel is my tutor for swinging and I am his for reading." There are moments when my eyes well with tears for being allowed to witness the strength, innocence, clarity, and love of the children.

Week Twenty

No-TV Week

Television should be treated like ice cream: as an occasional harmless event. But the worst sin of all remains the illusion that television can be harnessed for good purposes.

LEON BOTSTEIN

EVERY YEAR we had a "no-TV week" for our whole school community, parents included. A few of the new parents asked what were the parameters of this edict. My reply was, "Which words do you not understand – *no TV* or *week*?" I would have preferred a no-TV century. Obviously I had picked the wrong decades to teach without the influence of television. I was born long enough ago that the people who raised me had no exposure to the media, and thus television did not significantly affect my life until I was close to adolescence. Such was not the case for young children now. The average two- to five-year-old was spending twenty-seven hours a week in front of the TV; half of America's families didn't set limits to their kids' viewing; and one in four of the children in America had a television in their bedroom. By age thirteen they had witnessed eighteen thousand murders. Many parents had more verbal references from "Gilligan's Island" and "The Brady Bunch" than they had from the Bible or Shakespeare. By demanding a television-free week for our school community, we sent the message that the habituation, nay addiction, to the Blue Glow should not be ranked with necessary ingredients for life, such as breath, love, wholesome foods, and baseball. A few kids and several parents complained about this mandatory fast. I pointed out we had waited until the Superbowl commercials had aired.

In the minds of the Fayette staff, television was not evil, merely powerful. We felt that both the images presented and the way the human nervous system interacted with the media should be closely examined before plugging in. First the images. We preached that no one, especially children of any age, should as part of their passive entertainment view violent images or ones that produced an adrenaline response. For decades I had enjoyed adrenaline rushes – I had played rugby, climbed mountains, ridden my bike too quickly down steep roads. I was the guy who had tree climbing and rope swings as part of school. But these were real-world activities experienced through whole-body motion, not virtual thrills in couch-potato mode.

We had spent many years studying how human minds worked and developed. We knew that many of our inner operating systems, especially those of the young, were very simple programs. These circuits deep in the brain could not differentiate between real and virtual information. Seeing images of violence caused one to conclude they lived in a dangerous world. The mind-body system then developed the strategies, defenses, and endocrine-system responses to deal with such a world. Often this stance was at variance to the actual world they lived in. No razor blade was found in the Trick-or-Treat candy, nor were many children grabbed off the sidewalk in front of their home by strangers; few would ever see anyone shot or killed. I was aware that for children in inner-city ghettos many of these inhumanities were sadly a part of their world, but too many children were acting from the images of TV more than the reality outside their windows. We felt it important to break this pattern, if only for a few days.

We explained to the students that when our bodies' nervous systems, which had developed over millions of years, interacted with TV, which had been around for less than a hundred years, curious things happened. During those millions of years, learning was linked with whole-body movement and three-dimensional visual images. The observed images moved within nature's rhythms: heavenly bodies slowly crossed the sky, birds flew, water flowed, occasionally a saber-toothed tiger sprinted by. Lightning was the fast event. The observed world presented a continuum. With the advent of spoken language, areas of the brain were activated where sound waves vibrating the ear drums triggered inner images. In prehistoric times, the pace of the storyteller was synchronous with the small audience gathered around; the listener was in charge of their own inner visualization. Millennia later, written language brought activation to other regions of the brain. Scanning two-dimensional glyphs, letters in the West and characters in the East, triggered images in the mind of the reader. Text could be encoded and decoded at individual pace.

Television, on the other hand, being a visual medium, created the images for us, thereby causing an atrophy of self-generated visualization. If all TV images were slow sweeps of the camera lens over pastoral scenes, teachers probably would not have had so many problems in teaching academic skills. But the use of modern editing techniques where ever shorter, ever more discontinuous images were presented had a deleterious effect on our ability to process real-world information. These frenetically edited images were unintegrated, lacked context, meaning, and changed too quickly for young brains to assimilate. The recent technology allowing computer-generated or processed images to be morphed into ever more surreal visuals was another step away from real imagery. They also were input during a physically passive, optically locked mode. We knew that imagination, creative reasoning, mental and emotional operation, all in combination with physical movement, were needed for integrated cognitive development. TV viewing was counter to these needs. The passivity developed while locked into the tube transferred to the student's classroom mode.

Nature sends us continuous streams of photons reflecting from observed objects. Our optic-brain system evolved over the millennia with this as the sole type of input. Not so with TV. The hyperspeed sweep of an electron beam in a cathode ray tube generates a field of photons with properties not observed in nature. To illustrate this, cut a rubber band. Hold it stretched in natural light and pluck it.

Nothing of note is observed. Now repeat the experiment in front of a TV screen. Pluck the band while holding it both vertically and horizontally. The apparent standing waves are not part of the actual movement. They are an optical illusion generated by the discontinuous projection of photons from the tube. However, just because we can be tricked by optical illusions, it does not mean our more sensitive autonomic neurology is equally oblivious. TV viewing could at times be an enjoyable avocation, but we felt it should be balanced by whole-body activity, full-range eye movement, and sufficient time spent in inner creative visualization and contemplation. Part of the work in Marianne's studio was used to counter time spent in front of the tube.

Though the televisions were dormant this week, the sun still rose and our school days were filled with learning. Amelia continued to suffer from abdominal pains that defied diagnosis. Reese, who the week before had been quite sick, had spent the weekend at a gymnastics meet in San Diego. They both came to school on Tuesday with little energy and had trouble staying awake. I suggested they each gather enough pillows to make a comfortable bed and sleep during class, noting that their subconscious minds would probably hear the lectures and they wouldn't miss anything.

Ariel gave me a quizzical look – bed making in class was not in my standard repertoire of commands. I explained that the desired behavior must fit the circumstance and in this case both girls were quite ill but not contagious, so sleeping seemed appropriate. They improved their beds by covering themselves with the curtains from the doorways between the classrooms. We conducted classes in hushed tones and at 3:00 both seemed better for the rest. One more plus for a classroom with floor pillows. Imagine trying to create such a bed using school desks.

At morning break Rebecca and Rachel came to me to talk about their valentine tug-of-war. I asked if they could think of other ways they might have acted. Each girl voiced two alternate paths of behavior. I had them act out these strategies, reminding them that their reflexive reactions had not achieved their desired goals. When they were finished role-playing, I acknowledged that they had come to me with an open honesty, not asked for anything, and more importantly, I could see the warmth and understanding they now held for each other. Because of their transformation of hearts and minds, valentine exchange was reinstated. Off they ran to tell the others.

The Munchkins were busy reading reports, advancing their math skills, and learning French. Small abandoned piles of French vocabulary cards, math flash cards, and three-by-five cards with facts of countries or cute little animals were part of my morning cleanup ritual. In the Bigs' room the Bill of Rights, Sermon on the Mount, and laws of conservation of momentum and energy appeared in the week's curriculum. Freedom of speech, press, and religion; the right to bear arms, search and seizure, probable cause, indictment by grand jury, speedy and public trial, trial by jury, cruel and unusual punishment; the Beatitudes, salt of the earth, adultery in the heart, plucking the offending eye, turning the other cheek, loving thine enemy, the Lord's Prayer, the lilies of the field, pearls before swine, a house built on rock; and that momentum and energy cannot be created or destroyed, only transferred or transformed, made for a week of animated discussion. The ethics and concepts brought up would continue to be in our discussions for the rest of the year and, I trusted, with each student for the rest of their lives. These subjects were fundamental operating principles of our political, spiritual, and physical world.

Wednesday Reese stayed home but Amelia returned to school still in pain. She spent the day wandering from one pillowed nest to another in the various rooms. When our discussion of the Constitution interrupted her sleep, she headed for a quieter corner of the school. During physics I wrote problems on the board to keep the class occupied and headed to find where she was resting. I found her curled next to the wood stove in the studio with half a dozen kids, pirate-eye patches in place, chanting incantations over her.

Actually, they were maneuvering through the "arrow chart." Marianne had a chart on the wall with a matrix of arrows of different colors facing in the four directions. Saying the color of each arrow while moving the arms in the direction it pointed was the easiest level of using the chart. When I peered in, the task was to say the color across the color wheel and move the arms the direction opposite the arrow. Arms were waving in all directions, different colors being proclaimed. In the middle of this chaos stood Maggie, centered as always, unaffected by the arms and words of others, saying and doing the correct response for every arrow.

I asked Amelia if the chanting and waving seemed therapeutic. She said she couldn't feel any definite healing had occurred, but on the other hand didn't perceive any ill effect. As I left I hoped the group wouldn't make her part of the obstacle course they would be constructing and negotiating after finishing the arrow-chart exercise.

We believed that concepts as large as the Bill of Rights, Sermon on the Mount, and conservation laws of physics were too vast, difficult to grasp, and seemingly abstract to be merely read, noted, and relegated to short-term memory; they required attachment to real-life situations. To children brought up in the United States the freedoms and protections safeguarded by the Bill of Rights were assumed to be universal givens. By using examples from life in Hitler's Germany and Stalin's Russia we gained a perspective on and appreciation of the freedoms we were blessed with, but should not take for granted.

In considering the Sermon on the Mount, I told the kids I found the message of Jesus to be truly revolutionary. I asked if they observed many people living by his admonitions. They replied that most people didn't appear to follow his maxims. I suggested as an experiment they use some of his ideas in social interactions and observe the results. Referring to his admonition of giving your cloak to someone who has taken your coat, I asked what might be a modern scenario. Briana volunteered that if someone stole one of your Pokémon cards, you could give them another. She felt this would blow their mind. Interestingly enough, as we were discussing this in the abstract in the Bigs' room, the Munchkins were actually dealing with Pokémon in their room.

On Tuesday night Sam had left his extensive collection of Pokémon cards at school, and this morning when he arrived he found that a favorite and powerful card was missing. An informal investigation directed by Alison led to Robby's voicing that he might know where the card might be hidden. The card was found and returned. Sam wanted Robby punished. Alison reiterated that punishment was not part of our school and reminded Sam that if we did have punishment he would be near the top of the list for most time in the penalty box. By the time Sam had been in our school a few more years, he would hopefully turn the other cheek and give the other card. I trusted Robby would learn that pilferage was not the best manner of acquisition.

I started Thursday physics class by sharing Marianne's observation that Daniel was moving at a high rate of speed when he was traveling from shed to shed. I asked the class how we might calculate his speed. Matthew immediately had his hand in the air and said that by measuring the length of rope and the angle through which it moved, he could calculate the section of circumference of the circular path traveled. If he then clocked the time between sheds and divided the distance by the time, he would have the velocity.

I was delighted he had so quickly seen the steps needed for this approach to the solution. However, I pointed out that his measurements would be approximations and, more importantly, that I was uneasy about him hanging under the tree branch with a protractor measuring a swinging rope. Since the laws of conservation of energy and momentum were our main physics topic for the week and the reason I had advanced the subject, I suggested a different approach to the problem.

We agreed that Daniel gained potential energy by climbing from the ground to the shed roof and that this was transformed into kinetic energy as he flew mere inches above the ground at the bottom of his arc. We created an equation using the formulas for potential and kinetic energy. Solving the equation for velocity revealed that the only unknown quantity was the height climbed. We estimated that the shed was about two meters tall, plugged in the numbers, and found that Daniel was moving at six meters per second, or about fifteen miles per hour, at the bottom of his arc. An elegant example of the use of the conservation laws and the power of algebra in our real-world experience.

Coleman's bunny had reminded us of uniformly accelerated motion. Another image was used to visualize the conservation of momentum. We imagined our Boss and Vice-Boss, this year Forest and Matthew, floating freely in deep space. This set the stage for pure Newtonian motion – no gravity or air drag affected their movement. Forest was in charge of a remote-control–Nerf-popgun device strapped to Matthew. With it Forest could shoot Nerf balls of different masses at different velocities. By the conservation law, the momentum of each fired ball must be equal and opposite to the momentum added to Matthew. Momentum is the product of mass and velocity, so a two-kilogram ball fired at a speed of fifty meters per second would give Matthew, whose mass was fifty kilos, a speed of two meters per second in the opposite direction. A one-kilogram ball fired at one hundred meters per second would produce the same effect. After a short time the young physicists were creating problems that sent Matthew off in various directions at various speeds. The previous week we had tracked one object, a little bunny. This week we observed two objects traveling away from each other. Next week we would begin our study of collisions.

Valentine's Day was observed on Friday. Most arrived early for the exchange of cards. Though we did not have bells and whistles at school to guide our rhythms, I did run my class like a Swiss railroad. Friday mornings the spelling test began at thirty seconds after 8:00, holidays not excepted. All were in the card-exchange mode when I began the test. Everyone scrambled to their pillows. Cards flew, notebooks opened, no one complained or asked for the first words to be repeated. They all knew this was part of the fun of school. As I gave the spelling words Rachel passed me a handmade card. "Dear John," it read, "Happy Valentine's. Thank you for being so funny! Love, Rachel."

∽ Week Twenty-One ∾
Collisions

The first book that a child reads has a colossal impact.

JOAN AIKEN

AT THE END OF the previous week the Munchkins girls had said it was now warm enough to spend time in the Big Elm. After a short group discussion we collectively decided that afternoon break would be girls only around the tree, morning break for boys, and all other times coed. I told the girls I would rig another rope, creating a low, slow swing with a flight path parallel to our main high-speed shed swing. The prussic knot would allow each girl to set the loop of webbing at the height most comfortable for her feet. Daniel had already shown the boys that the loop on the shed swing was more fun used as a seat than as a foot loop; this freed both feet for stylish landings. However, as I rigged the new rope and prussic knot I didn't envision this swing being used that way. Since it was designed as a low swing, legs and bottoms would be dragging through the wood chips if used any way other than as a foot loop.

Tuesday morning I showed Daniel this latest addition to our rope world and explained how I thought it could best be used. During break times I monitored the tree area from inside our house by watching the movements of the top sections of the ropes. I noticed at afternoon break that the new rope was definitely not moving as I had planned. I went to investigate. Asha was seated, Daniel style, in the webbing loop eight feet above the ground. She was pushing off from the tree, swinging out and back, pushing off again. Definitely not the low, slow standing pendulum the girls had requested. Also, the flight path was perpendicular rather than parallel to the shed swing.

"Asha, whose idea was this?" I asked. "Daniel showed me how we could climb up in the tree and push off. This is really cool." I turned to him. "What happened to my plan?" He smiled, "This is a lot more fun for the girls." From the look on Asha's face and the line of girls awaiting their turn I couldn't deny his statement. "It looks like if they push off with too much force they will swing through the flight path of the shed swing," I observed. "Oh, I figured that out already," he said. "We time the swinging so we don't hit each other, and for safety I can tug on the tail of the rope and keep them out of each other's way." And so the new swing rope became part of our school equipment. How could I complain? The kids were putting physics into action.

Bible study for the week was the Gospel of John. All considered Jesus' turning water to wine, driving the money changers from the temple, healing the lame man at Bethesda, feeding five thousand with five loaves and two small fishes, and walking on the water to be dramatic events. John interspersed these tales with verses containing Jesus' philosophy and metaphors: will of the Father, body and blood, everlasting life. I pointed out that some people took these stories to be literal truth, others thought them metaphorical teaching tales, and still others completely rejected them.

Throughout our Bible study we had followed an ever-changing interaction of God with his creation. Beginning with his early experiences with humans, as found in Genesis, God discovered that people don't always do what you tell them and the option of wickedness was not always avoided. By Exodus he had learned better how to interact with people: wait until they were in a tough situation, carefully pick a spokesperson, and reveal a simple set of rules. With the Psalms of David, God had distanced himself from direct communication, leading to the musings and longings found in David's beautiful poetry. Finally, after this distancing from mankind, God sent his son to walk with the folks.

I never asked my students to belief or disbelieve the messages found in the Bible, or even to support my personal interpretation. I only asked them to be familiar with the text, to think for themselves of its message and possible significance, and to use the material as a topic for future ethical discussion with others.

Our week of physics focused on collisions. The two idealized extremes were completely inelastic and completely elastic impacts. In elastic impacts no energy was lost in the collision; billiard balls came close to this ideal. Bugs hitting windshields were an example of the rather inelastic type – not much bounce. Real-world collisions fell somewhere in between the two idealized impacts. We first studied inelastic collisions where momentum, but not energy, was conserved. I began by asking if they would rather be in a Volkswagen that crashed into a stationary locomotive or have the locomotive run into them in a stalled VW. Forest said he would prefer to avoid both options. I commended him for his admirable sense of safety, but pointed out in such a case there would be no dramatic introduction to our study of collisions and, secondly, these were only *gedanken experimente* so no harm would be done. Most students felt they would rather hit the train. I told them after an hour of calculating collisions between various masses they might change their answer.

For collision problems we didn't visualize bunnies or Nerf balls. We imagined iron cannonballs sitting at rest and different-sized lumps of gluey oatmeal hitting the cannonballs at various speeds. I couldn't conjure a more inelastic substance. After my leading the class in our mental imaging through a few of these, we all agreed the momentum of the moving cereal was transferred to the new heavier mass, a cannonball covered in oatmeal. But not all the energy was converted into motion because some was used in distorting the oatmeal spheroid. I proceeded to fill my board with equations transformed with a few simple rules of algebra. At the end we could calculate the velocity of the oat-covered cannonball for any combination of size of iron ball, mass of oatmeal, and initial speed of the hot breakfast cereal. Finding the kinetic energy lost in each collision revealed more energy of motion was lost when a small object collided with a large one than in the reverse.

Returning to our train and VW, we saw that when car met train the kinetic energy lost was converted into energy that crushed the car and injured its occupants. When the train hit the tiny car most of the energy remained kinetic – the car was simply pushed along by the train. Of course, a real train was so massive that when moving even slowly it possessed a considerable amount of kinetic energy. If only a little was transferred to the car, significant damage would result.

After two days of inelastic interaction we switched to the study of elastic collisions. Our images were pairs of idealized steel balls where no energy was lost as they collided. We plugged in different numbers to the equations. We found that in collisions of balls of equal mass with one moving and one at rest, the first ball stopped and the one at rest moved off at the first ball's initial speed. A big ball hitting a small one resulted in them both moving in the same direction, though at different speeds. When a small one hit a big one, the large one would be pushed forward a bit but the small one would rebound. Forest created scenarios where extremely large, rapidly moving balls knocked little ones faster than the speed of sound.

The class enjoyed creating their own problems and calculating the solutions. The standard textbook approach to physics had a few problems at the end of each chapter. These were solved and the student hoped to leave the topic behind except for the cramming needed before the final exam. In our approach, each student-generated problem led to the forming of another. The dynamic nature, the personal involvement, and the greater number of problems solved led to a deeper understanding of the material.

Each week in the HNW we faced a new sheet of Greek words. Tuesday evening as I scored the test on a list of Greek prepositions, it was obvious more time was needed on these slippery words. I turned to my computer, laser printer, and paper cutter, creating sets of flash cards. On Wednesday, instead of receiving a new set of words, the class spent their time in small groups quizzing each other with the disposable cards. A retest on Friday showed the time had been well spent.

Two hours twice a week were devoted to Latin and writing. Marianne studied Latin with half of the Bigs while the others wrote with Ele. After an hour the groups switched. Latin hours were intense study for all concerned. During the HNW each student operated at the edge of their ability, struggling with a new grammatical concept every week, a page of translation, and an ever growing vocabulary. The few oldest students, farthest along this arduous journey, could look only to Marianne for assistance. All the others had students ahead of them to assist with hints and help.

Being able to articulate the specific help needed was a valuable skill. "What is the ending for singular second-declension nouns in the ablative case?" Being able to explain grammatical concepts in a foreign language to another student demonstrated true mastery of the language, at least to that level. "How do I translate *to be about to seize*?" "That would be the future active infinitive, which is formed by adding *ur* to the fourth principal part of the verb before the regular ending and adding *esse*." "What is the fourth principal part of *to seize*?" "That you can look up yourself." The Latin hours in the studio were filled with young scholars moving forward, supporting each other.

Ele's essay classes were going so well she was able to devote alternate days to the writing of poetry. She began by having each student write a single line, then pass the sheets to the next student, who added a line. This way the pressure on each individual was much reduced. Some were surprised to see that the poems were quite good. After several sessions of group writing followed by discussion and critique, the young poets were ready to solo. Soon each student was writing well-crafted essays and composing poems revealing inner feelings.

Though our academics were the main focus of the HNW, we did not neglect lessons of socialization. Though the majority of our social teachings were with the Munchkins, the Bigs occasionally needed open discussion of their group dynamics. The present topic was group unity, behavior modification, and victimization. We constantly preached the value of loving-kindness in all interactions. When our young citizens wandered from this path, we carefully watched for the correct time to deal with the situation. If we moved too quickly, the kids wouldn't feel there really was a problem to tend to. If we waited too long, then too much pain would be felt and too much time spent in damage control. We had learned that a discussion group when all agreed a problem existed but no one had been excessively hurt was most effective. I delivered a preamble and turned the group over to Marianne, our master facilitator.

Normally Marianne would guide the discussion, allowing the children to set the pace and talk as long as needed. However, since we were in the HNW with much ground to cover, she drove immediately to the central issue when no one volunteered opening remarks. "A number of the boys are placing Jackson in the role of victim and a number of girls are doing the same to Kyrie. There is a difference between group social pressure used to create a unity and victimization used merely to put someone down." She cited the previous day's soccer game in which several boys had chided Jackson both when he made a good stop as goalie and when he had allowed a shot to slip by. She mentioned overhearing several snippy comments about Kyrie during the past few days.

The girls spoke of their situation first. All agreed Kyrie was often spacy and therefore an easy target. Maggie observed that Kyrie also was very perceptive of the foibles of others and often acerbic in her comments. Miranda suggested a person need not voice everything they thought. Cina added that possibly Kyrie was not aware of the several levels of message in her statements and that immediate feedback and honest discussion with her might be better than a cutting remark the next day. Kyrie said she could see these points of view and suggestions by the other girls. All felt the information was useful for their own future social interactions.

The discussion turned to the young gentlemen. Michiah observed that the previous year he had been in the same situation as Jackson was in now. When one was a second-year Big and feeling insecure with interactions with peers and the older boys, the tendency was to gather the younger classmates and the oldest Munchkins as a group of sycophants. Michiah related that from his experience this was a dead-end street that brought only misery to those involved, especially the ringleader. He said as he had worked on this in school and with his family, he had learned to separate his essential self from his behaviors. This led him to greater control and choice in his social interactions and created more individual and group happiness.

Many nodding heads indicated agreement with his insights. Several other minor points of interaction were mentioned by other boys. Consensus held that Hard Nine Weeks fatigue was a factor in eroding our harmony. I jumped in at the end to remind them of my maxim of always holding good form to the end of any event, pointing out that fatigue was always a factor in any extended activity and urging each to develop the habit of reserving energy for the end game. I concluded by reminding them to avoid the pattern where a group focused negativity on a single person.

Though the staff spent considerable time planning and preparing for each class, often the finest moments were created by circumstance and serendipity. Melanie was our expert at helping those children having extreme difficulty learning to read. We arranged schedules so that for two hours a week she could quietly read with the struggling ones.

Of our present students Daniel was having the greatest struggle. Alison's gentle support as his main classroom teacher, Marianne and Tara's work in the studio, and nightly reading with his grandfather were all contributing to the foundation necessary for eventual success. All the previous year, Daniel's first at our school, the mere sight of a book had sent him into despair. This year he had been slowly moving through the McGuffey primer.

Friday found Marianne and Tara away at a conference, which meant no one would be making lunch for the staff. Melanie volunteered to drive to Taco Bell. I pointed out she would miss her reading time. To keep with our schedule, we arranged the hour with the Bigs so a couple of them could read with the young ones. Daniel was sensitive about his lack of skill with the written word so I asked Michiah, our student with the biggest heart, to read with him.

As fate would have it, this was the day Daniel finished his primer. Michiah congratulated him, told of his own struggle learning to read, and explained how after the first painful steps with the primer reading became easier. As class broke for lunch, Michiah reported Daniel's success to some of the other boys, who added their congratulations and reinforced the belief he had jumped the largest hurdle. Daniel felt great and had been supported in a way no teacher could express. He came to me to report his success. I said the joy and mastery he was experiencing swinging was starting to leak into the other areas of his life. With a big smile he headed for the shed.

Around the popcorn bowl Friday several parents were relating how delighted they were with the physics thoughts brought home by their kids. They enjoyed the image of the colliding oatmeal. As we talked of these imaginary collisions I heard my name being called from the Big Elm. Upon arriving I found Nyssa, slightly dazed, seated on the ground with others brushing off the wood chips covering her clothes. She had walked through the gate without looking and was met by Daniel traveling at his normal swinging velocity. Someone asked if the collision was elastic or inelastic. Forest thought that from the look of her eyes quite a lot of the energy was still reverberating around in Nyssa's head. He judged the collision inelastic and helped Nyssa navigate toward the popcorn bowl. Physics had met real life.

∽ Week Twenty-Two ∾
The Brain

The Brain – is wider than the Sky –
For – put them side by side –
The one the other will contain
With ease – and You – beside.

EMILY DICKINSON

AFTER MORNING TESTS the week began with the writings of Saint Paul and the constitutional amendments of the twentieth century. Following the simplicity of Jesus' parables, Paul's epistles were a dramatic change of style and philosophy. I looked forward to the week of reading and discussion. The amendments dealt with income tax, extending the vote to women and then to younger citizens, the prohibition of alcohol, and the repeal of the Eighteenth Amendment. I also included the wording of the never ratified Equal Rights Amendment.

Setting aside the Bible and constitutional texts, I was preparing to turn to math when Forest asked about my meeting with a group of visitors the previous week. I said they had heard of our academic excellence and had come to observe and learn of the models we used in understanding child development. Jackson asked if I would tell the class about these models since he and his schoolmates were the ones most affected by our theories. I found this a reasonable request and mentally shelved my math lecture.

"To begin," I opened, "please understand that models are not reality, merely useful tools. We use two seemingly contradictory theories to describe you guys. One, 'the ego theory,' focuses on each person's awareness of their own identity. It holds that your ego is not an actual thing, but rather the name given to the process whereby you relate your unique individual inner patterns within the arena of external reality and the people around you. Being in touch with both your inner and outer worlds, your ego directs your thoughts and behaviors to fulfill needs and desires. At Fayette we assist each of you to form and strengthen a healthy ego so you will make decisions from your deepest values and personal integrity. We interact in ways to help you understand your own egocenter and make it flexible and appropriate. We honor each of you, your actions, and your life journey." Amelia said this helped her understand the staff better. She knew we were respectful in our interactions but now better saw why.

I continued, "The ego model is used to set the emotional and social tone at Fayette. When creating the specific activities, exercises, and techniques that make up the physical surroundings, the curriculum, and the studio work, we find 'the triune brain theory' useful. This model of the brain hypothesizes a tripartite division of the brain: the reptilian region in charge of basic survival, encased in the paleo-mammalian controlling of emotion, covered by the neo-mammalian in charge of thinking. The molecular and electrical interactions of these three areas create the consciousness of each human.

This outrageous model excited their interest: "You mean Matt and I have snake brains inside us?" "Marianne always talks of two hemispheres; why are you talking of three parts?" "How can you use two different theories when I am one person?" We are known for our engaged discussions and lectures, but this was exceeding the interest and attention of any previous hour I could remember.

"Let me take these questions one at a time," I proposed. "Operating with two such dissimilar models as the ego and triune theories is not difficult. Remember these are models and are not to be mistaken for reality. Just as physics views light with two theories-sometimes it seems better to think of light as discrete photons and at other times as waves-so it is when I interact with you. Sometimes I view you as mysterious vortices of cosmic consciousness visiting the planet and treat you with deference and honor. At other times I view you as just so many molecules and chemical reactions that I can easily manipulate." My smile showed I was using humor for effect. Picking up on this tone, Forest cajoled, "Tell us about Matthew's lizard brain."

"The Reptilian Brain includes the brain stem and part of the midbrain," I explained. "This region controls automatic functions such as body temperature and triggers automatic responses such as fight or flight. Matthew's lizard brain does not have much flexibility in its programming, so we at school must honor and work within its reptilian requirements. The safeties of our school environment are directed at keeping his inner lizard from triggering threat messages. When his lower brain signals the survival alert, his higher brain functions are shut down. Since learning happens in the higher brains, when Matthew is under perceived threat or stress, he cannot learn effectively. The many gardens and walkways around the school also honor the functions of this area of the brain. Do you really think I enjoy watering and weeding? The changing of the gardens over the seasons and the occasional moving of stumps and benches keeps your reptilian brains interested in the surroundings. When seeking to modify Matthew's behavior I don't speak harshly, as he would only retreat into lizardland. I want to talk and reason with his higher selves. At times I wish I could just pop him a good one with a big stick. Such as when he doesn't understand something I think is simple or when he leaves his papers on the floor. But, hey, I gotta work with the material I have."

Continuing to mix humor, outrage, and biochemistry, I went on. "You think I have ropes and swings because I like to see you play? Wrong! Our pendulum swing exists to excite your vestibular systems, the parts of your brains that detect motion. When swinging on the pendulum, the vestibular system is knocked out of balance and sends signals awakening and alerting the higher brain functions. The first few pendulum rides are interpreted as threats to the system. Your lizard brain freaks and calls for the release of adrenaline. This hormone decreases your ability to learn and remember, and therefore doesn't help me in the classroom. After several swings, however, since death or injury don't occur, your lower brain changes its signaling to that of pleasure and adventure. The hormones interferon and interleukin, among others, are called for. These have the opposite effect from the threat hormones and therefore help me in the classroom. Eventually, when simple swinging becomes boring, few pleasure hormones are released and you add variations to your swinging and again feel the surge from these happy hormones."

As they absorbed this new view of swinging I marched ahead. "Your paleo-mammalian brain, also known as the limbic system, is the seat of your emotions. Most of the brain development of the area occurs between ages fifteen months and four years. From this region the actual hormones called for by the reptilian brain are released. This region of the brain controls waking and sleep states, pain, pleasure, recognition of body language, memories of fear, and short- and long-term memory. With the development of the limbic system in early hominids, social bonds and relational patterns were formed, with characteristics such as altruism evolving. We feed and pay the vet bills of Max, Annie, Buddy, and Xylo so you will learn to be nice to them and then transfer this behavior to each other. The staff beams love at you, creates a comfortable social environment, and acts joyous so your middle brains will get trained in the habit of sending happy chemicals through your systems, making our jobs of teaching easier.

"The neomammalian brain, or neocortex," I continued, "is your intellectual creative brain. It is composed of left and right hemispheres, each with different functions. These are the two regions Marianne talks about and works with. Your left hemisphere deals with analysis, inputs data by seeing the pieces first, sees differences in patterns, is comfortable with planned events, and processes sequentially. Your right hemisphere is intuitive, sees the whole picture, sees similarities in patterns, is comfortable being spontaneous, and uses simultaneous processing. In art your left brain is concerned with the media, tool use, and technique; your right, with image and emotional tone of the work. In music your left brain

THE BRAIN 181

reads the notes, remembers the words, and holds the beat; your right feels the passion and the rhythm.

"Major development of the right hemisphere occurs between ages four and seven, that of the left hemisphere between seven and nine. Between ages nine and twelve you build a bridge between the two hemispheres. This is why you and the Munchkins act and see the world so differently. You have connected hemispheres and they don't. By the way, Maggie has ten percent more of these inter-hemisphere connections than Michiah. This is not personal, but holds for all men and women."

Jessica jumped in, "That's why Fayette's youngest students are seven. They are just starting to develop their second hemisphere. And at ten or eleven we become Bigs. We are connecting our brains." Forest continued her thought. "Don't tell me. At about fourteen our brains are wired and hormones kick in, and you send us off to other schools?" I nodded and smiled, "Yes, you are both correct. Also remember that the daily Brain Gym and your work in the studio is aimed at integrating all your parts. Your 'whole' is truly greater than the sum of your 'parts.'"

Amani raised her hand. "Speaking of the studio, Marianne is always talking about brain networks and a word I can't remember, but it starts with *m*." I switched from the big picture to the little one. "The word is *myelin*. Each of your nerve cells has a long, thin axon that conducts impulses to other nerve cells, muscles, or glands. When neurons are repeatedly used, the axon builds a coating of myelin that speeds transmission and protects the axon. That is why you do specific exercises repeatedly. Marianne has identified areas you haven't used much, and over time you build more myelin and therefore process information more quickly.

"Speed of brain function is improved with myelination but the complexity of your neural network is increased by the number of dendrites of each neuron. Dendrites are highly branched extensions of the cell that link with other neural cells. This complex branching network is always in a dynamic state. Unstimulated areas have little branching. Stimulating areas increases dendritic branching. Much of the work with Marianne and Tara encourages these improved networks. For example, by patching your dominant eye and doing visual exercises, the neural network is signaled to increase dendrites and myelination in the less used pathways. You have better academic performance and social skills not because of better character or genetics, but because you have better balance and integration between your sensory organs and the various areas of your brains. You have more dendrites and myelination in critical areas than most students because of the time and attention you, with the help of Marianne and Tara, devote to these critical neural developments.

"Remember yesterday when Amelia came off the roof with her face covered with soot? Most teachers would disapprove of, and surely not encourage, such activities. Since I view all of you using the triune brain model, my thinking went something like this: Sure, climb on the new shed – it will be good for Amelia's Reptile Brain to experience the changes in terrain. When her deepest brain had the urge to explore the stovepipe I completely understood. When she lifted her head after looking down the stovepipe and had soot on her chin, I told her to smear a full beard on her face. I knew this would make everyone laugh, which would trigger happy hormones in all your midbrains. These would excite your thinking brain and make it more awake so you would really listen as I talked about bronze tools in Scotland." With a better sense of their own neurology, all headed out for break.

The rest of the week was typical of the Hard Nine Weeks: we each had as much work in as many subjects as possible. As we finished our Friday popcorn we entered a weekend filled with homework. Fortunately, our brains, ears, and eyes were better aligned and we had more dendrites and myelin than we had two months before.

∽ Week Twenty-Three ∾
Tests and Celebration

*The greatest sign of success for a teacher...
is to be able to say, "The children are
now working as if I did not exist."*

MARIA MONTESSORI

THE FINAL WEEK of the HNW brought the conclusion of several topics and general celebration. Our study of the Constitution and prehistory had concluded the previous week, and now we were finishing our nine-week survey of the Bible, appropriately with Revelation. After all the hard work the pressure would ease for the remainder of the year. Not only had every student survived, but through the academic intensity each had increased their knowledge in each academic area of study and become more efficient at general scholastic skills.

While the majority of selections from the Bible gave precepts, metaphorically or directly, that could be applied to our daily lives, this was not so true of Revelation. The imagery was vivid yet completely removed from any mundane experience. We could not discuss ethical implications or tenets of faith but rather used the text to challenge our inner visualization skills.

As we read the chapters I made sure each student was creating their own inner video. For example chapter 4 gave the image of God on a throne surrounded by twenty-four elders also on thrones; four winged multi-eyed beasts were part of the scene. After everyone had their static tableau in mind, we reviewed the words in the text, which added action to the incredible scene: flashes of lightning, flaming lamps, an emerald rainbow, the song of the animals, and the prostration of the elders. I said this was the time to use all those hours of staring at MTV. The goal was for each student to create their own rich images, combining the words of the text with their own sense of sound, light, and movement. One of the aphorisms posted on several garden walls stated, "Explore the boundary between the sacred and sacrilege." I was probably near that boundary when I referred to Revelation and MTV in the same sentence.

Images well established were easily sustained and expanded. The next chapters brought the Lamb of God, the breaking of the seven seals, the four horsemen, and the silence in heaven as the seventh seal was broken. All now enjoyed adding scenes to their inner images: the seven trumpets of the seven angels, lots of blood, major astronomical events, lots of horses. By now the kids were saying the videos of MTV were lightweight compared to these. The images only grew: the woman giving birth, the dragon, the beast, the fall of Babylon, the new Jerusalem. We finished our journey through the Bible feeling more familiar with its styles and stories, understanding many of the rooted tenets of the Judaeo-Christian faiths, and still having no idea how John's vision in Revelation applied to our daily lives.

After months of deriding multiple-choice tests as a most inferior way to judge academic performance, I passed out just such a test. Two hundred questions, complete with a fill-in-the-bubbles answer sheet. Since students would be faced with these in future schooling, we used this time to practice the necessary techniques. After a few questions on content and procedure, the class settled into problem solving and bubble filling. Shortly I left the room to wander around the gardens. I knew that no one would cheat; each would maintain an excellent focus and attitude toward the task. When a school's structure, philosophy, practice and rewards were reduced to the lowest intellectual levels – that is, test scores and grades – students would automatically resonate to this system. Shallow, expedient thinking and cheating would be among the products. When a school embodied and rewarded self-integration, pursuit of knowledge, and personal ethics, cheating did not exist.

During the week Marianne and Tara checked with each student regarding their studio sessions. In May each would take a battery of diagnostic tests quantifying levels of improvement. These sessions were casual conversations. Since I wasn't needed in my classroom I puttered around the studio and overheard Katherine and Robby's talks with Marianne.

Katherine came to us last year with both ears and eyes not effectively signaling her brain. Her superior intelligence and iron will had made her a marginally successful first-grade student in public school, but at the price of extreme stress. She had had to develop compensating strategies in lieu of the direct inputs of ears and eyes. Our studio work first addressed her ears with phoneme exercises and then shifted to adding work with her eyes. When these pathways were better established, the focus of sessions moved to visualization.

As I rearranged bookshelves in the back corner of the studio, I heard Katherine say, "You know, Marianne, this last week I looked at the book I am writing and realized the words just didn't make strong pictures. I'm going back and adding all sorts of adjectives and adverbs." When Katherine headed back to class, Marianne dropped her professional stance, slumped on her desk, and cried. Seeing the actualization of potential after holding the image for a year and a half was an emotional, not intellectual event. I smiled and said, "Sit up. Here comes your next customer."

Robby had come to Fayette at the beginning of the year. The dominance tests revealed he was blocked dominant, meaning, for one thing, that his ears provided little information to his brain. After several years of schooling he still did not read. Since his ears did not aid him in school, he used his eyes to gather information. In his previous school, the label of cheater had soon been attached. Phoneme classes in the first months of school began building new neural pathways connecting ears and brain. The daily Brain Gym in studio and class added to intrabrain communication.

As I dusted clean xylophones Marianne asked him if he felt his perceptions had changed. He said, "Just the other day in music I could tell when my ears were really hearing the music and when they turned off. I could then think a little and they would come back on." Both Marianne and I knew Robby was not done with studio sessions but that he had taken the largest, most important step. Marianne asked how reading was going. "Last week while I was out shopping with my dad, I asked him to buy me a book Sam had said was really great. I was embarrassed when my dad gave me a big hug right in the middle of the store."

The penultimate day of the Hard Nine Weeks was Pajama Day. This one would live in the history of the school with a touch of infamy. Kids tumbled out of the cars still in their night clothes to be greeted by the staff similarly attired. James, who always rode his bike to school, pedaled in wearing pj's and a bathrobe. He spoke of the funny looks he had received on the way to school, especially a long, hard stare from a policeman. The pajamas gave a cozy feeling to the day. This was reinforced by the first significant snowfall of the season. The older Munchkin boys were full of excitement and energy before school, and I suggested they go outside and have a short snowball fight. Since this was the first snow of the year I reminded them of the rules: no hard packing and no throwing at the head. The most important rule was to avoid stepping on or gathering snow from the gardens. Tulips, daffodils, and various smaller bulbs were just beginning to emerge and needed to be treated with the best of care. The boys assured me they understood the rules and headed off for snowballing. I returned to warmer duties inside.

An hour later, with everyone settled into class, I ventured out to survey the gardens. Every one of the bulb garden beds had been stomped by young gentlemen's shoes. In the history of the school no one had ever hurt a single bulb. Joe Dimaggio's hitting streak ended at fifty-six games, our garden streak at twenty years. I called Alison and her class out to the wooden decks in the middle of the bulb beds. The prints in the snow spoke for themselves. Three different tread patterns were visible, those matching the shoes of Sam, Avery, and Daniel. I asked how this could have happened, especially after my explicit reminder minutes before their tromping.

Avery spoke of his need for fresh ammo. I cut him short. "First, you three are off the swing for a long time. Further consequences will come later." We returned to class.

After first break I asked Forest for his analysis of the effect on the school community. He said others felt sorry for the gardens, but the three boys seemed sad for the trouble they were in, not for the damage done. At lunch I gathered the three on the sidewalk with an audience of enough others to guarantee that word would spread to everyone. "You three are suspended for one day." This meant they would miss the celebration on the final day of the HNW. "Also, you will notice the three large planters now in front of you. Each of you, with your parents' assistance, will plant one of them and maintain it for the remainder of the school year. I will water for you on weekends and over the summer, but they are your responsibility the rest of the time." The part of me that was an educator was glad to have such incidents as teaching tools. The part of me that was a gardener would have taken the lads out behind the shed and applied the leather strap of my grandfather's generation.

Friday morning brought closure to many activities. Alison read the last Munchkin reports. Fourteen Munchkins each researching and writing eight reports, which were then read and discussed in class, added a tremendous amount to each Munchkin's body of knowledge. At the same time the Bigs scored their bubble tests. They exchanged papers, I read the correct answers, errors were marked, scores were totaled, and tests were returned to their owners. We spent a half hour analyzing answers and methods of problem solving. More than one mistake was made by merely filling in the wrong bubble. I suggested each study their mistakes and mentioned that sometime in the next months we might retake the test.

I concluded by reminding the class not to focus too much on their test scores, but rather on the knowledge gained on the Bible, Constitution, physics and the other subjects we had explored in the past weeks. Paraphrasing from the *Tao te Ching*, I reminded them "the knowledge that can be tested with bubbles is not the real knowledge." Balancing Eastern with Western thought, I added a quote by the English mathematician and philosopher Alfred North Whitehead: "Real education is what you have left after you forget what you learned in school." On that thought we closed our notebooks for two weeks.

Since the afternoon was to be spent in celebration, we scheduled our two hours of art and music in the late morning. The last of Alison's sketching classes was focused and skillful. When we returned from spring break we would be switching from sketching with pencil to working with brush and paint. Melanie set up the xylos in the rondo circle for the last time. The Munchkins were now comfortable with the eight rondos they had learned and moved around the circle without interruption or wasted energy. Their play at the Spring Concert would be a leap forward from their play at the Winter Concert. Of course this meant Melanie would write more difficult parts for them to play. Because they were young children I didn't reveal this fact, I only congratulated them on bars well struck.

Tradition dictated the Munchkins would see a video and have pizza the final afternoon while the Bigs walked to our favorite Northern New Mexican restaurant for lunch. Selecting a video for a group of young ones was never easy. When all movies with violence were eliminated, those already seen by most crossed off the list, those too uncool for sophisticated ten-year-olds rejected, there weren't many left to be found at Blockbuster. Some years before, we had hit on the answer to this problem. We now owned several European movies centered on the lives and adventures of children. We had found the Munchkins enjoyed these foreign scenes and customs, the weaving of the mundane and the mythical, and the commonalities with and the differences from their own lives. This year they settled into scenes from Ireland.

As Ele, the Bigs, and I walked the mile to the restaurant I felt proud of my students and pleased with the work they had done. Every one of the Bigs had curtailed extracurricular activities these past two months, many had lost sleep completing the increased amounts of homework, more than a few had had emotional storms at home. They had done this because we held to the belief that these nine weeks of extreme academic intensity would benefit them in the long run. I was honored and humbled by the trust they had placed in our staff. No one grumbled about the mile walk. It was accepted as part of the traditional triumph. They were happy with a burrito or taco plate and a dessert of choice, a small reward for the weeks of pressure.

The patrons of the restaurant did not see the kids through my eyes, however. Some asked to be moved to another room. The ones who remained did not acknowledge our presence. Here I was with a score of the finest young citizens in our city and no one cared. When adults wondered why kids seemed so disaffected from our present culture, the answer to me was obvious.

∽ Eleven Spring Weeks ∾

A SECOND Parents' Week began the final portion of our school year. From the intense level of academics of the Hard Nine Weeks we slowly eased the workload. By May, with all subjects well covered during the previous eight months and the weather warming, we climbed in the Big Elm more often, played ever longer baseball games in the afternoons, and rehearsed for our spring choral concert. The final weeks of school were filled with days of tie-dyeing, a potluck, a day at a waterpark, and melancholy as our oldest students prepared to leave us.

Week Twenty-Four

Parents Again

*All the time a person is a child
he is both a child and learning to be a parent.*

BENJAMIN SPOCK

Our second Parents' Week of the year found me in the garden. As parents came and went I enjoyed turning soil, trimming perennials, and planting seeds. Throughout the week the kids were well behaved and most parents had a good time with their projects. Looking over the garden wall, I was pleased to see many adults hanging around at the conclusion of their presentations, enjoying conversations with others and not just scurrying off to other duties.

Our school policy was never to counsel parenting skills. We were a school for children, not an organization devoted to family therapy. Interacting with the students was a full-time job in itself. Our role was to be a fierce advocate for each child, not a referee for parent-child disharmonies. The only exception to this policy was when my role was that of grandfatherly gardener. When parents wandered into that domain, sage advice and commentary – in the most general terms and holding to basic principles-was available.

Tuesday afternoon, as one parent was beginning to bake pizzas on our outdoor grill for the Munchkins, another parent who had just completed her time with the Bigs approached me as I planted spinach in a freshly turned bed. "I just don't know what to do with my daughter," she lamented. "Last year you told me adolescence would bring new challenges. Boy, were you right! She stays in her room with the door closed and listens to horrible music and watches disgusting shows on TV." Setting down my packet of seeds I took a long moment to consider the various emotions encoded in the mother's statement: sorrow at no longer having a little girl, anger at being tested, frustration at lacking the tools to deal with a difficult situation, fear of making the wrong move and alienating her only child. I mentally juggled whether to begin with the lessons of Sun Tzu, the Chinese philosopher and general, or the lessons of my grandmother. I decided to begin with my grandmother.

"You know that our grandmothers could deal with these situations in the blink of an eye," I reminded. "I find that now parents agonize for long periods and then often don't act or choose actions that make matters worse. Why do you think this is so?"

I could tell that my garden guest used my statement only to feel more inadequate and guilty so I quickly pressed on. "Our grandparents were not intrinsically better citizens than we are, but they lived in different times and situations. In those days children were raised in a network of relatives and close neighbors. Aunts, uncles, and cousins were a constant part of each child's life. Now often they live at a distance, are infrequently seen, and therefore are not a moral force helping to guide each child. You are not a poor mother, merely an unsupported one."

She smiled a little and said, "But our grandmothers didn't have to compete with rap music and TV." I put my arm around her as I remembered my grandmother's reaction to seeing a young Elvis Presley on our first television. I had never seen her so disturbed. Three weeks later she suffered a massive stroke and passed from our lives. In my mind at the time I thought these events were connected.

"You are right," I concurred. "In the olden days the barbarian was outside the village walls. Now we have let the enemy into our very homes. We have different challenges from past generations but we are not inherently less able." My inner gardener felt it time to switch to Sun Tzu. I held that our lives are a battleground, at least metaphorically. "In *Art of War* Sun Tzu tells us there are nine varieties of ground, three of which I think possibly apply to your situation: 'dispersive ground,' where the fighting is in your own territory; 'facile ground,' where one is penetrating a short distance into the enemy's territory; and 'contentious ground,' which is of great advantage to either side."

From the puzzled look on our mother's face I knew I needed to add a bit of modern commentary. "'Dispersive' is the happy world you lived in when your daughter was young, 'facile' is when you now enter her bedroom, 'contentious' is the several years in front of you before she becomes twenty-five and magically realizes that you were a pretty good parent after all. The great advantage Sun Tzu speaks of is the collection of life skills both you and your daughter can gain in your journey together through her teenage years." She asked how to handle these different situations. I smiled, "That's easy. Sun Tzu says, 'On dispersive ground, fight not. On facile ground, halt not. On contentious ground, attack not.' I have found this advice of noninterference useful in my dealings with family, students, and friends."

I could tell from her body language that our session was about ended and that I was not meeting her complaint in a way she had desired. As I picked up my shovel I concluded our talk. "Sun Tzu says, 'All warfare is based on deception.' In this case this translates as 'don't do the obvious with your daughter.' More importantly he reminds us that the true object of war is peace. This precept is too often forgotten in the heat of conflict."

Our father cooking pizza announced that "adult" pizzas were ready. I walked our troubled and now perplexed mother over to the grill to take a look. The proud cook lifted the lid to reveal pizza topped with broccoli. Inwardly I wondered how Sun Tzu would have dealt with my degree of disappointment. Outwardly I used what I learned from my grandmother. "Thank you so much for this marvelous pizza," I exclaimed. "I never would have thought of broccoli as a topping."

Wednesday's spring showers kept me from my garden, but bright skies on Thursday brought a return of outdoor activities to the school and my vegetable beds. Under the Big Elm large sheets of tissue paper, colored cellophane, and mylar were being cut and glued to create hot-air balloons. I was turning moist soil and crafting poles and string into climbing structures for beans.

A father joined me, and I knew that more grandfatherly advice would be dispensed. He did not begin with a complaint and therefore didn't draw from me obscure references to long-dead military strategists. He asked a most straightforward question: "What are your most effective principles for helping a child change the things they do that drive you crazy?" Without prologue I began, "To me the most important point to remember is to separate the 'essential self' of the child from the 'transitory behavior.' We too often find ourselves reacting to the latter and forgetting the former. In school when faced with a child needing a few pointers in social behavior, I avoid focusing on the twitchy body and the defensive emotional stance. I hold my thought and vision to the soul shining through their eyes. Bringing my full attention framed with a compassionate stance tends to quiet their body, relax the guarded posture, and increase the light of their eyes."

The father felt this was excellent advice but stated that he too often found himself using a voice that sadly reminded him of his own father's scolding. I laughed, thinking of the times my own father's tone seemed to come from my mouth. "I know exactly what you are referring to, but remember that these are merely habits. Habits are not part of our genetic coding and can be changed with sagacious practice. There is not a quick fix to replacing habits, but when you honestly know that you are using one that is not effective or fitting with your personal ethic, the work needed to modify it is well worthwhile.

"My second principle when faced with a behavior, in ourselves or in a child, we wish to alter or eliminate is to hold to the 'ideal' and not the 'problem.' In my observation energy tends to go where attention is focused. Therefore if you focus on the problem, it often entrenches. Focusing on the desired state tends to assist its manifestation."

As the first hot-air balloons were being carried to our parking area for maiden flights, we ended our talk and headed to watch the launches. The parent in charge of the balloon project was masterful at helping the young Montgolfiers assemble their lighter-than-air craft, but I calculated that the one hair dryer he had brought would be insufficient for rapid launches. I put up my gardening tools and headed around the neighborhood to gather all the hair dryers I could find. Soon limp sacks, as if by magic, were taking shape and then being released. Thanks to a very light wind they all descended a short distance from the launch pad. Each was quickly retrieved and returned for further launches. After dozens of flights, balloons, parents, and students left school, ending another day.

Friday, the final day of an excellent Parents' Week, brought another consultation in the garden. "You have raised four daughters, all of whom seem to have avoided the major pitfalls of youth and are now exceptional young women. How did you do it?" asked a father with two daughters of his own.

Continuing to rake a bed that would soon be ready for tomatoes, I replied, "It was easy – merely luck." His reply was immediate and fit right into my stratagem: "Luck! I don't believe that for one moment!"

"Oh, not the *luck* you are thinking of – LUCK the acronym," I explained. *L* stands for the first and most important principle, love: Demonstrate your love for them constantly. You may disapprove of certain actions and choices they make from time to time, but never stop loving them. *U* denotes understanding: They really are always trying their best to cope with their own growing and all the signals from a crazy world. Understanding the logic they use to arrive at their behaviors is the first step in helping them modify less-successful habits. *C* stands for communication: Never do anything to sacrifice communication with your children. The world they are venturing into has toxic and dangerous areas. Operate in a way that lets them know that they can always talk to you about anything and can call you on the phone anytime, no matter what situation they find themselves in. *K* is the first letter of kidding: Joke with your children, especially after delivering a teaching lesson or handling a difficult situation." Our father seemed pleased with my answers to his question.

Three o'clock arrived on Friday with everyone delighted with the projects and interactions of Parents' Week, the garden beds prepared for another season of growth, and several adults better armed to handle the challenges of parenting. A grandfatherly gardener smiled to himself as he reflected on the many lessons he had learned the hard way as his daughters had taught him how to be a parent.

Week Twenty-Five

Spring Training

Whoever wants to know the heart and mind of America had better learn baseball.

JACQUES BARZUN

WITH THE Hard Nine Weeks behind us the schedule in the spring weeks lightened. Instead of class beginning at 8:00 for the Bigs they were not required to be at school until 8:30, with instruction beginning at 9:00. Nevertheless, Tuesday morning at 8:10 all but two of the class were present and working on the puzzles in the weekly packet. We enjoyed being together and the work had been time tested to both add knowledge and give pleasure. The Munchkins rolled in glad to see each other, and by 9:15 both classrooms and the studio were in full swing.

In the spring weeks some of the subjects switched topics and others focused on solidifying the material raced through in the HNW. For example, Ele's writing switched and Marianne's Latin reinforced. Every year we spent some time on the art of note taking for research papers. We felt confident high school and college would provide our students ample practice in the writing of research reports so we highlighted the first steps needed in this discipline. I had always taken the standard approach of using encyclopedias, related books, and periodicals for reports, but this year Ele suggested a fresh idea. Each Big would interview a parent on their personal and extended family history and create a report from this information. As a warm-up, class time was spent interviewing fellow students on their hobbies. The first thing each learned was that interviewing others and collecting material were much more difficult than they seemed. By the end of the week each young researcher was excited by the project and ready for a weekend of interviewing.

Following the rigor of Latin in the HNW the pace could only slacken. In the spring weeks Marianne passed out fewer *grammaticæ* but did require longer, more difficult translations of Latin. The young Latin scholars became immersed in vocabulary, sentence structure, word endings, and most importantly, translating into flowing well-crafted English. The younger ones received help from the advanced students, but Forest and Matthew could rely only on each other and their Latin dictionaries.

After three soccer games a week since September we were excited by the switch to baseball, beginning this week with "spring training." Tuesday the Bigs practiced catching and throwing, while the Munchkins played a game of kickball that simulated the rules of baseball. The Bigs' practice did not include Forest and James. Thursday of Parents' Week they had ditched school for a day of skiing. All knew that skiing on a school day automatically placed one, or in this case two, in my doghouse. Part of me understood the urge to ski the uncrowded slopes when six inches of fresh powder had fallen the night before. Another part of me knew the rest of the class was in school working hard. And a third part of me was looking for help with some of the little tasks around school. Some years before, the "doghouse" had been created. Each year I explained to the Munchkins this was an idiom, not an actual building, and that only Bigs could be assigned this status. The Munchkins were always much relieved.

The two skiers monitored the Munchkin game. As I had anticipated, these denizens of my doghouse were great in controlling the kickball game. On Wednesday the classes switched activities. The Munchkins used the gloves for throw and catch, while the Bigs enjoyed a game of kickball. Our canine *casa* cohorts again monitored the kickball game, for a second day not getting to kick, run, or be on a team. In the third inning Forest pleaded his case to be able to join a team. "I'm graduating and this is probably the last kickball game of my life." I could not refuse and took over his pitching duties. As the Fates would have it he came up in the final inning with bases loaded and kicked a grand slam to win the game.

But back to our academics of Tuesday. The afternoon was devoted to physics and math, the former reinforced and the latter switched to a new topic. During the Hard Nine Weeks as we raced through new physics concepts, I had reassured the class that spring would bring review of the equations and properties of kinematics. A weekly review sheet with problems featuring Coleman's bunny, the boys in space, Maggie carrying cannonballs up a tall building, and other scenarios solidified the concepts and equations. Through the use of computer, laser printer, and copy machine, I was able to produce sheets based on the previous week's performance.

The task was quite simple. When all went well, I added variations to old scenarios and plugged in larger numbers to the problems. When the class was stuck, I stayed with familiar scenes and used simpler numbers. We also continued to work with metric conversions and scientific notation. Knowing that no new concepts would be presented gave the young folks reassurance as they worked to master the material.

While physics was old news, if ideas introduced in January could be called old in March, the math was new. After ten weeks of algebra in the autumn and nine weeks of arithmetic in the winter, we spent the first weeks of spring exploring different number bases. I had always been suspicious of devoting a whole year to the study of a single aspect of math. First, this does not allow for a young growing mind to develop different perspectives on the multifaceted study called mathematics. Second, the single-subject approach usually meant that in a school career each student received only one chance at each topic. Third, or tenth if thinking in base three, as we were about to do, math proficiency involved expanding concepts and improving ciphering. At Fayette we found our varied curriculum helped both skills.

Tuesday we introduced the concept that place value need not be based only on the number ten – any number greater than one would do. I explained that in our standard numbering system ten symbols were used and each column was valued ten times greater than the neighboring column on the right; the close linkage to the metric system and scientific notation was noticed by the class. Base three had only three symbols and each column was three times greater than its right-hand neighbor. Base five used five symbols, with each column five times its neighbor. Here was an excellent example of one simple principle with a different manifestation for each base number used.

After my demonstration on the board of converting a few numbers into other bases and changing a few from various bases into base ten, exercise sheets were passed out and pencils and brains engaged. Wednesday we extended to bases above ten, using letters for the extra needed symbols. Thursday brought the special and easy-to-cipher relationships between bases two, four, eight, and sixteen. Friday we made sure everyone was comfortable with all these different transformations and spent a little time going around the room counting in different bases. The numbers 1, 2, 10, 11, 12, 20, 21, 22, 100 began the counting in base three; 7, 8, 9, A, B, 10, 11, 12 was a correct sequence in base twelve. The thinking needed to switch from base to base and the ciphering done mentally or on scratch paper were tremendous exercises in math skills.

The Munchkins also were expanding their math abilities and perspective. I had never liked standard math flash cards for they trained young students to say one number and assume they had completed the required task. The next card was unrelated to the previous, so young minds were being conditioned to take small, discrete, halting steps and not see the broader picture. The actual applications of math were never like this. To remedy this concern, I used computer and printer to create multistep flash cards, where two numbers were multiplied and then a third was added or subtracted. My theory was that if the young ones were taught to take at least two steps at a time, they would then be able to move easily into multi-step math problems. I asked Melanie to test the cards with the Munchkins and reminded her to perform the multiplication first, followed by the addition or subtraction.

An hour later we met at break over cappuccinos. Melanie reported that the cards had been well received but that Sam had asked why the multiplication came first. I explained that by convention the higher operation was performed first, then the lower. "You mean it is just an agreement?" she queried. I said that was all it was, like agreeing to drive on the right. "What if you want to add first, then multiply?" I informed her that in this case parentheses were used, adding that in not wanting to confuse our young students I had not yet made such cards. She responded that she thought they were comfortable enough to try including operations with parentheses, so I at once leapt to the task. Finishing my cappuccino at the computer, I had the new cards ready before break was over. I included a few with division to see how the Munchkins would feel with the complexity of four operations and parentheses.

After school Melanie said the advanced cards had also been enjoyed. Many had stated that these cards were much more fun than the standard flash cards. Eliza informed Melanie that though she had not learned division yet she knew the correct answers for the cards. The eagerness and joy of learning of the kids, Melanie's attention to their needs and words, and the computer and laser printer had all combined to seize a moment of chance, producing a quantum jump forward.

The final two days of baseball spring training were devoted to batting practice. Each day Alison pitched to her Munchkins in one corner of the park and I pitched to the Bigs in another. As the manager in the movie *Bull Durham* said, "Baseball is a simple game: you catch the ball; you throw the ball; you hit the ball." This week we worked on these skills.

Of course, baseball is an infinitely complex game extending far beyond these fundamentals. For our group of kids to enjoy soccer we needed only to roll out a large ball and they could have a great time kicking and chasing it around. There might be little resemblance to World Cup soccer but all finished tired and injuries were rare. Baseball for us was a quite different sport. Bats, balls, gloves, and bases had to be hauled to the field. We had to explain concepts such as positional play, intelligent base running, and countless other factors, decisions, and skills. Then there were the safety issues. Bats and balls were potentially deadly if not used by rigidly prescribed rules. While soccer was a rather steady-state game – the ball was usually moving and constant running around was required – in baseball, not much happened for periods of time and then the action could develop explosively: line drives whizzing, runners rounding bases, fielders scurrying, basemen awaiting throws, teammates cheering. Everyone looked forward to our games of baseball.

The week ended with our art and music hours – again one familiar and the other changed. In music we sang as usual, though the selection of songs began our work for the Spring Concert. Our Americana medley this year would be mining songs. I took class time to discuss the historical background and the meaning of the words found in such songs as "Sixteen Tons" and "Dark As a Dungeon." The concept of working for the "company store" evoked much discussion, indignation, and sorrow. The idea of being controlled by the company, who set wages low and rents and food costs high, disturbed many. Forest asked about the difference between this oppressive system and slavery. I pointed out that one could freely walk away from an Appalachian mining town, a choice not open to slaves. The previous year we had sung a medley of railroad songs the kids enjoyed but did not really ponder. By contrast, the mining songs already were evoking more thought and deeper feeling.

Our art, like our sports, switched from a simple game, sketching with a pencil on paper, to a more complex activity. All tables and surfaces in the classrooms were now covered with newspaper. Containers of water, scores of expensive brushes of various sizes, art paper, and palettes of paints were passed around – we had opened up our Romanian-inspired painting classes. Several years ago our school had been privileged to sponsor young Romanian artists visiting Santa Fe. These children lived in a remote mountain village and produced internationally award-winning folk paintings. They and their brilliant teacher had come to Santa Fe to hold classes with local children. We had incorporated their techniques and exercises into our art program.

Our first lesson was to create as many shades as possible with a single primary color and white. (Actually the first lesson was to avoid splashing water, spilling paint, or damaging brushes!) Soon the class was engaged, and as with all subjects at Fayette, the veterans gave tips when needed to those just beginning. The second half of the hour was spent with a very small brush, working on fine control of thin lines and tiny dots. In the coming weeks these and several other techniques would come together in complete paintings.

Around the popcorn bowl everyone was happy the spring rhythms had finally arrived. As we approached the last two months of the school year we were a tightly knit community, each proud of their scholastic endeavors of the past seven months, and we collectively sensed that this momentum would carry us through the end of the year. Ever diminishing amounts of schoolwork, many long baseball games, preparation for our Spring Concert, and several entertaining year-end activities would fill our time and hold our interest.

~ Week Twenty-Six ~
More Flash Cards and Freebies

The essence of teaching is to make learning contagious, to have one idea spark another.

MARVA COLLINS

WE CAME TO SCHOOL eager to play four long games in this our first week of actual baseball. Our style of baseball was high scoring, zany, enjoyed by young and old, and played with passion. Former students always asked how the games were going; our alumni attending local high schools could be counted on to ditch a few days and join us. Since college semesters ended before we finished the school year, various young adults could be found in the outfield the last weeks of May.

Though afternoons we viewed ourselves as a baseball team, we were still a school in the mornings. Tuesday morning I checked with Melanie to see how the multistep flash card drill was going with the Munchkins. She said some of the kids who had had trouble with standard cards were more proficient with this multiple step approach. She suggested creating some with two additions or subtractions, not just one. Since most of my math time was spent with the older kids working on algebra, Pythagoras, or number bases, I had not been attuned to the idea that increasing or decreasing an answer by one or two was a sufficient and appropriate step for young ones. Another cappuccino, another set of flash cards. These were added to the collection, and Melanie worked through the Munchkin class, three students at a time.

As the hour ended all the Munchkins except Eliza, were delighted at their mental ciphering – the time ended before Melanie could cycle around to her. Young ones rightfully demand fairness and equal attention. As Melanie was assuring Eliza she would be in the first group the next day, her mother came in to hang out at school. "Eliza, why don't you take the cards and show your mother how they work?" Melanie suggested. As the rest of the children ate snacks, swung, or climbed on the garden walls, Eliza and her mother sat in the garden, surrounded by daffodils, sharing flash cards. Eliza clearly explained the order of operations, the meaning of the parentheses and the various facts needed. This was quality time.

After lunch we assembled on the bricks ready for the first ball game of the year. Everyone had a glove, we had the right selection of bats, and my pack held the bases, scoresheet, several balls, my beloved old mitt, and sunscreen. Everything was in order except the weather. Living in the high desert meant wet weather was not often a factor. On the few days the weather service predicted rain the forecast could usually be ignored. We had often walked to the park under dark clouds to see them disappear before the first pitch. Not this day. As we stood on the bricks the clouds darkened, thunder clapped less than a half mile away, and seconds later we were pelted by hail. We scurried inside to play card and board games. I gave a silent prayer of thanks to the gods of weather for pounding us while we were still on the bricks and not luring us to the park and then releasing tons of hail.

Ele's writing class with the Bigs had marvelous energy. In past years report writing had been "endured"; now it was being enjoyed. Each student returned with notes from their first interview of a parent. Ele spent a session explaining the use of note cards, notation systems to aid order and organization, and bibliographic conventions. This year our writing program had been most successful. We had written scores of five-minute writings to free the mind and hand. Each student had then crafted nine paragraphs, after which Ele extended their skills into essay writing. She had also drawn from each a collection of poems and now was maintaining their enthusiasm late in the year with report-writing skills.

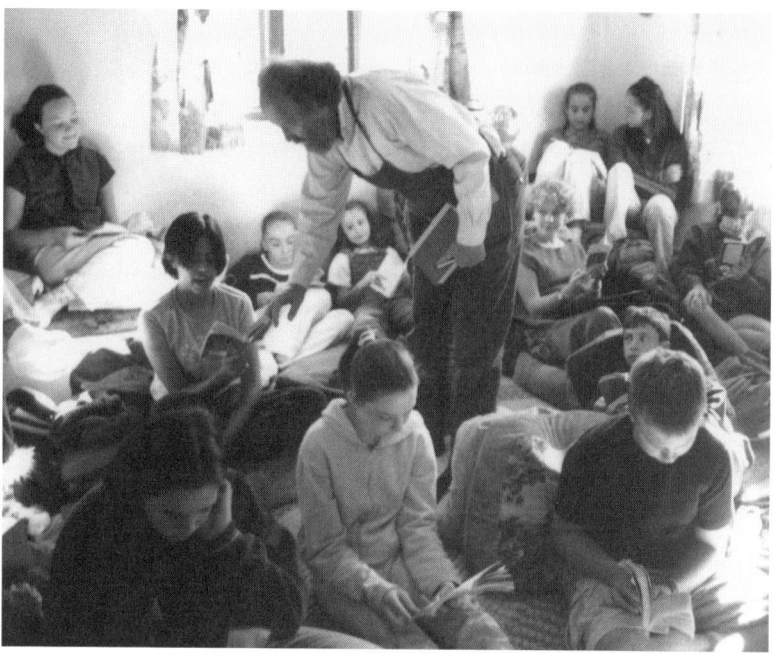

In math, after a week of considering numbers in bases other than ten, the Bigs were ready to begin operations in these other bases. We found that the smaller the base number, the fewer flash-card facts were needed. For example, in base three, leaving out the trivial cases of adding zero to a digit, we were faced with only three facts to remember, many less than a Munchkin struggles with in learning the base-ten facts. Of course, the answers seemed like they were from *Alice in Wonderland*, for in base three, one plus two equals ten and twenty two plus twelve was one hundred eleven! We had addition and subtraction work sheets for all the bases under ten. After demonstrating base-three and base-five operations on the board, the Bigs added and subtracted in base four, six, seven, eight, and nine without further instruction.

One of the subliminal beauties of math is that a set of inviolate principles underlies changing conventions. The class was excited to find their mathematical tools and understanding were operating on such seemingly strange grounds. Carrying and borrowing in addition and subtraction were seen in a new light when dealt with in different bases. After two days we were able to consider multiplying. On Friday I announced that the weekend assignment was to add, subtract, and multiply as many numbers as possible in all the bases less than ten. On Tuesday we would begin exploring division and operations in the bases above ten, rather more difficult terrain.

Two sessions of Greek calligraphy, scripting letters and then words, were a warm-up for the return of a favorite activity in the Bigs' room, the study of *The Iliad* in its original language. Alison wrote a paragraph from Homer's epic on the board. Each student copied it in their best Greek script, noting words they recognized. With Alison's help the class then worked through the complete translation. Discussion ranged from grammar to mythology to philosophy. These paragraphs were a marvelous finish to the year's Greek classes. The following year, after learning two hundred Greek words not studied this year, the class would end with paragraphs from *The Odyssey*.

Wednesday the weather was fine for baseball. The most asked question as we walked to the park was, "Will I be a 'freebie'?" Since we had players from ages six to fourteen and wished for everyone to enjoy the game and contribute to their team, we had added a few rules to the standard game of baseball. Batters, who by tender age or lack of skill would make an out at most plate appearances, were given "freebie" status. A freebie advanced to first base no matter what their performance at the plate. They never struck out, could not be thrown out at first, never flied out. With this single rule our least proficient often became our most valuable.

A culture had developed around the freebies. Many young boys didn't want to be a freebie even when they struck out regularly; many girls wanted to remain freebies even after they started smashing line drives into the outfield. Graduating from freebie status was a rite of passage. The consensus of the two teams determined the status and when it should change. Anyone mired in a horrible slump could be a freebie for a few days.

We arrived at the park with all the gear, including a shovel and old newspapers. We played in the far corner of the park, and over the years the prairie dogs living in the adjoining vacant field had extended their domain into our playing area. In this case the grass was truly greener on our side of the fence. In past seasons the few holes had not bothered our games. However, this year as we were playing soccer, we noticed that our baseball area was becoming a large suburb for our little friends.

During past baseball seasons our zaniest plays had been when a fly ball disappeared down a prairie dog hole. Runners would circle the bases while fielders frantically reached down the hole searching for the ball. We averaged two of these inside-the-park home runs a year. Now, with the increased number of holes we knew our meager supply of balls would disappear well before the end of the season. Therefore the day began with Forest leading a group of Munchkins around the field stuffing newspaper into each hole. During the game members of the team at bat shoveled the mounds flat and filled the craters.

With the field in reasonably good condition we were ready for our first game. I divided the players into two teams. Every day the rosters were different. One day two friends hung out together in the outfield and the next day were on opposite teams. This daily division precluded any "us versus them" mentality. With teams picked, Lauren and Reese performed the "hands up the bat" ritual determining which team batted first. Lauren's hand covered the knob at the top of the bat so her team headed to the scorekeeper to register their lineup. Our rules stated that no more than two freebies could bat consecutively so lineups usually had two freebies followed by a power hitter.

Meanwhile, Reese's team took the field. Teams were not limited to nine players; usually they had around sixteen. We positioned five infielders: each baseman played on their bag and we added a rover between first and second, creating defensive symmetry with the shortstop. Players fielded different positions each inning, and one

Munchkin per inning was allowed on the infield. The rest of the team covered the outfield, usually in small chatting clumps.

At the beginning of the season, I pitched and Alison caught the whole game. This way I controlled some of the variables. I pitched slowly down the middle of the plate when a team was far behind and saved my good stuff for big hitters on a team well ahead. Alison enjoyed being catcher because she relished blocking runners at the plate. Since most of our players were returning students, the few new ones were surrounded by constant good advice. The game was safely and smoothly played. From the smiles as we walked back to school, I sensed we had begun a grand season.

In order to counter the tendency of springtime tardiness we had a policy that should one of the Bigs be late for school, that day's ball game would be shortened. Thursday Sylvan rolled in ten minutes late, and we faced an added hour of class time. The class berated him enough to express their feelings without going over the line of abuse. Usually only a few late arrivals and the subsequent shortened games were needed to bring a promptness to the class.

Avery arrived at school with six-packs of pansies, thereby completing the flower-stomping boys' task of providing three filled planters. The boys could now return to the swing. Daniel found he had lost a level of skill during his three-week hiatus. Alison pointed out to him the same thing had happened to his reading skills and that was why he should read every day. Point taken, the boys picked up swinging again with gusto. In the garden, the tulips and daffodils showed signs of the damage but appeared to have flower buds and now three planters of many-colored pansies graced the front of the school. I was well satisfied with the results.

At afternoon break, as I made my rounds I found only three children on the ground, and they were jump roping. The rest of the students were swinging around the Big Elm, sitting on shed roofs, climbing various walls, or traversing along the aspen-pole fence. In most other environments they would be yelled at for such behavior; here we were comfortable even with our feet off the ground.

Our shortened ball game was high spirited. Instead of time spent on instruction before the game, we quickly picked teams, set line-ups, and talked about safety as we played. Every Munchkin runner had a "coach" run with them. The first responsibility of the coach, who wore a glove, was to protect the young one from being struck by the batted ball. The second task was to instruct the young runner in the art of base running: when to advance, when to tag up, the meaning of such maxims as "Two outs – run on anything." Occasionally during tight games with fast runners on base behind a Munchkin, the coach would pick them up and carry them around the bases.

In the fourth and final inning, with the score tied, Sylvan was on third with James at the plate. Last year's scouting report had listed James as an abysmal to poor hitter. Thus the fielding team felt confident, the team at bat despondent. To everyone's surprise James hammered my second pitch into deep left field. Many congratulated him on his first ever game-winning hit. I gave Sylvan a pat on the back for scoring the game winner and suggested he set his alarm ten minutes earlier.

Friday was bitterly cold, prohibiting baseball. We used our time well with longer singing, art, and an hour of board and card games. During our singing hour we were joined by our favorite guest, Archie, a cowboy friend who played guitar and knew hundreds of folk songs. The plan was for him and Alison to play guitar for our mining medley in the concert. Most of our practice was a cappella, but we all enjoyed Archie and his guitar.

While each class sang, the other was painting with Tara. This week's exercise explored the mixing of primary colors. Small studies were produced with reds blended through oranges to yellows, blues changed to greens and on toward yellows, and a couple of blues to violets to reds. In only the second week everyone's mixing of shades had improved. Many young artists were also becoming comfortable with the tiny brushes. We pasted a dozen representative works from the week on a sheet of newsprint taped to the wall. The young artists could be found standing around, commenting on different uses of technique. As a bonus, over the weeks, the walls of the school would fill with color.

In our curriculum we strove for process more than product. For each child, knowing how to learn was more important than what they learned. We encouraged student input into the rhythms of schoolwork. The Latin Betas, after talking amongst themselves and with advice from Forest and Matthew, asked Marianne if they could postpone further grammatical lessons until next year. Briana, their spokesperson, focused on their study of prepositions and verbs. She stated they had mastered the difference between the ablative of place and the accusative of motion toward; they understood the ablative of means, indicating the instrument used in an action; and they could successfully find the ablative of accompaniment in sentences. However, they wished to save the next step, the ablative of agent, for the next year – the two older boys also had told them passive voice was quite difficult. The group suggested they spend the rest of the year solidifying their present understanding, focusing on translations, and saving the big steps for the beginning of next year.

These were the types of exchanges we encouraged at Fayette. Marianne readily agreed. I added that I had been considering starting Latin with the five Munchkins who would be joining the Bigs' class the next year. The Betas said they would be glad to shepherd the new five. Jessica suggested we keep it a surprise, tell them on Tuesday right before Latin class, and wait to see the looks on their faces. Vowing secrecy, we headed for the popcorn.

∽ Week Twenty-Seven ∾
New Latin Scholars

*What is really important in education is not
that the child learns this and that, but that the mind
is matured, that energy is aroused.*

SØREN KIERKEGAARD

TUESDAY I greeted everyone in my kilt and an Hawaiian shirt. Let me explain. In spring when the weather warmed up again, I switched from my standard of starched long-sleeved Oxford shirts to my collection of Hawaiian shirts; the kilt this day honored Cina's thirteenth birthday. My outfit was admired by staff, students, and parents, though with some chuckling and shaking of heads. As the five oldest Munchkins came on the bricks they were informed that a surprise awaited them. People have different reactions to the word *surprise*. Dorothy was excited, Sam looked worried, Avery reserved judgment. I told them that by 9:30 they would know what was happening and it was nothing to fear.

We waited as the clock swept past 8:30 to see if our ball game would be shortened. Fifteen minutes later only James was not present. Since he rides his bike I called his mother, asking when he had left the house. She said he had just departed, having told her that school did not begin until 9:00. I informed the class the game would be shortened and took our Boss aside for a conference. We wanted to play a full game and also had three situations to be dealt with: James's tardiness, a field full of prairie dog holes, and the large quantity of neighbor-dog droppings on and around the infield. After a few minutes' thought, Forest saw the best solution and announced to the class a long game, assigning James to the new role of pooper-scooper for the day. We settled into class.

At 9:30 Marianne called for her five new Latin students. Ten Munchkin eyes opened wide, five mouths dropped. A personal tutor awaited each new Latin scholar as they entered the studio. The hour class went smoothly, and our five new students headed for first break wearing big smiles.

In math hour we found to our collective amazement that long division worked in different number bases. Using our experience in the three other arithmetic operations and the principles of division, we were soon performing long division with a single-digit divisor. I used the metaphor of walking in a strange city using a street map as a navigating tool. After demonstration, questions and answers, and some practice, I asked the more proficient to move to two-digit divisors. We ended class with everyone agreeing to solve some problems during homework time.

We returned to the ball field well established in the game's rhythms. Since our games were used as teaching tools, we kept everyone busy with many roles. In addition of the standard challenges of fielding, throwing, catching, hitting, and base running, each team when at bat needed to have coaches ready to run the bases with each Munchkin, someone behind the plate backing up Alison, the correct person on deck, and a person shoveling and carrying dirt to fill prairie dog holes. Any task avoided cost the team an out. When a team was in the field, the pressure was lessened, especially for the outfielders. Standing in small groups chatting was standard practice for our outfielders. Players from previous years invariably asked if the outfielders still made chains of the dandelions. I sadly informed them that the city had poisoned the plants, so one of our favorite activities was no more. James did a great job putting doggie droppings down the prairie dog holes before the shovel crew sealed them off.

Though the games were always fun and winning never the goal, pressure was a factor. Fielding a ball with runners whizzing around the bases and deciding where to throw was a form of pressure. So was batting in critical situations. Amelia came to bat in the top of the final inning with two outs. As I prepared to pitch she complained of the pressure she felt. I informed her this was not pressure – her team was ahead by three runs – and that she should relax, keep her eye on the ball, and swing naturally. I gave her a slow pitch down the middle of the plate, which she lined into left. No pressure. Her team won the game when in the bottom of the inning a pop fly was caught for the second out and Walker, the runner at second base, became the final out when he didn't tag up. As we collected the equipment I asked Maggie, his coach, why she had not kept him on the bag. "I yelled for him to stay but he ran anyway," she explained. I counseled that grabbing the back of the collar was an effective way to keep a Munchkin near the bag.

On Wednesday, proud parents of the new Latin students thanked us for both throwing their young ones into Latin and doing it gently. At home the new scholars had proudly declaimed the first mantra of every Latin student: *amo, amas, amat*. Dorothy's dad said she was wondering how to say, "I love Dad" or "I love you." Setting my eyebrows to their most formidable scholarly slant, I informed him pronouns were not to be trifled with in Latin – they didn't show up until "Grammatica XXI." I added that *patres* and *matres* were third-declension nouns and still a long distance away for our neophytes. Switching to a big smile I informed him that by next week his daughter would be able to say, "I love the trumpet," and they might use this phrase until the advanced grammar allowed fuller expression.

Some of my best teaching topics were delivered to me unexpectedly. The day began with a car-side visit with one of our mothers just returned from a distant seminar for medical professionals. The presenter spoke of questioning Harvard graduates immediately after they had shed their caps and gowns. His question: "What causes the seasons?" Surprisingly, all those asked had wrong answers, the most common being, "We are closer to the sun in summer." His concern was not just the ignorance but the holding of a belief countered by evidence from common knowledge, that is, it is winter in Rio when summer in the Big Apple. Thus we observe a contradiction that should defeat the proposed hypothesis. He lamented that today's education based on rote learning did not lead to the practice of critical thinking. Teaching should be directed toward developing realistic models explaining reality and adding to each person's current body of knowledge. Instruction should not be aimed at good multiple-choice test scores.

Teaching that integrated new facts with previous information, ever improving each child's mental model, had long been a tenet of our school. The previous week's science lecture had finished our discussion of kinematics. As I listened, an idea flashed through my mind: applying our principles and habits of investigation and observation to another area of physical phenomena would be a great strengthening exercise before we continued with our review of kinematics. I returned my attention to our car-side chat.

Our returning mother said that after the main lecture the participants had broken into small discussion groups. The topic of discussion was the difference between the majority of teachings, where unlinked seemingly random bits of information were presented and students then rewarded or punished for regurgitative skills, and the lecturer's view that all information should be integrated into an existing body of knowledge, where critical thinking was encouraged. Each member of the discussion group in turn had complained and railed against the disconnected thought processes of their students or employees. Our mother had commented that her daughter's elementary school seemed to be incorporating all the points she had heard in the seminar. She observed that no one at the table was interested in this and merely continued complaining about current education. I thanked her for sharing this with me and headed for class.

Whether or not professional folks in a distant city cared what we did at Fayette in no way affected our philosophy or course of study. I began class by asking, "What causes the seasons?" Jackson offered, "The seasons are caused by the Earth's axes." Inwardly I smiled, knowing we were already ahead of some Harvard grads in this area; outwardly I gave a dramatic frown. "Can't be, – Earth has only one axis, not several axes." (There is never a time not to be correct with Greek singular and plural.)

Kyrie mentioned rotation around the sun. I congratulated her for bringing us a step closer to the true model but coaxed the discussion toward the differences between rotation on an axis and revolution around the sun. We used our skill with inner imagination and visualization to tie the information to each of our own bodies of knowledge. I had everyone close their eyes and first visualize spinning around, then running on a circular path around a friend, and finally combining the two motions. To make knowledge truly one's own it must be registered in the body, not just passed through the favored hemisphere of the brain.

My next statement was tangential to our main topic: "One body never revolves around another – they together revolve around a common point. However, when one body is much more massive than the other, the point of revolution can lie within the larger body." I pointed out that the Earth-Moon system revolves around a point within Earth, though not Earth's center and that the tides on the far side of Earth are caused by the centripetal force generated by this eccentric motion. These tangential leaps added over the year countless morsels of information and also kept us mentally alert as we jumped to and from the main topics.

From this aside we returned to the seasons. We continued with pieces of theory and observable fact until we had a good working model of a planet rotating on its axis, evidenced by the sun's daily apparent motion, and revolving around the Sun, a supposition reinforced by seeing Orion in our winter sky and Scorpio in the summer's. Forest then introduced the critical factor, the tilted axis. Now the seasons, equinoxes, solstices, the Arctic circle, the Tropic of Capricorn, the extremes in length of day or night with increased latitude all became part of a unified model, not random troublesome vocabulary words. I was always grateful for such morning talks with parents.

At lunch I asked Alison how the morning had gone with a young visiting child and why her class had done math all day long; it had seemed to me that the two might be connected. Mom and Dad, on their visit, had loved our little world and so their son was our guest for the day. He had survived a standard first grade but after the first two months of second had disenrolled and been home schooled. We would be his next experience with school. A shy boy, staying close to Mom, had walked onto the bricks. The two of them had stayed together in Alison's class. Our Munchkin gentlemen used the presence of visitors to act out more than usual and brought little focus to their hour of math assignments. Alison never raised her voice or threatened; she used more subtle and effective methods. In this case, math all day.

As for our young guest, I could not tell if he liked his visit or not. I asked his mom to call me in the evening and tell me how his day had gone. After lunch we bid good-bye to our visitors, headed for the park, and enjoyed a spirited game. In our evening phone conversion, Mom related that she had said to her son, "In my heart I think Fayette is the right school for you." His response was, "In my whole body I know Fayette is my school." Our enrollment for the next year was now complete.

Friday we had just enough class time so all understood their weekend homework assignments. We then focused on singing and art class until our final ball game of the week. In art each student continued gaining comfort with the paintbrush and the mixing of colors. This day's exercises and experiments explored the adding of black to the primary colors. The studies produced were most dramatic. We found that while lots of white had to be added to the primary colors to change tones noticeably, only very small amounts of black created significant change. I thought, but did not say, this might be a metaphor for light and darkness in life.

Our ball game brought the return of Harold, Matthew's dad, to the field. We always encouraged parents to come and play. Moms could bat but dads only played in the field. Few found the time to join us but Harold had over the past years played many games with us. I looked forward to his return because he enjoyed pitching, which meant I could move to the infield for a few innings. The Munchkin girls were even more pleased to see him – with no dandelions to pick, teasing and chatting with Harold had become a favorite outfield activity. The game followed its regular course: many runs, a few great catches, several dropped balls by young gloves, good cheering and focus by players on both teams.

In the bottom of the final inning with her team trailing by one run, with two outs, and with runners on second and third, Amelia came to the plate. I asked if she remembered what I had told her during her final at bat on Tuesday. She nodded. As I rubbed the ball in my hands and rocked back and forth on the mound, I smiled and said, "This is *real* pressure." After two weak swings, she lined my third pitch toward Forest at shortstop; he bobbled the ball and made a wild throw toward Alison covering the plate. Two runs scored. Both teams applauded Amelia for her game-winning hit, gathered the gear, and headed back to school.

ॐ Week Twenty-Eight ॐ
Nerve Endings

If they make you go where learning is flying around, some of it is bound to light on you.

SATCHEL PAIGE

WHILE IN the grocery store, the gym, or the pub, folks often asked how I was doing. Eleven months of the year my reply was direct and heartfelt: "After twenty years of teaching, I am enjoying my life, my teaching, and all the children around me more and more each year." When queried this time of year, however, I would reply, "In the month of April, don't ask school teachers how they feel."

By April the months of lesson planning, paper correcting, tone setting, unnumbered little exchanges, and constant personal interactions had fatigued the nervous system. Soon my system would register this feedback and switch to another mode, where the signals were damped down and numbed. But on Tuesday I could still feel every impulse and was grumpy and irritable. Having taught for decades, I was familiar with this state and knew how to best survive it. I avoided making big decisions, I didn't overreact to situations, and I waited for the week and this transitional feeling to pass. From Alison's look as she came on the bricks, I knew we were in perfect sync.

Nevertheless, these was an unspoken rule at Fayette that whether teachers' nervous systems were fresh or fatigued, classes, collateral activities, and the needs of each child remained the primary focus. As Ele taught writing, Marianne Latin, Alison French, and Tara ran studio sessions, Melanie and I introduced each student to their xylo parts and partners for the Spring Concert. Most of the year small groups rotated from class to studio sessions, a pattern of which Alison was not particularly fond; she preferred to settle in with her young charges and focus on their class work. However, she recognized that these sessions were beneficial for each child and that the removal of learning blocks in her students made her job of teaching easier, so she generally accommodated the rhythm of the school with good cheer. But today I knew that her students scurrying to xylos and to Tara's groups, combined with the state of her own nervous system would not make her happy.

At break I asked her how the rhythm was going. She said things were fine but that she'd added a new rule to her class. They had been reading and reciting poetry in class as students came and went. That had been working OK, with minimal disruption. Some reentered quietly and settled into the flow, while a few shuffled and ruffled papers before settling down. Then suddenly Sam burst through the curtain and in a loud voice interrupted the reading of a poem with, "What's happening in here now?"

Alison's response had been to institute a new pattern. No one returning to class from other activities could simply burst in. From now on they would each wait at the doorway until the poem or thought was completed. Only then would she invite them in. I congratulated her on this addition to student deportment and on being able to use the pain in her nerves for creative purposes.

I had the easier task. Since my class was working on its own, I moved back and forth between studio and school calling groups to sing and also assisted Melanie as she taught each player their xylo part. At the concerts many in attendance were amazed by the confidence and proficiency of these young ones as they stood four or five at a time in front of the choir, facing a chapel full of friends and family, and led us in our singing. Only I saw the hours of patient attention Melanie gave to each player. They each approached the xylophones with a different combination of musical abilities, personal fears, and aural and physical development. She wrote parts to match their abilities; coached each in keys, rhythm, chord triads, and playing together; and generally helped them build the self-confidence that allowed them to stand before hundreds and play well and actually enjoy the experience.

By 1:00 all players had been introduced to their parts. On most days baseball would have been next on the schedule, but this day rain had fallen steadily so we faced two more hours of class work. But first we had a treat in store: we would be celebrating Melanie's birthday. In twenty years this was the first time weather would force us to sing "Happy Birthday" indoors. At times like this I realized that we really do live in a desert!

As we gathered in the study I knew that an important point of procedure would be raised and debated. Would treats be given youngest to oldest, or oldest to youngest? Forest pointed out that Melanie was "old" and therefore the line should be oldest first; the Bigs agreed. Dorothy countered that Melanie was a teacher in the Munchkins' room and therefore the youngest should get their popsicles first. Good-natured discussion swung between these two opinions until Daniel asked to be heard. "Since there are fewer Munchkins than Bigs, we more often are last in line. So for Melanie we should be first." No one could disagree. We sang "Happy Birthday" in full voice, received our treats, youngest to oldest, and then settled in for our extra class time on a rainy day.

Both Alison and I used an hour of the afternoon for grammar. In her room grammar exercises consisted of sentences written on the board and the class stating the parts of speech. The youngest pointed out the nouns and verbs, while the more experienced ones handled the nasty prepositions and adverbs. Young grammarians learned to enjoy the challenge of unpuzzling the parts of speech.

In my room we diagrammed sentences. Each weekly packet had twenty sentences highlighting an aspect of grammar. I would diagram a few on the board during the week, and by the following Tuesday each student would have done ten others. Early in the year the topics were simple, such as compound nouns or sentences loaded with adverbs. Later in the year we focused on verbals and clauses.

I had told my class that this week's grammar would be a surprise. When I passed out the weekly packet all immediately turned to the grammar page. Eyes widened and then smiles broke on their faces. "These sentences are in Latin!" Maggie asked if I also wanted the sentences translated into English. "No, do the work in Latin." James commented that the different endings made it easy to tell subjects from objects. They eagerly commenced working.

After grammar we switched to math. Though we had introduced the concept of different number bases less than four weeks before we were now wrapping up the topic. Students brought up areas of confusion and others commented on their techniques and strategies for solving the various types of problems. Some were concerned with what they still had not mastered. I expressed my delight at our collective ease with the topic and how the thinking and ciphering had strengthened each student's math skills. All had been trained by our school philosophy and practice not to hide ignorance. We had witnessed ample demonstration that directed effort paid off, that we were each surrounded by many others eager to help, and that if one sensed a large perceptual block in their own inner working, Marianne was always ready with exercises to remove the glitch in the system. In such an environment vast amounts of complex material could be assimilated by the whole group in a surprisingly short time. The day ended with smiles all around.

Three mornings a week my days began with the ritual straightening up of the school. I followed the same pattern every day. I started in my classroom, picking up the papers and pencils left from the previous day. (I figured with Matthew going to high school the next year this task should be cut in half.) The daily schedule was then written on the board. The bathroom was next with a mandatory wipe of the toilet; this year the boys all had had excellent aim, making my job easier. In the study I reshelved the encyclopedias left scattered. Some years before, I had found myself beginning to resent this task and then had thought to reframe my reaction. Now as I reordered the books I held to the idea that they were being used and enjoyed. After a check of paper supplies and the emptying of pencil sharpeners, I moved to the front room. Any lunches left on the shelves were broken down into compost, recycling, and trash.

Clothing and lunchbags left the previous day were dumped outside the school below the bulletin board.

I had performed this ritual hundreds of times. My time alone before school allowed me not only to check systems but also to be in prayer, contemplation, and gratitude before facing the busy activities of each day. Only one thing could modify this ritual: if too many jackets and sweaters were left at school. In the past when this had occurred I'd dumped them on the entry bricks so everyone, especially parents, would see and hopefully retrieve them. This week my irritated nerve endings led to creative change. Wednesday, as the first cars arrived, seventeen jackets were lying neatly on the sidewalk, carefully placed with cuff touching cuff as if holding hands. The chain stretched along the whole front of the school. Another Fayette tradition had been born. Parents smiled as they saw the new display and, more importantly, jackets were retrieved.

Different traditions were being formed elsewhere on the school grounds as well. The Big Elm was an area for constant but ever-changing social and physical interaction. The Munchkins had found they were not happy with the morning and afternoon single-gender sessions; the before-school, lunch, and afternoon times were in a gray area and therefore still contentious. A short meeting brought consensus: Tuesdays and Thursdays would be girls only; Wednesdays and Fridays were reserved for boys.

With this established, creativity blossomed. Tuesday the girls developed a new game called "Don't Hit the Teacher." I had been walking to the studio deep in thought when Nyssa, on the new high swing, flew back toward the tree, kicking me in the head. Since that time the various bobbing girls, when seeing a teacher come through the gate, would synchronize their pushes from the tree to create a safe corridor of time and space.

The boys were busy too. Wednesday the Munchkin gentlemen discovered a new game quite unlike the girls'. They built a launch platform by stacking several sections of pine stumps normally used as garden seats. Experimenting found the best location and height for this platform. One boy pendulumed from there, and another launched a moment later on a different rope from another stump behind the Big Elm. They then collided, fell to the ground, laughed, and rolled in the wood chips. This went on until Alison called them to class.

Of course, my encouraging such behaviors often made it harder for Alison to have quiet, focused class time. Over our cappuccino at break she related that the boys had complained they were always in trouble in class and the girls never were. She suggested they switch roles for a day. The girls could act rowdy, complain about the work, and generally mess around. The boys could enter the classroom quietly, open their notebooks to the correct page, and become engrossed in academic activities for at least a half hour before changing state. After a moment's thought, the boys had agreed such a change would be boring and that they would rather continue listening to her reprimands.

Our three baseball games of the week were filled with many hits, much running of the bases, several outstanding catches in the outfield, and a new player, Matt's father, Micky. When parents joined our game for the first time, we coached them on a few rules of safety. We reminded each never to throw the ball with full force; that way if they hit someone in the head it would not cause injury. We told them never to run full speed for fly balls, but to just let them drop – most ball players were not used to an outfield full of Munchkins and prairie dog holes. And, most importantly we told them we would coach them on the various unique rules of our game, but that it usually took several games before they understood the proper plays. After our coaching session and a few innings in the outfield, I handed Micky the ball and let him pitch an inning.

With a new pitcher I usually played second base to be in a good position to give the call of the situation as each batter came to the plate and to coach our rookie pitcher. Micky pitched well to the first two hitters, giving up two singles – we liked lots of hits and runs. With runners on first and second and Walker coming to bat, I called, "No outs, freebie at the plate, force play at second or third."

Walker bounced the third pitch to Micky, who turned and made a good throw to first, beating the runner.

However, Walker, being a freebie, stayed on first. Micky had a puzzled look. I trotted to the mound and reminded him that freebies can't be out from their plate appearance and this was why I had called "play at second or third." I reminded him that he now had bases loaded and no outs. The next batter was not a freebie so my call was, "No outs, tag at any base – any base." Forest at shortstop fielded a sharp grounder and fired to Alison for a forced out at home plate. Bases still loaded, one out.

Another freebie, Nyssa, stepped into the batter's box. I jogged to the mound. Amelia, our scorekeeper for the day, confirmed that the team at bat was trailing by five runs. I told Micky, "You have a freebie at bat, but the rule is that with bases loaded, no freebie. The team is trailing so you have to hit Nyssa, putting her on first base and forcing home a run." His eyes widened and he had a look of disbelief. "I don't mean you need to clock her in the head with your fastball,' I explained, "just roll the ball at her feet. She knows what to do." He bowled to her. She, with a look of defiance, kicked the ball back toward the mound and jogged to first. All runners advanced, scoring a run. James came to the plate and drove the ball deep to left for a grand slam. Game tied.

Micky and I again conferred at the mound as James rounded the bases. I congratulated him on fine pitching. Giving up hits that evened the score was considered good pitching in our game. He asked what to do if faced with a freebie up, bases loaded, and the team in the lead. "You strike them out with your best stuff."

Two innings later the game ended with the potential winning run left standing in the on-deck circle. As we walked back to school, players talked about the more noted catches and hits in the game. A week of singing and baseball had been therapeutic for my nerves. I was grateful we had most of our academics behind us and could look forward to days of playing, singing, and climbing in the final weeks of school.

Week Twenty-Nine

Parent Conferences and Spankings

*Every education teaches a philosophy;
if not by dogma then by suggestion,
by implication, by atmosphere.*

G. K. CHESTERTON

We rarely scheduled parent conferences. When parents asked how their child was doing in school I used one of two standard responses. The first was, "All the kids are doing great." The second was more pointed: "Have I called you recently to discuss a problem?" We observed the children all the time and were aware of the first signs of personal, social, or academic troubles. Handling problems identified in their first stages was much easier than allowing them to fester before addressing them. Most corrections were woven seamlessly into the fabric of school without parental involvements. If an unattractive situation or unwanted behavior became entrenched, we sat down with the parents and coordinated our efforts. We averaged four such meetings a year, and now one was needed.

Tuesday morning as the kids were dropped off I was out watering the sidewalk gardens. This way I was sure to catch Miranda's mom so we could schedule a conference. Normally Miranda hopped out and Mom was quickly off to work. Today they both climbed out of the car, Miranda in tears. We headed to a garden bench for an immediate meeting.

Miranda enjoyed participating in local children's theater. She had missed all classes the previous week with performances and had had many rehearsals the week before. No homework had been done for fourteen days. She had thought that by working all day Monday she would catch up. However, at 10:00 Monday night she had gone to bed with much work still to do and knowing I would be passing out more papers as soon as class assembled. That was when the tears had started to flow.

As we sat in the garden I asked why she was so upset. She said she felt the combination of the amount of work and my being angry with her was more than she could bear. I pointed out I wasn't upset and explained that my role as teacher required me to pass out endless papers and demand their timely return. I continued by saying that my role as teacher was a thin exterior and that with my whole being I enjoyed every minute spent with her – I always looked forward to our time together, especially our kidding around at break and on the sports field. I then asked if she had learned why avoiding homework for two straight weeks was a poor strategy. Her eyes were still red, but the tears had stopped and a smile was beginning to show. Mom thought that over the next week they could catch up on the overdue work. I found this a reasonable solution.

As Miranda entered school to join her friends and Mom drove away, another of my students and his dad walked on the bricks. The boy was wearing a wrist support and the dad a look of rage.

Our new community ice rink had provided Santa Fe with opportunities not before available. Men my age could play hockey again, the first time in decades, and then be seen limping around town with strained muscles. Kids could skate and fall, or in the case now being presented to me, one of my students could push another, causing a hard fall, strained wrist, and angered dad. I confess I was happy to be in the role of wise impartial elder, not of adult in charge when a child was hurt.

I asked the dad if he had talked with the other boy's parents. "No, I wanted your advice first before I just yelled at them." My advice was to treat the incident as a learning opportunity, for both boys and both families. A small sprain was sufficient for those concerned to pay attention, but minor enough not to cause long-term harm. My belief was that if we learned from small lessons we avoided larger ones. I said his son could use this incident to strengthen his balance and zone of safety, both on the ice and metaphorically. I suggested that if Dad could set his rage aside while talking to the other family, they might hear the message that their son was developing the trait of hurting others. Merely yelling at them would simply cause them to close their ears. He smiled and said, "So, you want me to be diplomatic?" I nodded, patted him on the shoulder, and headed into class.

I began with a disturbing announcement to the Bigs. Melanie had called Monday night saying we had a problem with the use of the Loretto Chapel, our traditional venue, for our concert. The fire marshal had informed the chapel's owners that he wanted no more than 139 persons in the chapel at one time, which was too limited for our needs. It looked like the children's voices would never again bounce from the vaulted ceiling, bathing the packed house of family, friends, and entranced tourists. I asked Melanie to consider doing two shows there instead of one and also to explore a change of location. The children wanted to know what had caused this decree. I pointed out that the fire marshal was afraid the combination of a large crowd and a fire would be dangerous. James asked how the marshal intended to burn limestone block walls. Forest added he felt certain no parent would build a fire under a pew. I let the kids vent some of their discontent before I passed out the week's papers.

Mocking the fire marshal had long been one of our joys. The Bigs' classroom had an exterior door thanks to the marshal. Every time a gust of winter wind blew under the threshold, the two students sitting in the doorway grumbled. I would remind them to thank the marshal for the fresh air. Years before, he had come to inspect our school. Adobe walls, new electrical outlets, and a wood-burning stove exceeding code brought him no areas to demonstrate his power. He racked his brains. "I see you have only one exterior door; you need another." I asked for his reasoning. "A car crashes and explodes in flames in the school's only doorway. The kids are trapped. I want a second door."

PARENT CONFERENCES AND SPANKINGS

Over the weekend a donated door and the assistance of a carpenter friend brought the school into compliance. Anyone who thinks an adobe building is a pile of mud bricks that can easily topple should try knocking a doorway in an adobe wall. Four times we scheduled appointments with the marshal to inspect the new door. Four no shows. Fifteen years later we still wait. So we gently mock.

Normally the weekly papers for each subject were passed out at the beginning of the subject's class time, but these weeks before a concert were not normal weeks. I passed out packets, physics review sheets, and math after our fire-marshal talk, and told the class to work on everything and help each other.

As the students settled into their work, the players of the first two xylo pieces and I headed to the studio to work with Melanie. One group practiced their parts under Melanie's instruction while the other sang accompaniment. I played for absent students. Early morning phone calls had alerted me to an active flu bug. Five children were home in bed, so I learned many xylophone parts. After Melanie was satisfied with the session, these students returned to class and two more groups headed for the studio. Amelia, one of our better musicians, was absent. I found myself struggling on a tiny glockenspiel with a page full of notes.

At 1:00 satisfied with xylo practice, Melanie left in search of another site for our concert. We headed to the park for baseball, greeted by good and bad news. The good news was the return of Ken, our sometimes judge, to the pitching rotation. Though his two children were now in college he still came out every season to play with us. The bad news that was the weatherman had forecast thirty-mile-per-hour winds and his predictions proved to be accurate. Munchkins leaned into the wind, our carpet bases kept blowing to the outfield, short pop-ups were blown into long fly balls. Seeing clearly was difficult with all the dust in the air.

I was proud of the kids for staying focused on the game without a single complaint. On the outside I was projecting a humorous bravado in the face of the elements. Inside I was questioning whether we had crossed the invisible line of safety. I hoped the wind would increase a few knots and I could cancel the game. The wind gods seemed not to be listening, for the winds neither increased or decreased. We played on. After four innings I declared the game over and we gathered the gear, headed back to school, and finished the day with board games.

Wednesday morning as Amelia and her dad arrived, I approached the car signaling for a moment of their time. Using my zany John Madden persona, I waved my arms and declaimed Amelia wasn't allowed to miss any more school. If necessary I would drag her out of the house, for I was going nuts trying to play her xylophone parts. She and her dad laughed and said they understood my position. Students came, parents left, the school day began. We all cycled through the studio and classroom until time for our ball game.

Winds like Tuesday's usually did not last long, but they often brought changed weather. This was the case today: by the second inning of the game we were playing in snow flurries. For me, this wasn't so bad: living eight steps from my workplace had its advantages. As the day got colder, I added more and more warm layers of clothing and by game time was properly dressed for the conditions. Robby, on the other hand, had come to school in shorts and T-shirt; he played the game in this outfit. Michiah, showing he was a veteran of our system, gathered a jacket from the lost-and-found pile as we headed to the park. Again no one complained about the nasty conditions but all were delighted when I declared the game over after four innings.

Thursday brought little wind, warmer temperatures, and a new location for our concert. Fortunately, Santa Fe had more than its share of old churches restored for tourism and musical events. Melanie informed me before school started that the director at the Santuario de Guadalupe warmly welcomed our use of this old adobe church. We would be losing our familiar sound at Loretto but gaining better all around acoustics. Melanie blushed as she related the director's only concern: the last school group to use the church had been the local Waldorf school, and the kids had torn up

PARENT CONFERENCES AND SPANKINGS

seat cushions and vandalized a few other items. She assured him our behavior was in no way like theirs.

I gave a huge laugh when she related this to me. Years before when her daughter was a student here, Melanie was the music teacher at the Waldorf school. In casual talks on the bricks she would complain about the restrictions she worked under and how she had many ideas she could not implement. One spring day I said, "Your daughter will graduate from here in a month. Why don't you quit Waldorf and start a music program here? You can do anything you want. The staff and I will support you to the fullest." The next autumn she became Alison's assistant and our music teacher.

When Amelia and her dad arrived that morning I again raced out to the car. "I've changed my mind," I told them, "keep her home. I've been practicing all night and I think I can be the star of the show." We laughed. Using a wide range of emotion, tone, and body language allowed for different messages and communications than were possible in the narrow bands of politically correct style and manner. Humor, at times bordering on the absurd, was one of my standard tools of interaction. My love of life and the freedom to access a wide range of personal expression were embedded teachings. My wearing a kilt thirty days a year added to this message.

In our society I could get away with such humor. Other devices, such as physical affection, were currently still taboo. On Tuesday at the end of my conference with Miranda, my desire had been to hug her, kiss her forehead, and send her to class. I would have hugged and kissed Mom too. Instead, by the conventions of our culture, I remained seated two feet away, hoping the sincere tone of my words conveyed the care I truly felt for her. It is interesting that while I might not be allowed to hug and kiss them, I was allowed to spank them.

As with so many things at Fayette, I created a unique style of spanking. This year we had begun using hand-held stop signs to increase the safety of our crossing of the busy street between school and park. The combination of self-directed kids, the years of experience of the younger staff members, and my bike crash had allowed me to miss most park duty during the soccer season. During baseball season though, I played every day and so found myself with stop sign in hand. In school I didn't like objects with only one use, nor did I like time not filled with many and varied lessons. Walking to and from the park merely toting a sign seemed to violate both maxims.

Somewhere in the second week of baseball, as we all walked down the sidewalk I asked Robby if he had been spanked recently. This stopped his chatter. We could almost hear the gears of his mind grinding various thoughts and searching for a safe answer. My tone and his observations of the past seven months that I was often the jokester and never the ogre suggested to him that a new game was being born. I gave him a gentle pat on the bottom with the stop sign.

On Friday as we gathered on the bricks before the game, five Munchkin boys lined up, turned around, bent over, and awaited their pregame good-luck pat. As we walked to and from the park I tried to coax others into receiving their first swat. I always remembered to give myself a couple of good ones as I encouraged the reluctant to join our latest game.

As planned my spankings led to comment and discussion on the way to and from the park. From Dorothy, "You barely touched me with the paddle; I don't think that was a spanking." "Why would I want to use a lot of force?" I countered. "Who would want to hurt a child?" From another, "You laugh and are silly when you spank us. That's not how my spankings have been at home." "So maybe it's the energy of the adult and not the physical act that is scary? As you know, when I want you to change your behavior I have better ways than to yell and hit." A boy said, "My mom uses a hair brush." "My mom doesn't believe in spanking," declared a sassy one who could use *some* form of behavior modification at home. Another said, "I was only spanked once, and then my mom cried."

ᔰ Week Thirty ᔱ
Uncle Matt

*All children are artists, and it is an indictment
of our culture that so many of them lose their creativity,
their unfettered imagination, as they grow older.*

MADELEINE L'ENGLE

THE RIGID STRUCTURE of our daily schedule continued to relax. Instead of various hours for specific classes, work for the week was passed out Tuesday morning and individuals or small groups picked what to do when. The constant movement to and from the studio for concert practice demanded this mode of class time, but even without concerts we would have switched to this more self-directed style in the final weeks of school. After eight months of teacher-directed assignments, often focusing on narrow aspects of specific fields of knowledge, now was the time to widen, synthesize, and allow each student to unify the many parts and pieces in their own unique expression. By the use of general review sheets in each subject, every student was able to explore where they had mastery and where their mental models needed a little help, ideally provided by a fellow student. I spent very little time in the classroom. I could be found playing xylophones for absent students, singing with other small groups, hanging around the Big Elm, and enjoying the baseball diamond. These were signs that now the whole school community was in a self-regulated mode.

In Tuesday's ball game, for the first time in the season I played in the outfield. Ken and Harold pitched and controlled the infield, and the kids were comfortable with the game. I used the opportunity to spend some quiet time in center field doing what outfielders do: think of things other than baseball. While a couple of freebies were at bat, I thought of each rope in the Big Elm and which ones should be replaced before the upcoming climbing week. As Jessica fouled off a couple of pitches, I decided to replace the old transverse ropes, thereby adding a few hours of work to the weekend. Forest's bases-clearing home run to left field didn't affect me directly so I mentally ran through planning for our year-end potluck, graduation dinner, and school trip to the water park in Albuquerque. My thoughts were interrupted as I watched a fine fielding play by Jonah at shortstop, but I quickly returned to my musings. As Reese ripped two fouls down the third-base line, I ran through logistics about our new concert site: schedule a meeting with the director, measure the risers we were borrowing for the stage, remember to determine how much floor space the xylos actually would cover.

Satisfied I was ahead of the curve with each of these activities and hadn't forgotten anything important, I turned my thoughts to my biggest problem: what to do in art. Alison's sketching classes with pencil and paper had been excellent – her own enthusiasm while sketching radiated to the kids. However, she was less excited when faced with the mess of brushes and tempera paint. Tara had been great managing these materials but was a touch phobic about her own artistic talents. Now that we had practiced the techniques of mixing shades, tones, warm colors, cool colors, browns, and grays, the time had arrived to be creative. As headmaster I had until Friday at 11:00 to give someone a directive. This Tuesday, standing in the outfield in the third inning, I was clueless. Then I turned to see our piper coming across the grass trailed by another gentleman.

Maybe not every school needed a piper, but one with as much Celtic tradition as ours did. The sight of our piper always lifted my spirits. As they joined me in the field I was introduced to Zoe and Sam's uncle Matt, who, as Providence would have it, taught art to children in New York. "Nice to meet you. What are you doing Friday from 11:00 until 1:00?" As Matthew sharpely grounded out to Jackson to end the inning, I walked to the mound with one less unsolved problem.

Wednesday morning before heading for the studio I asked the class if they had any questions on the weekly work. Lauren wanted help on a physics problem; Heather asked for clues needed on the word puzzles in the packet. I was delighted. They each articulated the missing piece of information required for the completion of their tasks. We jumped quickly from topic to topic. A few of the week's diagraming sentences had nasty structures. Forest was stumped by the final steps of one, and asked to see it on the board.

Finding the subject and predicate presented no problem, neither did the fact that they were followed by a predicate adjective, not a direct object. While this point of grammatical difference was confusing for many folks, because of our Latin, it was quite clear for all in our class. The predicate adjective was itself modified by an infinitive, Zoe pointed out. I congratulated her on her certainty with verbals. The verbal was in turn modified by a prepositional phrase, and the object of the prepositional phrase was a noun clause. So far so good.

With the diagram strung out across the board, most were still comfortable as we came to the crux, the final two words of the sentence. Forest remained stumped, and no one else raised their hand with suggestions. At these times I never merely gave the correct answer but demonstrated the process leading toward solution. "This looks sort of like the direct object of the clause, but it doesn't quite fit the rules. What else could it be?" The whole class was silent. I was about to let the exercise go, satisfied with the advanced grammatical thinking of these young scholars, when Miranda raised her hand. She was the youngest in the class and in a small unsure voice said, "It is the object of a preposition, where the preposition is implied." The class was stunned, Miranda correct, and I awed. Some of us headed to the studio to sing with the Munchkins.

Nyssa was sick so I played her two xylophone parts. I noodled the notes of "Lavender's Blue" and then her partner, Rachel, instructed me on the correct rhythm, the intro bars, the coda, and the pauses between verses. Melanie gave us a little extra time, knowing I was building on our relationship and "putting money in the bank." The next year Rachel would be in my class and I wanted a good pile of assets before I started handing her papers, demanding work, and coaching social skills.

I next teamed with Rebecca. Of the innumerable lessons we experienced in our concert preparation, one of my favorites was that mistakes inevitably would be made but the song would keep moving along. We learned that focusing on missed words, wrong notes, or misstruck bars only increased the possibilities of future mistakes; returning to the flow of the whole group was the best path.

I had observed that when Rebecca struck the occasional wrong bar she would cover it with her hand to silence it. This of course upset her timing for the rest of the verse. While Melanie instructed others, I spoke with Rebecca about better ways to be in harmony with the piece and whispered that I was going to intentionally mis-hit a few. I asked her to watch how I just kept playing and the little mistakes would not even be noticed by the other players, Melanie, or the singers. Rebecca would also be leaving the Munchkins to join my class the next year and I was laying more foundation for next year's class.

Rebecca had a habit of striving for perfection. I often said, "Angels may be perfect; we humans definitely are not. We make mistakes; honor yours and learn from them." As we left the studio for lunch I was pleased our integrated school structure allowed me to enjoy the activities of the moment and also to be preparing for the next year. I didn't know that during our afternoon ball game I would already be drawing from my account with Rachel and working with Rebecca on her perfectionism.

Later as we walked to the park, I noticed that Rachel had a book in her hand. I didn't say anything about it but just began the game. In the third inning two singles placed runners at first and third. No batter was at the plate as I prepared to pitch. Invoking our rule that each batter was responsible for timely plate appearances, I pitched a perfect strike to Alison and cried, "One out." In the past this had caused scurrying by the next batters, but today no one moved to the batter's box. Another strike: "Two out." Still no batter. One more and the cry, "Three outs: change sides."

In twenty years of Fayette baseball I had never recorded three outs on three pitches. Analysis revealed that Rachel, the initial tardy batter, had been reading and not paying attention to the game. The next batters, Maggie and Reese, had tried to get Rachel to move rather than run to the plate themselves. Ken, our philosopher, chuckled at the lessons learned on the diamond that had nothing to do with hitting and fielding.

The next inning Ken pitched and I headed for the outfield. As I surveyed the defense I saw Rebecca at third base. We preferred those Munchkins not yet proficient with the glove to play rover or shortstop. This way throws to the bases could become catches for outs, not missed balls leading to extra bases. Also, the hardest-hit balls were those pulled down the third-base line. I weighed these factors against my constant desire to honor, not diminish, each child's spunk and courage. Three options were open: remove Rebecca from the base, do nothing, or lay on a bit of coaching pressure. I chose the last. "Rebecca, if you stay on third be ready for balls coming at you. If they come from the outfield they will come fast and hard."

She held her ground. Matthew whistled a drive by her. Fortunately she was so tiny that the chance of being hit was small. The next batter, Jackson, lined to me in center. Matthew rounded second; I fired to third. Rebecca had Matthew and the ball both headed for her. She held her stance and got leather on ball, though it didn't stay in the glove. Matthew scored as the ball skipped into foul territory.

After the game, as we walked back to school Rebecca sheepishly apologized for dropping the ball. I told her I admired her courage for staying with the play and that next season with more practice she would be catching everything thrown her way. She smiled. I yelled ahead to Rachel, "What is one thing ball players never bring to the game?" She turned, set her feet, gave me a stare that would make Ty Cobb proud, and said, "A book." I was enjoying my class of next year already.

Though our baseball games, practice in studio, and classwork filled much of our time, the Munchkins were still making great use of the Big Elm, the ropes, and the sheds. Thursday Daniel directed the launches and timings of the swings. During their previous games of collision, the boys had discovered that near misses led to the two ropes entwining and two boys revolving in ever faster circles, especially if a friend pushed them. After perfecting the twining from the piles of stumps, Daniel launched from the shed to increase the energy in the system. The girls watched and on Friday worked out the feminine style of contact. One girl would pendulum from the shed and another would push off from the trunk of the Big Elm so they could high-five each other as they passed in midflight.

This was also the day several Munchkin girls broke through their fear of swinging. Those who had never swung from the shed and those who had done it but once and had not liked the sensation huddled together. They decided this was the time to step through their discomfort. After months of gentle swinging around the Big Elm and watching others enjoy the pendulum, they mounted the shed and one by one entered the ranks of swingers. They did this on their own, with no encouragement from me or others. Rachel, Dorothy, Asha, and Katherine each stepped from the shed and learned to enjoy the feeling in the stomach and not to be paralyzed by it. Their timing for this change was excellent because the following week was spring climbing and all day Thursday the Munchkins would be in the tree.

Friday at 11:00 found Uncle Matt teaching art to the Bigs. I had shown him the tools and techniques we had worked with and he settled into instruction. He gathered the kids around, started mixing colors as he talked, said his first shape looked to him like a bird, added features, talked, mixed, brushed. He demonstrated how if one was careful, a color could gently be applied over another, even while still wet. When asked what he wished them to paint he said, "Whatever you want."

Uncle Matt became an instant hero. After several weeks of specific exercises the release into freedom was exactly what the young artists desired. The Munchkins received an hour of his time with equally satisfying results. Now our art classes had ideas and projects to finish this year and also begin the next. After class Uncle Matt commented that the children were the most respectful group with whom he had ever painted. He was also delighted that the older ones had not lost their sense of creativity. In his experience each year in school eroded creativity in children. I thanked him for his time and hoped he would visit again.

As we stood around the popcorn bowl I was pleased with our past work, the current week's activities, all members of the school, and our collective alignment as we approached the final four weeks of school. Our year's academic work had been superior, our citizenship and good will exemplary, our concert had a home, our baseball was great, and our tree was ready for climbing. I had no problems to deal with, so I could have a little fun.

As Robby's dad pulled up to the curb, I strode purposefully to the car. Leaning over the sunroof, I said I had a problem to discuss. Parents always feared the worst when confronted by their child's teacher. "Robby is swinging at pitches out of the strike zone. I'm going to keep pitching him junk until he stops swinging at bad pitches." Dad was reacting to my tone and not my message. "I will talk with my son and work on this at home." I switched body language and tone of voice, smiled, and winked. "Isn't it great the kind of problems I have to deal with?" His shoulders relaxed; he grinned, laughed, and wished me a quiet weekend as they pulled away.

∽ Week Thirty-One ∾
Spring Climbing Week
The path up and down is one and the same.

HERACLITUS

ON TUESDAY MORNING, the first of the Bigs ran excitedly to the Big Elm. Daisy chains of carabiners hung on the fence, colored webbing was neatly piled on a bench, ten harnesses waited for a week of action. Several more ropes than usual hung from the tree. We were ready for Spring Climbing Week.

The Bigs looked forward to three climbing days and the Munchkins one. The Bigs were divided into two groups: one was around the tree, while the other was in class. In the autumn the groups had been divided by Latin abilities; this time the split was by gender. The Big boys were scheduled for the morning, the girls for the afternoon. After a few minutes devoted to safety reminders I told the boys they could begin climbing, expecting them to race to the pile of harnesses. Instead, most of them, lunch boxes in hand, headed to the bench under the tree and started eating. After snacking, a few began climbing but with little excitement. Forest refreshed himself on the technique of prussicing and then returned to his lunch. At the end of the year my policy was to cease to impose my will on student activities. The boys apparently needed food more than the thrill of climbing. I wondered if this tone would continue for the whole week. After three hours of much eating and little climbing the groups switched.

The quiet around the tree lasted only until the change of groups. The girls raced from class to put on harnesses, and soon ten girls were in the tree, climbing to high branches, exploring the new traverse ropes, chatting with each other, coordinating the use and sharing of the protection loops. Cina tried the prussic ascent and enjoyed it; as she descended others awaited a turn. I asked if they would like three prussic ropes instead of one. A loud cheer sent me to the rope bag to cut and tie more prussic loops. For the rest of the day the three ropes were never empty. Girls going up, girls coming down. Several of the group had never enjoyed the heights of the tree, climbing, and certainly not rappelling. The security of the prussic ascent was to their liking and soon they were farther off the ground than ever before.

Afternoon climbing brought a change from the morning session – the winds had begun to blow. Spring winds in New Mexico were never steady breezes – they came in strong gusts. Tuesday was a typical day. The girls in the tree were cooled by a ten-mile-per-hour zephyr with occasional cannonades of thirty miles per hour. Folks who spend most of their time on the ground think trees sway back and forth. However, from the vantage of a six-inch branch thirty feet above the ground, one soon learned the branch's swaying was linked with a twisting motion. This complex movement was mirrored in the pit of the stomach. Reese, highest in the tree, held tightly during the gusts and climbed during the still times between.

Wednesday the girls climbed in the stillness of the morning and continued their efforts and excitement of the previous day. Briana and Miranda had enjoyed the prussic ropes the day before and asked if two could prussic together. One of the joys of our climbing environment was that, as in Marianne's studio, the children invented activities. In her studio, when they suggested a new activity she judged whether it added to brain-body integration. If so, it then was included in the ever growing collection of games and exercises. Around the tree, when an idea was suggested I mentally checked to see whether it violated any of our rules of safety.

After a few moments of thought about kids prussicing together, I gave my approval and added another leg loop to the rope. Soon, as other girls watched from above and below, Briana and Miranda were ascending, giggling, squirming around in midair, and generally having a great time. They soon learned that coordination and teamwork were key. After their climb and descent other twosomes enjoyed the new exercise.

During their break from classwork the boys stood around the various gardens and sat on far walls watching the girls. I called Forest to join me as I monitored the tree. I told him I hoped some of the girl's intensity might rub off onto his lads. I also hoped they would have eaten most of their food by the afternoon and wouldn't spend so much time on the bench.

In the afternoon the boys enjoyed climbing, rappelling, and prussicing, though none were successful at the double prussic. Each pair would get about two feet off the ground and then their energy would go into aerial wrestling and laughing, not ascending the rope. With lunch boxes empty they did in fact spend more time climbing. Matt and Jackson had the best of both worlds – they clipped their lunches to their harnesses and spent an hour snacking high in the tree.

For all these years no one had doubted my statement that climbing ropes were strong. Using the pieces of the old rope removed from the tree, I thought the boys might like to test my belief. Every climbing rope had a brightly colored outer sheath that received the wear from the tree and damage from the sun. The majority of strength of the rope came from the strands of nylon making the inner core. Thirteen mini–nylon ropes were bundled in each 10.5 millimeter climbing rope.

I cut the sheath from one of the discarded ropes, extracted one of the thirteen strands, tied a loop, clipped it to a main rope, and asked for a brave volunteer to hang from the loop. No one stepped forward. I pointed out that if it broke, the fall would be only four inches onto the wood chips.

Forest then nominated Sylvan, our lightest, to clip on. The thin strand held. Jonah clipped on and the strand held them both. Three were held, and a fourth. All were amazed at the strength of nylon. As a fifth joined, finally the strand snapped, and all fell the four inches to the ground in a heap of laughter.

For the next hour other strands were tested and ruptured, each failure bringing more laughter. Matthew noticed each strand was actually three smaller ones twisted together. He separated out a single strand and found even this impossibly thin filament could hold his weight, though not the weight of himself and Forest. Zoe cruised by on the way to studio practice. As she silently surveyed piles of boys hysterically snapping nylon, her look seemed to say that males probably come from a planet much farther away than Mars. I told her of the strand testing. Her math wheels spun in her brain and she said, "These tests indicate all the kids in school could be supported by one rope. Amazing." She disappeared into the studio.

My watch showed parents would soon be arriving. I suggested we clip five boys to a single climbing rope as a strength demonstration for the parents. One of our rules of climbing was that only one person at a time should be clipped to any one rope. The boys asked why I was suggesting they violate one of our cardinal rules. I pointed out they would not be using the rope for climbing protection so the rule did not apply. Much talk of who clipped where, in which order, and how they would be protected getting into position proceeded the actual event. Soon five lads looked rather like a living squirming totem pole.

Parents began to gather. Forest and Matthew then joined the pole by clipping to the loop closest to the ground. Parents' eyes widened; our demonstration of the strength of nylon was succeeding. James calculated the combined weight: 770 pounds. I handed Coleman to Forest and stepped on the pile myself. Now the rope was holding 1000 pounds. I announced this to the boys and parents, reminding them that the rope could easily hold twice the mass. All were impressed and had increased their trust in our climbing system. We were halfway through the week of climbing. The next day, during which the Munchkins would be climbing, would be our most challenging.

Munchkin Climbing Day began at 5:30 A.M. As related to me later by her mother, Asha jumped out of bed, quickly dressed, then stomped up and down the hall waking the rest of the family, all in the hope of hurrying the beginning of climbing. On the school front, by 8:30 Big girls were helping Munchkins into harnesses and the Big boys were hauling the young ones to the top pulley. In the autumn this initial activity had been accompanied by much tension and some protest. Now all were eager for the ride. Discussion and analysis revealed that the physical sensations were the same as in the autumn but that each was now interpreting these signals differently. They were enjoying the thrill and not panicking, engaging both brain and body. A valuable lesson.

Some Munchkins liked the added thrill of rapid descent, so while they were still high in the tree I let the rope run freely for a few feet before gripping it tightly. These kids came down in three or four quick drops. Others were still learning the joys of heights and interferon rushes, and were gently and steadily lowered until they were near the ground. I would then let the rope play out before braking their drop inches from the ground. Everyone enjoyed the first activity of Munchkin Climbing Day.

Next we turned to the business of climbing fundamentals. Alison clipped herself into the ropes attached to First Notch in the tree. Each young climber tied the belay rope around their waist, climbed to Alison, and then down-climbed, returning to the ground. This reminded them they were in control and increased their trust in the rope and my belay.

After each had completed this exercise and watched the styles of the other climbers, we switched to a more difficult task, the rappel. The previous climb was repeated but this time while wearing a loop of webbing holding a locking carabiner and a rappel device, and with a pair of leather gloves jammed in the climber's pocket. Standing in the notch, protected by my belay and with Alison's gentle help, each Munchkin arranged all this gear in the correct configuration. No easy task. To rappel one must defy the messages of the body. The climber must lean back into space relying on the equipment, not balance or grasping fingers. Often a novice rappeller spent ten minutes struggling with the commitment to the move. I held a tight belay, while Alison spoke quietly. For me the ten minutes of inactivity with my hand cramping seemed interminable, but the time spent was some of the most worthwhile. Each child's first rappel was a major step in their growth, confidence, and maturation.

During our autumn climbing, some had given up on the rappel, removed gear, and down-climbed. More than a few tears had been shed in the notch over the years. This day we had dry eyes and no down-climbs. Asha talked with Alison about her tears of autumn as she arranged her gear and gracefully rappelled. These passages gave each child irrefutable proof of their growth.

Rachel, who had not liked any climbing activities at the beginning of the year, had enjoyed the pulley haul and spongy drop. She now approached the rappel with a determined effort. I held the belay for quite a time until she finally committed to the descent. As she touched the ground she asked if I would be willing to belay her a second time, for she felt a second rappel would help her master the technique. Though my hand objected to the task, my words gave her permission. My heart swelled to be a witness to the courage of a young one as she grew.

The Munchkins were eager to emulate the Bigs using the new prussic ropes. The previous two days during break they had watched the ascents of these ropes. Now they equally enjoyed the activity. Daniel, our master climber, donned harness and headed for free climbing in the highest branches. Sam joined him and, with Daniel's coaching, joined the club of those comfortable with play at great heights. Robby tried to follow them but found, as many others do, that his body, which was superior at sports played on terra firma, refused to move when more than ten feet off the ground. I had observed this many times. A great athlete who is at ease playing against an opponent, battling over a ball or puck, in a game played within boundaries, can be uncomfortable when the game becomes internal to self – when there is no one to beat and no lines defining the field. Robby returned to the ground.

As 3:00 approached, Rachel and Katherine came to me with a request. Could they free climb up to Second Notch and wait for their parents? In previous years I would not have let two inexperienced climbers venture to new heights without veterans surrounding them. Now, after watching many children in the tree, I had increased my trust in the tree, our safety system, and the kids themselves. I nodded that they could harness up and climb. Together, comforting each other, they climbed to the notch, clipped into protective loops, and awaited their parents.

Unfortunately, Katherine's folks never saw her. They were busy elsewhere and had asked Eliza's dad to pick her up. He, being a veteran observer of our rhythms and knowing how long it would take these novices to safely descend, said he would run a few errands and be back in twenty minutes.

In the morning Rachel had asked her mom to come early, around 2:30, to watch the end of climbing. By the time Mom arrived at 3:15, Rachel and Katherine had been above ground for longer than they had planned, were tired, and had nerves that were close to used up for the day. With Mom on the ground, Rachel's attention was divided between climbing safely and focusing on her mother. Alison made sure Rachel was always clipped into a safety rope.

As Rachel slowly descended the tree, I asked Mom if she was feeling pride for the remarkable accomplishment of her daughter. "Actually, I was thinking she would fall to her death at any moment." I gently chided her for lack of trust in the brilliance of our safety system and her equal lack of trust of the hydrogen bonds across the polyamide molecules of nylon. "On second thought, that was my umbilical cord speaking. I would actually like to try climbing one of these days." So ended a great Munchkin Climbing Day.

Friday climbing with the Bigs was filled with great energy. At the end of the day, as the last climber left the tree I was relieved to end Climbing Week. Our concert in two weeks also would require extreme attention, and there was a desire to let down my guard for the week between these activities. Fortunately, I followed my own advice and held good form through the last day of school. As I relaxed over the weekend, I did not know that the coming week would in many ways be even more challenging than Climbing Week.

ஒ Week Thirty-Two *ൟ*
Los Alamos Fire and Pete

You gain strength, courage, and confidence by every experience in which you really stop to look fear in the face.

ELEANOR ROOSEVELT

NORTHERN New Mexico is the home of two small but world-renowned communities, Santa Fe and Los Alamos. Though separated by only thirty miles and the easily fordable Rio Grande, no towns could be more different. Santa Fe is as ancient a city as can be found in America; Los Alamos did not exist sixty years ago. Santa Fe is home to many folks exploring alternative healing and inner consciousness; Los Alamos is home and workplace for many scientists and technicians exploring the inner realms of nuclear energy. Santa Fe probably has a greater mass of crystals than any community on the planet; Los Alamos has a greater mass of plutonium than any other. The more extreme members of each community reminded one of pre–Civil War abolitionists and slave holders – not much thought of middle ground or understanding the other's point of view.

Our school sat on the Mason-Dixon line. Some families working in Los Alamos were attracted to our school for the superior academics, especially our math and science. For them our perceived "touchy-feely" atmosphere was a secondary benefit. Some folks in Santa Fe sent their children to our school for the great vibes, the spiritual foundations, the loving-kindness, and the Zen-like gardens. The excellent curriculum was for them secondary. Our school had long prided itself on the collective harmony of families coming from different races, cultures, religions, sexual preferences, and economic levels. All parents could drop off their children knowing they would be loved, honored, and protected. Parents would chat socially with each other on the bricks after school, focusing on points in common and avoiding differences. This week these patterns were challenged.

Tuesday began as other weeks had before spring concerts. All semblance of regular class activity had disappeared. Performers with xylophone parts in the first half of the show gathered in the studio for two hours of practice, followed by those playing in the second half. In the morning I passed out the weekly packet, a fifty-question physics test, and several math sheets to those remaining in the Bigs' class. After giving the instruction, "Do a bunch of this when you have time," I headed for the studio.

Rehearsal went well, including the addition of a new verse to an old song. We had been enjoying singing "Surfin' USA" so much I had asked if anyone could write another verse to lengthen the song. At break Briana and Amelia came to me with a rough version. I suggested what to keep, what to rewrite, and how to open their minds to the whisper of the Muses. They returned ten minutes later with the completed verse. I printed some copies on the laser printer, passed them out in rehearsal, and soon we were singing a longer version of a classic song.

Earlier in the morning Daniel had asked if the boys could swing in the tree. I reminded him we always rested the tree for two days after a climbing week but that Pete had promised to come on Thursday and swing with the kids. They always enjoyed it when Pete played with them around the tree. His work as a news cameraman for a local station gave him flexible hours, and he had scheduled some time off to be with his young climbing buddies.

At 1:00 we headed to our first baseball game in eleven days. Climbing had been great, but we had missed the action of our ball games. As we walked to the park I kept my eye to the northern horizon – the National Park Service had announced a planned burn in the forests adjoining Los Alamos. Decades of fire suppression had created dense forests of towering ponderosa pines. Now forestry policy had switched to a strategy of small burns designed to reduce the fuel load. I knew that the drought of this year and the annual spring winds did not seem to create the best environment for a "controlled burn." The biggest fear in Northern New Mexico was that a forest fire would breach the nuclear labs at Los Alamos and release sufficient plutonium to make the area uninhabitable for a hundred thousand years. We paid close attention to every fire in our northern mountains. As we played I saw no signs of smoke. The game ended with a great throw by Robby from center field catching Forest at home plate.

Wednesday we again had large rehearsal groups in the studio and some work in the classroom before our afternoon baseball game. Later, when we walked to the park a small cloud was visible on the northern horizon. This did not bode well, since there was no moisture in the air and therefore this was not a rain cloud. Also, the winds had been blowing since dawn and were now becoming quite strong. Ken showed up and we pitched alternate innings. Each time I jogged to the outfield after my inning of pitching I noticed the cloud kept towering higher in the sky. From the size of the pyrocumulus cloud, I knew a huge fire was raging out of control; from its location, that Los Alamos was burning; from the winds and forecast, that this fire would not be contained for days. Fortunately for us, southwest winds were blowing the smoke away from Santa Fe. As long as they remained this way we would not have to deal with consequences at our school. A shift to a north wind would bring hard decisions to the school and each of our families. Whichever way the winds blew, I knew Pete would not be coming to climb with his young friends.

As we walked back to school I told the kids that this was serious but there was no need to panic – many very intelligent and dedicated people had worked hard to insure the safety of the nuclear material. James's father, a local plumber, had worked installing safety equipment. Former school parents were scientists working at the labs and had no desire to bring harm to family, friends, or neighbors. I suggested the kids watch the evening news for they would be guaranteed dramatic images. I promised we would devote morning class time to explain the situation, any rumors they had heard, the facts as they were known, and anything else they wished to discuss in order to give them a clearer view and a sense of safety.

Thursday we assembled at school having spent Wednesday night watching TV and seeing scores of homes in Los Alamos burn to the ground. The fires had been too large and the winds too strong for the fire fighters to establish a fire line. The town had been evacuated and the news pictures had been taken from helicopters. Then as we had watched the early evening news, we had seen pictures taken from a car driving between rows of burning houses. Most dramatic.

This morning when I asked the kids if they knew who had been brave enough to drive near the fire and sneaky enough to get through the police lines, they exclaimed in one voice, "Pete!" No longer was the fire impersonal and abstract. The man who had tied all the knots in the most critical ropes in the tree was on the scene, always near the most intense action.

Our morning discussion centered around plutonium, fact and fear. In our spectrum of parents we had a few who didn't believe anything the government ever said about nuclear safety. My role was not to refute the beliefs of others but to present the information as I understood it. It was a fact that none of the lab buildings had burned during the night and therefore no plutonium had been released; the fires had been in the residential areas of town. Discussion turned to the chemicals released from the burning homes. We talked of the modern materials used for construction of homes and the chemicals found inside: insulation materials, plastics of all kinds, cans of paint, cleaning products, and hundreds of other items that when burned could be hazardous to health. I pointed out most smoke was comprised of small, relatively harmless molecules and the more dangerous chemicals were found in the heavier ash particles that would over time be transported by water into our rivers.

Forest said he understood that lots of plutonium had been released from the burning trees – he had heard that they had picked up plutonium during the building of the atomic bombs in World

War II. I thanked him for bringing up this important point, and we proceeded to separate fact from rumor, with the understanding that we would never have total certainty in this or any human event. I noted that during the first years of nuclear experimentation, safety of the materials had not been well understood and some uranium had been handled more haphazardly than now. Some trees held trances of uranium in them, but the canyon with the most contamination had not burned. As for plutonium, I pointed out that during the war it had been an extremely rare substance so we shouldn't fear that detectable amounts of this historic plutonium would be dropping on us. I reinforced that this was still, for us, a hypothetical subject for the wind was continuing to blow the plume of smoke away from Santa Fe.

Our final preconcert music practice was great. We were singing better than ever, united as one voice. Twice Melanie's eyes teared. As we sang "Dona Nobis Pacem," I too started to cry. This ended our practice for the concert. Our left brains were now comfortable with the words and notes of the concert. Friday and again Tuesday would be full rehearsals when we would run through the show in the exact order of the performance. During these times Melanie would address our right brains, telling us of the many nuances, slight variations from verse to verse, and changes of pace in parallel phrases. None of this could be found in the songbook, but it was what brought the power to the music.

That afternoon, as many worried about hypothetical harm from the fire, we played our baseball game, which always carried the possibility of actual harm. Regarding throwing to the various bases, we taught the habit of throwing to the outside of the bag, away from the runner, and never at head height. In the third inning, Miranda ran toward second base on a grounder to Forest at shortstop. He fielded the ball, but didn't set his feet so he threw off balance and too hard. The ball bounced off Miranda's skull. From my position in the outfield I saw it strike above her temple and knew that in a few minutes she would be fine. I said a silent prayer to Ken, who last year had convinced me our time playing with a standard hardball was over. He brought a half dozen high-tech balls that had a softer core and distributed impact over a few more milliseconds. I called for a pinch runner, put my arm around Miranda, and walked her off the field. I then reviewed the play and importance of controlled throws with Forest. The rest of the game was injury free. One more day of school remained in the week, but the forecast had predicted winds from the north.

The forecast was correct. Friday we awoke to a cold north wind and a slight smell of smoke. The phone started ringing. I encouraged families to bring the kids for at least the morning and the rehearsal. I said the winds would be gentle until noon and therefore little smoke would reach us until then, and the fires would also be small until the winds increased. Two families had not been seen since the fire exploded. One family had left town Thursday night. Another chose not to come to school this day. We were down eight kids for rehearsal: five avoiding the fire, two with pinkeye, and one with stomach flu. Though we wished all students would attend the final rehearsals, we never wanted to impose our will on families, but rather to give them a clear statement of the school's schedule and activities. They could then make their own decisions on attendance or absence. In talking with the families of the absent students, we told them anyone missing both this and Tuesday's rehearsal would not be in the performance on Wednesday. I did not want to place unnecessary pressure on young children, and I knew that missing both rehearsals would mean they would not hear or practice Melanie's final instructions and thus would have a hard time being part of our unified sound. Though some were missing the rehearsal, we added one singer.

With Los Alamos and the bedroom community of White Rock evacuated, many residents found housing with friends in Santa Fe. The schools were closed and most of the kids were spending the days watching TV. James's mom called to see if the boy staying with them could come to school. She added that he sang well. I of course agreed. As we packed into the Bigs' room for rehearsal, James and Andy arrived.

I worked my way across the crowded room, put my arm around Andy, and said in my sternest teacher voice, "You haven't turned in any papers to me this year." With perfect timing and sincere student tone, he said, "I'm sorry. I will try to do better." Here was a young gentleman who had been displaced, might not have a home to return to, was in a room full of strangers, and still had his poise and sense of humor. Speaking for the whole school I said, "Welcome to our little world."

We all sang well; Andy joined right in. I played the xylophone parts for the missing kids. With the many absentees, each section had missing voices, but the high section was most depleted. Daniel told Melanie he would join the thinned ranks. This was the same Daniel who during all previous music sessions had only mouthed the words. As the three-part song began, a new and beautiful sound was heard: a choir-boy voice with excellent pitch. Though Melanie continued to give cues to each of the sections and held the beat, I saw she was struggling not to cry.

If asked, Alison would say Daniel's time in the Munchkin room, where her quiet voice and patience had helped him heal his scars, had contributed to this moment. Marianne would say her studio work had helped him connect his ears and brain. Melanie would say two years surrounded by others singing had helped bring him to this breakthrough. I would say all the time he had spent swinging in the Big Elm had empowered him with the confidence to express himself in other ways. We were each correct in the small picture. In the larger view, though, none of us would ever know the mechanism by which young children blossomed and stood forth in their own strength and beauty. We did know it was for moments like these that we worked in the school.

Several parents came and picked up their children before noon. Others called several times to talk with their kids. A few parents came feeling the need to share their fears with others. One chose to come wearing a gas mask; I noted she didn't bring any for the children. All morning I had been asked if we would play ball at 1:00. My answer had always been, "I don't know. I will make the decision at 1:00." I could tell, though, that the kids were beginning to feel uncomfortable with all this swirling, conflicted energy and the increase of smoke as the winds picked up, so I called everyone into the classroom for a talk.

I began by acknowledging that much fire, smoke, and talk were in the air and in order to be extra safe we would not play baseball that afternoon. "A little smoke is not what most folks are concerned about," I said frankly. "The fear is that the government won't tell us of radiation leaking from the labs if the buildings burn. Fortunately we at Fayette have a direct contact to the best information. Pete, who you all admire and trust, is at this moment with the governor, who is his friend and skiing partner; our congressman, who is one of his rock-climbing partners; our two senators; the secretary of the Department of Energy, who was for years our local congressman; and the Director of FEMA. All the experts monitoring the fires, the detection instruments, and the data are reporting to this group. I talked with Pete this morning, and he said that if anything went wrong anywhere he would call me with his cell phone and tell me the real information. He has not called, so let's enjoy the rest of the day."

It was amazing how quickly the tension in the room disappeared. Some kids headed for the tree, some played chess in the Bigs' room, some colored in the Munchkins' room. Two hours later all of the students were relaxed and happy as their parents came to pick them up. One mother berated me for my upbeat attitude in the face of the fire and the imminent danger. I merely smiled, thought several things, said nothing, nodded, and walked away. As the last child left, I began my prayers to the weather gods that they would halt the winds or at least bring a south wind Tuesday and Wednesday for the final rehearsal and the concert.

Week Thirty-Three

Spring Concert and School Potluck

The music is found between the notes and the words.

DIZZY GILLESPIE

TUESDAY MORNING as Melanie called us into the Bigs' room for the final run-through of the program, four Munchkins were missing. I found them in the study room. To create space for our rehearsal, the pillows in the school had been piled in the corner of the room. The missing Munchkins were lying on the mound of pillows complaining of vague head and stomach aches. I told them to relax, breathe deeply, and when they felt better to join in the rehearsal. By the end of the third song the four had become eight. Normally for final rehearsal we ran straight through the program with no retakes or commentary by Melanie. But this day was not normal. I called a time-out, had everyone sit, and asked the eight to join us for a short talk.

"We have for the past days experienced the emotion of fear, sometimes in ourselves, sometimes in our homes, and definitely in the community as a whole," I said. "We, in this room, are seeing and feeling the effects of fear. Some of our youngest have taken in what they have overheard and are distressed. Our singing has lacked the unison and beauty we usually experience. Being familiar with fear and its effects is a valuable lesson, but fear is not the only powerful emotion. The opposite is a feeling of power and security. As we sit here, the wind is blowing the smoke away from us, the labs are safe, and we are one day away from show time. Let's all return to the power we feel when we sing well together. Those of you feeling ill, go back and relax on the pillow pile, and listen to the beauty of the rest of us singing. Be comforted by the words and melodies. Join us when you feel better."

The young ones left and the rest of us did a session of Brain Gym exercises to assist balance and integration. The break helped. We sang better and could feel we were again building strength. Between songs I checked on those on the mountain of pillows, using quiet words and wiggling a few toes. Daniel and then Nyssa joined the choir. Our rehearsal ended with four Gregorian chants and three other songs speaking of God's peace, blessings and protection. As we sang these hymns, one by one the Munchkins rejoined us, and we finished the rehearsal a group reunited and revitalized.

After rehearsal the Bigs caravaned in several vehicles to the concert site to check out the acoustics in our new location and to set up the instruments. A few lucky ones loaded the instruments in our old Chevy van and piled in with me. The van had only the two front seats, making it ideal for hauling large loads. Many years before, we would throw in some school pillows and a bunch of kids and have a great time. Now, with parents wanting their children seat belted, the van rarely was used for school business.

Our rehearsal and my talk had helped change the energy among the students, but I knew more work was needed to overcome all the fears – it was time for zaniness. As we drove I asked Forest to crawl back to the bass xylo, slide the alto over to Cina, and pass the tiny glockenspiel to Amelia, riding in the passenger seat. As we slowly drove the final few blocks through downtown Santa Fe, tourists heard a moving rendition of "Surfin' USA," complete with harmonies and instrumental accompaniment.

At the Santuario the instruments were soon positioned, and we tested our voices in the unfamiliar acoustics. As we sang Melanie moved around the room, declaring the sound fuller and more distinct than in the former chapel. Unfortunately for us we could not hear the others in the choir as well as in the Loretto. Sound tests completed, we returned to school to find the Munchkins laughing, chatting, and jumping rope. As they left for home the children were much closer to the relaxed state needed for our concert than when they had arrived in the morning.

SPRING CONCERT AND SCHOOL POTLUCK 257

Wednesday morning the smoke was still blowing away from Santa Fe. After everyone had arrived at the Santuario, we gave the Munchkins a tour of the building, let them play the xylos to get a feel for the sound, and then sang a few of the more difficult songs. Melanie satisfied, Alison and I led the procession to the bathrooms and drinking fountains. In this half hour before the concert, Alison and I quietly reminded each child to hold their excitement and energy and release it during the show; though the location had changed, our rituals remained the same. As we reentered the now filled chapel, I handed each singer a songbook and most touched my gold tiepin. We took our positions, followed Marianne in a few minutes of Brain Gym, and awaited Melanie's cue.

Beginning all concerts with the same Islamic and Hindu chants not only set the desired tone but also allowed us to begin on familiar ground. These we followed with a Navajo prayer sung first in unison and then in three parts. This selection was intentional: the conscious analytical mind cannot simultaneously track three different parts. As we sang, thought was suspended and feeling took over. Before the audience's left-brain faculties reengaged, we began our "political" song, Dylan's "The Times They Are a Changin'." We sang as one, and with passionate conviction, "There's a battle outside and it's ragin'....," "your sons and your daughters are beyond your command...." "the first one now will later be last...."

Changing the tone, we next put five Munchkins on the xylos and sang a few children's songs. Our Bach cantata followed, demonstrating our proficiency at true choral music. Then we moved into our Scots and Gælic section. Two Gælic songs well known in Scotland and a few fast-paced work songs we'd learned from Deirdre earlier in the year brought us to the final selection before intermission. As our piper led us in our Gælic version of "Amazing Grace," few in the audience were not moved; many eyes were moist.

Feeling pleased with our efforts, we moved into our intermission traditions. The kids sat, we passed water bottles around, the staff walked around checking on all, many touched the tiepin. After ten minutes we stood, Marianne led us in a few more centering exercises, and we were prepared for the second half of the show.

The audience settled in again. Alison sat with her guitar and Archie joined her; we were ready for our Americana medley of mining songs. We began with "Clementine" and followed with "Dark as a Dungeon," John Prine's lament in waltz time, in which "Mr. Peabody's Coal Train" hauled away not only coal but also the town of Paradise, brought us to Merle Travis's "Nine-Pound Hammer." Hearing Munchkins sing that such a hammer "is a little too heavy for my size" produced the expected humorous effect. The medley concluded with "Sixteen Tons." Both audience and choir enjoyed such lines as "cain't no high-toned woman make me walk the line."

Now it was time to switch gears again. Forest, James, Cina, and Zoe stepped to the xylos and donned the silk flower leis hidden in the music stands. We were ready for "Surfin' USA." The audience rocked, and Briana and Amelia's verse brought spontaneous chuckles. Gregorian chants followed as we approached the conclusion of the concert. We ended with our three hymns, sung in rounds: "Ego Sum Pauper," "Tallis Canon," and "Dona Nobis Pacem."

In past years these had finished the show, but this spring's program mentioned an unnamed final song. After the last note of "Dona Nobis" faded, we quietly began "We Shall Overcome." Tears and a standing ovation demonstrated to the kids the power of their unified voice. Back at school a relaxed ball game ended the day.

When the kids arrived at school on Thursday Ken's court was in session. The crime was "Murder One." The Bigs were excited. Unlike the year's previous case, my bike crash, they were able to create the players and scenario of this drama themselves. Since Jonah had departed for a river-rafting adventure, he became the murder victim. Amelia, desiring the starring role, became the accused. A team of three crafted the details of the murder: two shots from a .45 during a robbery at the local Starbucks. Amelia retained Ariel and James as defense attorneys. Michiah and Reese prosecuted. Several others were in charge of creating the physical evidence as well as the props needed for the drama. Many volunteered to play the roles of various witnesses.

Forest pointed out that no one was left to serve on the jury. Zoe voiced a radical idea: a Munchkin jury. All the Munchkin girls were eager to serve. The boys asked if they could use the time to climb in the tree. As I headed for the tree with the young men, the jury was sworn in. The trial had begun.

The young jurors took their new responsibility seriously and soon realized that they held the most power in the day's drama. They would decide the case, and therefore all the efforts of the witnesses and attorneys were directed toward them. They began by asking the important questions. "Is it OK to talk with each other?" Now the Bigs were teaching: "Certainly, the more deliberation the better, but jurors can't talk to lawyers, the accused, or the witnesses." Eliza asked what the word *deliberation* meant. Ariel explained. Dorothy asked if they all had to agree on a verdict. Ken informed them that in murder cases their judgment had to be unanimous. Another word entered their vocabulary.

As the trial moved through its early stages, more new words tossed around by the Bigs rained down on the Munchkins: *allegedly* (so they say, but nothing's proven yet), *implicated* (involved somehow, but exactly how, if at all remains to be seen), *perjury* (it's bad to lie any time, but it's a crime to lie in court), and *defendant* (in this case Amelia, who is presumed innocent until proven guilty beyond the shadow of a doubt). The Munchkin jury took this all in and the trial moved forward.

Once the lawyers realized the exercise was to round up witnesses to counter the testimony of other witnesses, the true duel of imaginations began. The prosecution's star eyewitness, Heather, fingered Amelia at the scene of the crime, pointing to her in court, describing her clothes and eye color. During cross-examination, Ariel tested Heather to determine just how much someone could remember after seeing somebody for only a few seconds. The Munchkins seemed convinced that such testimony could easily lack credibility.

The defense then presented exhibits of movie tickets for *Little Mermaid II* from the local mall's theater complex, as well as a receipt and credit-card slip from Gadzooks, a clothing store in the mall. James argued that these demonstrated Amelia was hanging around Villa Linda Mall at the time of the murder and that any fool knew Starbucks was at another mall altogether. The prosecution, after a brief recess to create a new character from the pool of players, called Amani, a cashier at the movie theater, who testified that Cina and not Amelia had purchased the tickets. The defense quickly countered that Cina was Amelia's pal and had simply bought the tickets for both of them.

The teaching value of court was its formal structure. Court was not a bunch of kids all talking at the same time, throwing ideas and opinions around. All players had to keep track of their own roles and also follow the performance of the other players. The lawyers had to take notes on what to ask later. Everyone had to be quiet most of the time; listening became the main activity. Amazingly the Munchkins were very attentive, riveted on every word.

After nine witnesses the case was turned over to the jury. They sequestered in the sauna courtyard abuzz with all the inconsistencies in the testimony: "He said her eyes are green, but they're really blue-green." "She said she was wearing gray pants, but then the next witness testified they were black." Nothing had slipped by them. After surveying and weighing all the testimony and looking at the physical evidence, each member of the jury had to vote for guilt or innocence.

Dorothy, the jury foreperson, informed Miranda, the bailiff, that they had arrived at a verdict. All, including the boys in the tree, gathered in the Bigs' room to hear the decision. Amelia and her attorneys stood and faced the Munchkins. "Not guilty," Dorothy announced convincingly. Amelia whooped and hugged Ariel. Michiah and Reese grumped in the corner. Everyone then headed out for break time in the various courtyards and gardens. I found Eliza and asked her how she had arrived at the verdict. "Simple. Who in the world would want to be hanging around Starbucks committing murder when

SPRING CONCERT AND SCHOOL POTLUCK

they could be at Villa Linda Mall shopping at Gadzooks and seeing *Little Mermaid II*?" Case closed.

Friday morning Fayette became a vocational school teaching the finer skills of raking, scrubbing, and vacuuming. The oldest boys set up serving tables, arranged more stumps for seating, and spread rugs under the shade of trees. Tara directed the Big girls in setting up the recycle and reuse containers. By noon the school was ready to hold a potluck for more than 150 people. After the potluck we would all drive to Albuquerque to enjoy an evening of minor-league baseball.

Our own baseball game in the afternoon was a full nine innings, filled with action. By the end of our season all were playing much better ball than a few weeks before. The older players had honed their skills, but the greatest improvements were in the youngest players. Walker had begun his rookie season with excellent bat speed, but contact with the ball had been another matter. As with most Munchkins, when he was at bat the outfield relaxed and the infield moved in a couple of steps. After tracking hundreds of pitches over the season, Walker had begun to show signs of much improved hand-eye coordination. In the third inning the skills came together. He lashed a wicked shot past Reese at third; the ball skipped down the line and rolled to the far sidewalk. After this demonstration all the fielders paid good attention during his plate appearances.

Though adding to the skills of athletic young gentlemen was a joy, our greatest pride came when a young lady, especially one who had never enjoyed sports, embraced the game. We applied no pressure, demanded no level of performance. Playing the whole season deep in the outfield watching the prairie dogs was fine. Staying a freebie for years was OK. Each player was encouraged to remain in their own comfort zone. They picked the time to step up their level of play and involvement. Our task was to recognize when they were shifting their paradigm.

Asha shifted hers on Friday. She played in the infield, not merely to have a better view as balls whizzed by, but to trap them and throw to the bases. Her hitting also improved. As we walked back to school after the game I mentioned she seemed to be enjoying baseball more. Her smile showed she was – but she was not finished with breaking old patterns.

Back at school as we gathered for the potluck, the kids asked if they should have a climbing demonstration for the parents. I pointed out that when we had done this the last two years no one had seemed to pay much attention. Miranda's explanation was that in the past boys had climbed to the top of the tree and simply hung out; none had played to the crowd. She suggested having six girls begin this year's demonstration. I concurred. As the crowd assembled for the potluck, the girls donned harnesses and soon were hanging upside down on the prussic lines and doing flips over the traverse ropes. As Miranda had predicted, this time the crowd paid attention.

Asha asked me if she too could hang out on the traverse rope. "But you have never done the traverse," I reminded. "In fact you have never climbed above First Notch. Is now the time for your breakthrough?" Five minutes later she was on the traverse, smiling like the Cheshire cat. I strongly believed that our task as parents and educators was to patiently wait for each child's quantum leaps. And when they were ready to take the step, never to say, "Now is not a convenient time."

The boys wanted to be part of the action too and asked if they could swing. With gate and ground monitors in place, they demonstrated the pendulums and landings on the shed roofs. Matt asked if he could show his grandfather his climbing skills. Harnessed, he quickly climbed to the top of the highest rappel. I stood with Granddad to explain what was occurring. He scanned the tree but didn't see his grandson. "You're not looking high enough," I counseled. "He is that pair of legs half hidden in the very top of the tree." I did take pause when his eighty-year-old heart skipped a few beats. As Matt expertly glided down the rope his granddad swelled with pride and relief. Matt unclipped, hugged his grandfather, and headed for the food line.

I was now ready to receive compliments from this elder on my fine climbing system and its benefits for our youth. Instead he said,

"Marianne must be an angel." I could not agree more, but had no idea the direction this would lead. "Her work in the studio must be magical. I was worried about Matt – his development and his reading. He seems a changed person, so mature and self-confident. And he not only can read but enjoys it."

When we all finished eating and talking, families started to head for the ball game. One task remained: to get everything cleaned up. Tara's system had been working well – different containers for compost, aluminum cans, plastic ware, and reusable cups were being correctly filled. Only the serving containers needed washing. As I circulated through the crowd hinting that a little time in the kitchen by a few would help us all, several said they were off to the game; some not going to the game spoke of tasks awaiting them at home; a few whined that they had cleaned up last year, making this someone else's turn. Such behavior did not anger me. Over the years I had been conditioned. Upon entering the kitchen to survey the work left undone I found two parents, bless them, and Asha cheerfully scrubbing away.

With all in order we headed for Albuquerque. Everyone enjoyed the game; the home team won, and then we drove safely home. A school day that had started at 7:00 A.M. ended at 11:00 P.M. In those sixteen hours the staff had directed a cleanup crew of thirty, played nine innings of baseball, hosted 150 people, monitored the tree, and watched an exciting professional baseball game. But as I drifted toward sleep, my thoughts were on one little girl.

↢ Week Thirty-Four ↣
The Final Week

Aloha Oe, Aloha Oe,
A hui hou kakou.
Farewell to thee, farewell to thee
Until we meet again.

LYDIA KAMEKEHA LILIUOKALANI

AS WE GATHERED on Tuesday all sensed the end of a great year. Never would the school community be the same. Our student leaders who had held a strong beat for nine months would in September be at various high schools, and new faces would add their flavor to the class. We each faced the prospect of three months without time together in our small society. Early in the morning many of the Bigs sat around the tree watching the Munchkins' last climbing day of the year.

At 9:30 the Bigs headed to their classroom for a viewing of *Midsummer Night's Dream*. Earlier in the year after we had finished our reading of the play, the Michelle Pfeiffer–Kevin Kline version had not yet been available at the video stores. Instead we had watched the 1930s Hollywood production with James Cagney as Bottom and a very young Mickey Rooney as Puck. But young people never seemed to feel fulfilled watching black-and-white movies, and though they had enjoyed the older version, I had promised them we would view the latest interpretation before the end of the year. All were eager to see actors and actresses with whom they were familiar perform the play.

For the last hour of Munchkin climbing we played jungle ball. The older ones who had flown the year before were first to launch, with the young ones watching. Several of the Bigs took turns being the "ball" for the Munchkins. Selflessly one would jump for awhile, missing some of the movie, then head to the classroom and another would appear, harness up, and send Munchkins flying. After her first flight Eliza said, "That was really freaky." "It is designed to be," I informed her. "Glad you enjoyed it." She jumped in line for another launching. By the end of the session most of the Munchkins had flown.

Tie-dyeing was the special activity of this day. Twice a year, during holiday crafts and now the final week of school, we tie-dyed, an event eagerly awaited by most students, the staff, some parents, a few friends, and the neighborhood. Over two hundred items, from socks to sheets, were transformed from white to rainbow colors. For the first years of this activity the staff had spent considerable time instructing and assisting the students with the various folds, rubber bands, and strings. A teacher had constantly monitored the outdoor dyeing table to avoid puddles and to make sure the dye created the desired effects.

Now, years later, our only time spent was in mixing the chemicals and filling the dye bottles. The veteran students instructed the rookies and visitors in our collection of patterns, ties, and techniques. The knowledge had been stored in the collective consciousness of the school community. Our parent guests took note that the various kids who helped them came and went, but the flow of information continued uninterrupted.

Wednesday was the final day of climbing for the Bigs. Some of the kids who had never crossed the traverse ropes used the guidance and encouragement of fellow students to overcome their fear at being supported by only hand and foot ropes. Seeing children who in September were quite uncomfortable at any height off the ground but now were moving across slender ropes thirty feet in the air was an inspiring sight.

One of the parents who had finished tie-dyeing wandered over to the tree. She asked about the etymology of *dye* and *die*. I smiled as I looked at her pink and blue fingers and then up to the ten climbers in the tree and asked, "What do you think brought those two words to your mind?" A short run for the *Oxford Dictionary* revealed that the cubes used in gambling came from the Old French, the word linked with death from the Norse, and the coloring agent from Old English. Three different Indo-European roots homophonically linked had given just one example of the confusion faced by students learning English.

The last hour of climbing for the Bigs was of course jungle ball. James was worn out after launching only half of the eager flyers, so Briana, remembering her dual ball efforts with Amelia in the autumn, convinced Heather to join her in this activity. They both clipped to the rope and Briana said, "We will jump on the count of three." She counted to three – several times. Neither jumped.

After some complaining by Miranda, standing in the doorway awaiting flight, Heather climbed down and Forest took her place beside Briana. He counted to three and jumped. Briana, still in the hesitation mode, didn't jump with him and didn't have both hands holding the rope above the carabiners. Miranda flew; Forest and Briana landed in a heap, her finger pinched between the two carabiners. Pete, who had dropped by to watch, and I conferred. I said that if we used only one carabiner fingers wouldn't be pinched. He countered that it was better to have an occasional pinched finger than to ever have someone really crash from the tree and get hauled to the emergency room.

Jungle ball and the year's climbing ended twenty minutes later with no more injuries. I was relieved as I pulled the belay ropes through the pulleys for the last time. Climbing added so much to the spirit and development of each student, but the price was having disaster only one careless move away. As I coiled the ropes and returned them to the rope bag, I was glad one pinched finger had been the most serious injury in our year around the Big Elm.

While the Bigs were spending their last time in the tree, Alison took the graduating Munchkins out to lunch. Upon their return each was escorted by one of the Bigs through the curtain separating the two classrooms. Though they passed through the doorway several times every school day without giving it a second thought, this was truly a rite of passage and for each Munchkin a scary one.

For ten- and eleven-year-olds moving less than ten feet and switching to a teacher who had been with them daily as sports coach, fellow choir member, and general jokester seemed terrifying. But their terror was balanced by their pride in joining the Bigs. They knew they would be leaving behind all vestiges of fairyland and in September would encounter Latin, Greek, and algebra.

Every year I took the Big graduates to a private dinner at a restaurant of their choice. No ceremony, no parents, just a quiet dinner together before they entered the roll of the Fayette alumni. Wednesday night Forest, Matthew, and Zoe joined Ele and me. We talked of little events during our time together. Sadness always sat with us at these dinners. For years I had given each graduate a book of wisdom. Part of my ritual of the last week of school had been to go to a local bookstore specializing in sacred works. From the hundreds of books a few always seemed to jump into my hand – teachings of Buddha, words of the Dali Lama, poems by Gandhi. Books that took up little shelf space, that could be opened at random and scanned for a few simple lines to be held in mind and heart during the day. I passed these out between the main course and dessert.

Thursday morning brought a huge motor coach to school. It towered over the school building, took up half our narrow street, and delighted every student. In past years we had caravaned a half-dozen vehicles to The Beach, a water park in Albuquerque. This year a parent had suggested exploring the possibility of renting a bus to take us all. Money from our fund-raising in October paid for the bus and admission to the park. We piled on and were off for a day of fun in the water. While riding we calculated that the space in the coach was larger than either of our classrooms.

We enjoyed our four hours of play at the water park. From a base camp stocked with sunscreen and snacks, we broke up into small groups and tested the different water activities, from the "Lazy River," which slowly circled the park, to the four-story-tall water slides. We observed that the other schools in attendance had broken up into groups of the kids who played and the teachers who sat.

At Fayette, by contrast, staff and students played together. Ele, Coleman, and Walker headed to the small-kids' area. Coleman was not yet comfortable with water sports, and having Walker for a guide helped him begin to enjoy the small slides and shallow pools. After a time the lifeguard came over, had Walker stand by the height standard, and declared him an inch too tall to be in the kiddie pools. Ele brought her two charges back to our base camp. Seeing this, Eliza said, "I'm an inch shorter than Walker – I will go with Coleman." Turning to Walker I said, "I guess if they think you are too big for the small area, they think you are ready for the big slides and pools." Sylvan said he would be happy to introduce Walker to the slides. Off they went.

As each of us climbed the stairs of the four-story-high tower leading to the top of the highest slides, we longingly looked over the side wishing we could throw over a few rappel ropes, knowing of course that we couldn't. The groups kept changing partners – Bigs with Munchkins, teachers with various kids, alumni where they were needed – one big happy group with no cliques or factions. On the ride home half were asleep and not too many square inches of skin were bright pink. As the bus returned to school, the parents were awaiting our arrival. Thirty-six children had climbed on the bus in the morning and thirty-six stepped off upon our return. We had not lost a one. As we waved good-bye we were down to one day in the school year.

The morning of the year's final day was spent packing pillows and books into the corner of one room in preparation for summer the fix-up/clean-up. The afternoon was devoted to our final baseball game, which, attended by many parents, was interrupted by an award ceremony and a short pizza party. This year's awards of Zuni fetishes were given to Ken and Harold, for their pitching, fielding, and joking with the little ones in the outfield; to James, who rode his bike to and from school every day – rain, snow or shine; and to our Boss, Forest, who so well held the valuable and difficult link between staff and students. As Forest sat down to applause, I had

Maggie stand for a moment. She would be Boss come September, and I wanted everyone to be thinking of this change, especially Maggie.

The game was as spirited as always, with many great plays and a sufficient number of zany events on the base paths. The final out of the ninth inning was a collision at second base, which knocked me head over heels and left the score tied. Since I was in no hurry to have the game, the season, or the school year end, I suggested we play until the tie was broken but left the decision to the graduates. They huddled, conferred, and ruled that the game should end with no one losing. I could not but agree, and we returned to the school for final hugs, good-byes, and tears.

As we said good-bye to Forest, Matthew, and Zoe, we knew that though they would not return as students, they would take part of Fayette with them. An ancient tale speaks of a time when tea was reserved for the elite. A group of people who desired to drink tea were debating the reported properties and powers of the drink. After much inconclusive arguing a wise man ended the discussion by saying, "Those who taste, know. Those who have not tasted, cannot know." Each graduate had tasted being comfortable with their own self, tasted the joy of acquiring knowledge, tasted the warmth of community where members honored and supported each other. They each left with a taste no person or force could ever take away.